T0333140

MAN AND HORSE

MAN AND HORSE

Four Thousand Years of the Mounted Warrior

ANDREW SINCLAIR

First published 2008

The History Press Ltd
The Mill, Brimscombe Port,
Stroud, Gloucestershire, GL5 2QG
www.thehistorypress.co.uk

British Library Cataloguing in Publication Data.
A catalogue record for this book is available from the British Library.

ISBN 978 0 7509 5034 3

Typesetting and origination by The History Press Ltd
Printed and bound in Great Britain

To SONIA GRAHAM and all the Borderers with their rich history and song.

An asterisk in the text denotes that there is a corresponding illustration in one of the plate sections.

Contents

Maps	8
From Asia to King Arthur	11
Islam and Norman	31
Crusade and Cossack	41
The Creation of the Reivers	51
Harry and Burn	67
Ballads of Circumstance	85
The Prickly Pride	93
Women of Courage and Circumstance	106
Kirk and Destruction	118
The Social Bandits	134
The American Horse	145
The Scotch-Irish	159
Warriors into Outlaws	169
Print the Legend	179
Horse Culture	193
Outback and Backlands	203
Commandos and Camels	217
The Machine and the Hunt	235
Dressage	253
Appendix	263
Acknowledgements	268
Notes	269

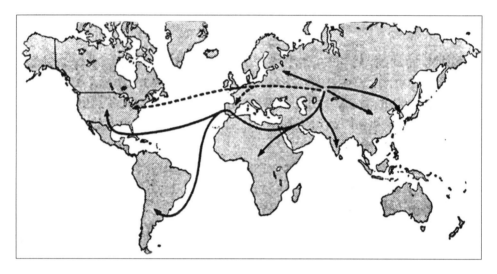

SPREAD OF THE HORSE CULTURE

The heavy line indicates the general drift of an Asiatic variant of the complex through Africa to Spain and thence to the steppes of the New World; the broken line, to the west, indicates the path through Europe to England and thence to the colonies located on the Atlantic seaboard. Note that the two horse cultures met on the Great Plains of North America. (From Walter Prescott Webb, *The Great Plains*, 1931, and derived from Clark Wissler, *Man and Culture*, 1914.)

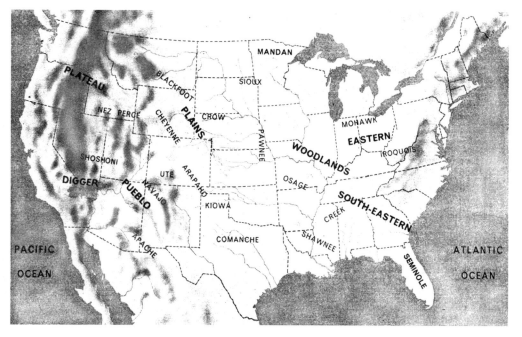

The Distribution of the Main Tribes at the Time of the Arrival of the Spaniards in Central and North America in the sixteenth century with Cattle and Horses.

CHAPTER ONE

From Asia to King Arthur

The land makes people, even though people aim to make the land. The clans and tribes of the plains and the steppes had to accept the elements of their survival. The folk of the forests and the rivers and the valleys might sow their crops and build their settlements. Yet between the harsh flats and the moist farms, there would always be a conflict. The margins of understanding would lie on the borders of these two cultures, the hunters and the herders set against the growers and the dwellers. How could the range ever be reconciled with the wall, or the *pampas* with the fence?

For the prehistoric men in the caves, the horse was merely another kind of food, along with the bear and the mammoth. The cradle of the original horse cultures was around Lake Baikal, one of the large waters left in the midst of Central Asia, after a vast inland sea had dried or drained into the ocean. To the south lay the arid dunes of the Gobi desert, while to the west reared the chains of the Altai and Tien Shan mountains. Valleys of beech and cedar and fir trees to the north were trenches before the forests of Siberia, while towards China and the east spread rugged and barren territory. The wildflower spring grasses of the steppes became brown stubble in the summer drought and turned to icy snow in the winter. The Turks and the Mongols and the Tungus of the nomadic peoples had to move with their beasts to feed or die.

The early Mongol tribes were split between the hunters of the forest and the herders of the plains, although the hunters kept some cattle and sheep, while the horsemen also sought out game. Indeed, the war tactics of Genghis Khan and the Golden Horde were honed in great circular drives, in which thousands of mounted warriors tightened the net of fear about all living creatures, driving them into the killing ground of the Great Khan. On the steppes, the quarry was antelope and wild pigs and donkeys, pierced with arrows or javelins, thrown from horseback. The wild meat and most of the herds of cows, ewes and goats were slaughtered in October, because there was no fodder. The flesh was frozen, while the wool was woven into cloth, and the hides cured into armour and boots, tents, saddles and quivers.

The culture depended on animals, particularly the horse, even on the sweet or fermented milk of the mare. And, indeed, a famished Mongol would even lightly slash the jugular vein of his necessary pony to drink its blood *in extremis*. Although small and squat, the steppe horse had a strong neck and a thick hide and elastic powers of endurance through storms, defiles and crags. It required half the fodder and water of the later chargers of the military knights of Europe. The Mongol cavalry rode with remounts, the faster pony for warfare, the slower for carrying arms and provisions. With the invention of the stirrup and the bridle and the bit, warriors would be able to use their carriers as shooting platforms for their small curved bows, plucked so quickly that they could even loose eight arrows in the air before one fell. Their tactics were encirclement and feint and retreat, before a final assault on a scattered and demoralised enemy.

The trails of these herding and raiding tribes would take the horse to India in the south and China in the east. By the Yangzi river, the shaft burial chambers of the Han dynasty with their thousands of terracotta warriors held squadrons of clay cavalry, but also ten chariots and twenty-nine equine skeletons and eleven hunting dogs to escort the imperial majesties on the path to paradise. Equine burial also reached the Caucasus mountains and the Ukraine and Asia Minor in the lands towards the sunset. The ancient Scythian kings were gutted and sewn and preserved with herbs and wax, before they were entombed in a vault under an earth mound, guarded by the strangled and stuffed bodies of fifty cavalrymen along with the bones of their mounts, as an escort to the hereafter.

The cult of the horse extended to Asia Minor, where the Hittites made the light chariot a triumphant weapon of war. Until this time, the lack of writing left no records of such a mobile strategy. But in their campaigns against the Pharaohs, the Hittites and the Hyksōs even occupied Upper Egypt, introducing about 1600 BC the means of a long-range counterattack, the horse and the strong compound Asiatic bow. When the invaders were routed, two Pharaohs struck back as far as Syria, mounted on their swift-moving missile carriers, a driver in the front, an archer and javelin-thrower at the rear. At the battle of Megiddo, Tuthmōsis led his army 'on a chariot of gold, equipped with his panoply of weapons like Horus, brandisher of arms, lord of action'.

At the later struggle of Kadesh, Ramessēs II glorified his role, fighting in his golden corselet 'like Ba'al in his hour' behind his great pair of horses, named Victory. He started at a gallop into the ranks of the foe and found himself surrounded by 2,500 pairs of horses pulling all the enemy champions. 'They were three men to a pair of horses in each chariot, while there was no captain with me, no driver, no soldier, no shield-bearer; my infantry and charioteers melted away before them, not one of these stood his ground to fight.' Although Ramessēs declared in his paean of self-praise carved on a stone relief, that he routed the Hittites single-handed, actually he was saved by a flank attack by his men, while Hittite clay tablets even claimed that Ramessēs suffered a defeat. The graven words of history are so often the propaganda of the past.

The lance and the bow and the bronze dagger and the shield were the weapons in the age of the chariot. Light auxiliary archers were mounted for surprise attacks, but their day was yet to come. In the courtyard tombs of Salamis in Crete, models of horses and chariots of the sun were freighters to the hereafter. The largest of the Cretan tombs of the 7th century BC had two chariots and six horses sacrificed before its stone temple door. Inside the war vehicles were iron-tipped arrows, a quiver and a shield and a sword. They suggested the need for another battle to reach the afterlife. Other carvings or monuments or vase paintings within the ancient Greek sphere of influence showed the connection between water and carriage and sun. The Episkopi sarcophagus depicted a funeral chariot gliding over waves as if a boat. At Kalochorafiti in the Messara, a memorial showed a ship with fish below, while above, a horse-drawn chariot was descending, illuminated by sun-discs and rays.

Moreover, to cattle-herding tribes, the worship of the bull made divine the beast, particularly in ancient Anatolia. There, the mother goddess Cybele gave fertility and inspired oracles and was the spirit of wild nature. Her cult induced ecstatic visions. Her lover Attis was castrated and died and became in myth, as the later Mithras, a sun god. In her rites, 24 March was the Day of Blood, with the sacrifice of many bulls in her temples. Their genitals were carried up in a vessel for use in the ceremonies; later, these testicles would adorn the tunic of the Greek goddess Artemis, the virgin huntress and mistress of childbirth, while the bovine balls ornamented the tops of Ionic pillars and friezes in the Temple of Apollo at Didima. The date 25 March, however, was the Hilaria or Day of Joy, when the beef was consumed in gargantuan feasts.

In their ceremonies in ancient Crete, young men had leapt over the horns of huge bulls, while the mythical founder of Athens, the hero Theseus, redeemed the sacrificial victims of his city by killing the Minotaur, the shag-headed and hoofed and tailed monster at the heart of a maze. That great beast was the offspring of Queen Pasiphae, who had lusted after Poseidon's Bull of the Ocean, meant for sacrifice and not for her bed. Her husband King Midas was the son of Zeus, who had changed himself into a white holy bull to ravish Europa and give a name to a continent.

The Minoans from Crete were the trading partners of the Egyptians. And at Saqqara, near the Nile and the ancient capital of the Pharaohs at Memphis, the persistent bull cult of the Eastern Mediterranean can be viewed in one desert place. Near the original step-pyramid designed by the high priest Imhotep in the 27th century BC, there is the Serapeum, the catacomb of the bulls sacred to the divine Apis, a creative force through which life reached this world. He would later be called by the Greeks Serapis, in a combination with the god of dying and rebirth, Osiris. Off dark vaults, side chambers hold twenty-five huge granite sarcophagi weighing seventy tons apiece. Buried within the tombs for 1,400 years were the mummified corpses of the sacred cattle kept by the priesthood; one pickled beast remains in the Agricultural Museum in modern Cairo. And outside in the desert, a circle of Greek philosophers, now headless, can still be seen, as if in silent approval of the crowds of pilgrims who came there for healing by incubation, or to pay for the oracle to interpret their queries or their dreams.

The worship of the beast dated back to the Babylonians and the Assyrians. The vengeful Bull of Heaven sent by another primal earth goddess Ishtar had been killed by Gilgamesh, who had spurned her divinity and lust. The genitals of the animal were eaten by many worshippers, while a bath in its blood would become a pagan precursor and response to the Christian communion of the Blood of the Saviour. One ancient text stated, 'Reborn into eternity through bull sacrifice'.

Shrines to Apollo and Artemis and their mother Leto were built in swampland to the north of the Athenian colonies of Colophon and Ephesos on the Asian mainland off the islands of Samos and Chios. According to the historian Pausanius, the Clarians claimed to be descended from the Cretans, where Minoan culture stretched back to the 4th millennium BC with its labyrinth and its bull worship. Two

Serapeum altars with drainage to blood baths below have been excavated, but not the hecatomb of the stalls of the sacrificial bulls. And at Claros stood a blue-marble navel stone, the 'ομφαλοε the origin of this earth, also a sundial, to mark the passage of that deity across the sky.

The temple there was so famous as an oracle that the Latin poet Ovid, in exile by the Black Sea, wrote of Clarian Apollo. The inquirers went underground to a vaulted chamber, where a male priest drank from the holy well and answered the question he was posed in a gnomic way. His trance may have been aided by the opium poppy or crushed bay leaves or methane gas from the neighbouring marshes, for shrines to Artemis were located on the margins of land and water. Alexander the Great consulted the oracle before founding Pagos or Smyrna, whose inhabitants had this answer from the priest:

> You shall live three and four times happy
> At Pagos, across the sacred Meles.

And so they did for millennia, although Alexander died young, before he could see his new city grow, while his cavalry tactics would inform the Mediterranean world for many generations.

At neighbouring Ephesos, bulls' heads decorated the assemblies, while a Temple of Serapis lay in the corner of the Agora marketplace. This was a convenient way to combine a place of worship with an *abattoir* and a butcher's shop. And at the hilltop city of neighbouring Priene, the holy area of Demeter, that spreads between the horseshoe theatre and the holy mountain, contained a sacrificial pit. When the killings of living offerings were made to the divinities of the Underworld, the gore from the slaughtered animals was poured over the worshippers – a literal washing in the Blood of the Lamb.

The Mesopotamian, Egyptian and Hellenic mystery religions would become the forerunners of Christianity in some of their beliefs and ceremonies. The fertility rites were matched in the contemporary Orphic mysteries of Dionysus, the overlord of wine and the spirit, whose inscribed seat at Claros is still to be seen. He was a similar god to the Egyptian Osiris and Attis and the Phoenician Adonis. They all died and were born again to become divinities of life and death, giving human beings an assurance of their own immortality. In Greek legend, the body of the child Dionysus was eaten by the Titans, who boiled and spitted and roasted his flesh. This was a communal and cannibal feast.

The Titans were then destroyed by a thunderbolt from heaven, and humanity was born from the ashes. An element of this ancient blood sacrifice would reach the Christian religion.

The celebrants of Dionysus also ate the raw flesh of animals, as he was said to have done: the savage hunter as well as the maker of wine. When his follower Orpheus, with his lyre, was torn apart by the frenzied Bacchantes, his sacrifice was a prelude to eating the divine flesh and drinking the blood in an orgiastic mystery, at which some healing cures of the disturbed and the sick were reported by Plato. The singing head of Orpheus was said to have been washed up at Lesbos; an event celebrated by Milton in his *Lycidas* – another version of the speaking heads of the Celtic gods and Christian martyrs.

The way to heaven was through an ecstatic vision of God. An ascetic life of penance culminated in a religious celebration, in which wine and narcotics were used to induce the vision of the divine. The early ceremonies of the Orphic cult may have included Minoan and Anatolian sacrifices, where the blood of sheep and goats was poured from a jug into a cauldron in the ground. Later Orphics in Roman times were attracted by the Christian communion, when wine was translated into holy blood as a means of absolution, of freeing the spirit from the flesh.

Migrating west across the steppes, the Scythians had reached by 1000 BC the Caucasus and the Crimea and eastern Europe. Four hundred years on, they met Greek colonists on the Black Sea. The interaction between these city-dwellers and the nomadic hunters and herders was significant. On the imperial principle of divide and rule, Scythian archers were recruited as the Athens police. Seen as noble barbarians, they were above partisan squabbles, and as they were slaves, they obeyed those who had bought them. Aristophanes may have lampooned them in his anti-war play *Lysistrata*, in which the violent and anti-sex women stripped the foreign enforcers of their formidable curved bows. On their home ground, however, they were as feared as they were reviled. Incorporated in far places by the Greek and Roman empires for their prowess, the Scythians were shown in their fighting methods on the golden comb from the Solakha burial mound. On that memento, a helmeted and greaved and mailed horseman with his sheathed sword and plunging spear and trousers and boots evidently sprung from the bearded cavalry of the northlands. Such a weapon of a hairdresser matched the nearby grave objects of a Scythian king, which included a bow-case with arrows, and two large shields.

The steppe tribesmen built their own fortified capital on the lower Dnieper river, while the Greeks learned mobile cavalry tactics, which would consign the chariot to obsolescence. The father of Alexander the Great, King Philip of Macedon, killed the Scythian monarch Atheas, who had extended his power as far as the Danube. The armoured royal cavalry of the 2,000 Companions would become the main strike force of Alexander in his future conquest of Asia as far as India. The chief enemy of the Greeks was the Persian Empire. According to Herodotus, the conquering Cyrus the Great had no cavalry and had to create his own mounted troops. In southern Persia, the Karmanians went to war on donkeys. The equipment of these new hussars was listed as a horse and harness, a saddle-cloth and an iron cuirass, a helmet with a felt neck-guard, a shield and an iron club, two javelins and a bow with a quiver holding 130 arrows. While the king himself was still mounted on a huge command chariot, the new heavy cavalry proved its efficacy when Xerxes, the successor of Cyrus, invaded Greece. At Plataea, the mobile invaders cut off the supplies of the Greeks and harassed their line of battle without quite breaking the ranks of the hoplites. In his counterattack on Asia, Alexander would surpass them in mounted action.

Before he invaded Persia, Alexander secured his rear by crossing the Danube to force a truce on the raiding Celts, who were to carry the horse culture further into Europe. After his success, Alexander asked his beaten foemen what they most feared. Instead of replying 'Alexander', they said that they were afraid of the sky falling on them. And so it appeared to the Persian King Darius, when Alexander crossed the Hellespont with 7,000 horsemen, led by the heavy-armed Companions and another 2,000 Paeonians from Thrace with their long light lances. The infantry was composed of 12,000 Macedonian pikemen and shield-bearers, trained in the porcupine phalanx, marching with the same number of Greek foot soldiers. These were supported by two battalions of archers and some 8,000 skirmishers with their slingshots and javelins and stabbing swords, led by the faithful Agriânes. Curiously enough, the core of the Persian troops were Greek mercenaries, recruited from the occupied colonies of Asia Minor and paid from the riches of the treasury at Babylon.

If the initial Macedonian advance into Phrygia had been savaged by hit-and-run tactics, as the apostate Greek general Memnon suggested, Alexander's forces would have been harried into retreat. But on the Granikos river, the Persians stood and fought with 5,000 heavy cavalry on either wing and massed infantry in the centre. Alexander attacked with his light and heavy cavalry, the Paeonians and the Companions. The whole affair was a hacking match of battle-axe and sword, but a final charge of the Greek lancers broke the enemy horde, and the battle ended in a massacre, while Alexander only lost a hundred of his horsemen.

Again on the narrow coastal plain near Issos, a flanking charge by Alexander's cavalry turned on the infantry at the centre, and King Darius himself was forced to flee, leaving his queen and family behind him in the royal tent. In the final climatic conflict at Gaugamêla, another cavalry charge backed by the phalanx at the run broke through a gap in the Persian centre and made Darius flee on a speedy mare. Turning back, Alexander and the Companions had their fiercest combat against the retreating Persian horse, which had broken the Greek lines and now had to fall away after their ruler.

These three pitched battles showed the genius of Alexander in using his horsemen to exploit any weakness in the array of his enemies. Yet now he adopted the mobile tactics, which would have defeated his long advance. He slashed at the remnants of the Persian forces all the way to Babylon, which was abandoned by Darius, taking to the northern mountains with the last 2,000 of his Bactrian horse and his Immortal Guards.

After the winter, Alexander resumed his strategy of strike and surprise. He had to capture or kill Darius. He forced the blocked mountain passes by taking small tracks over the hills in order to attack the enemy in the rear, as the Persians had done to defeat the Spartans at Thermopylae. At Persepolis, Alexander paused to burn down the Palace of Xerxes in revenge, it was said, for the Persian sack of Athens. Here he formed a new regiment of light horse, Asiatic javelin-throwers, and struck after Darius to Ectabana, which the King abandoned, choosing to seek refuge in the wilderness beyond the Caspian Gates.

Alexander's pursuit was relentless, covering nearly 40 miles a day, with his men and horses falling and foundering in his wake. With his advance guard of the Companions and the Lancers, he pushed on day and night, only to discover that Bessos, the leader of the Bactrian cavalry, had made Darius a captive. Alexander overtook them in their flight and found Darius bleeding to death from his wounds in his prison carriage, drawn by mules. Alexander honoured the corpse, commanding that it should lie beside the tombs of other Persian Kings.

What Alexander had demonstrated was that speed and cavalry strikes could destroy an empire. The only defeat suffered by his generals in their long and many campaigns up to the Indus river, where they had to turn back after fighting elephants, was by the nomadic light cavalry under Spitamenes. The Scythians had come from the steppes to the mountains, and at the height of their power, their clans held the wide spaces from the Carpathians to the Don river, and east as far as the Caspian Sea. Sending a column to relieve the besieged city of Samarkand, Alexander found his men wiped out by Spitamenes and 600 mounted archers; the Greeks were ambushed and harried into a massacre. Alexander himself had to relieve his beleaguered garrison, but his Scythian foe had disappeared into the wilds beyond pursuit.*

As the US cavalry on the Great Plains and the British lancers on the *veldt* would later deal with Comanche raiders or Boer *commandos*, so Alexander sent out mobile columns against the Scythian horse, while concentrating their women and children in fortified towns, leaving only scorched earth to feed the enemy. Provoked into a pitched battle against a Macedonian column, Spitamenes lost some 800 riders to a mere forty Greek dead. His starving forces became deserters and killed their commander, sending back his head to Alexander as a trophy of his eventual victory.

One of the bequests of the young emperor Alexander at his death was the strategy of combining the heavy cavalry with the light horse of mounted archers and lancers. His imperial successors would learn again the same lessons. For if we choose to forget the examples of the past, our bitter experience will make us the pupils of our mistakes. The Romans founded their empire on the armoured infantry of the legion. Yet from the earliest days of the city, three hundred mounted lancers, the *equites*, were enrolled, later supplemented by 2,000 more horsemen, pledged to serve in ten campaigns. In the imperial period, the *equites* became an aristocracy, ranking only behind the senators. While they filled many administrative roles, some 400 posts annually were made available, so that they could form an officer corps in the Roman armies.

When the Carthaginian army under the command of Hannibal crossed the Alps, the Celts of northern Italy were almost engaged in the first Sack of Rome. Mostly tall men, they fought with a spear and a long shield and sword, also with bows and slingshots, while Livy described their 'wild outbursts . . . and hideous songs and varied shouts', as they charged into battle with their war chariots. Their horsed warriors both struck from the saddle with its four pommels for stability, and they dismounted to trade blows on foot. Often, two men went into combat on a single steed, one to stand and one to go on riding down the enemy. The chiefs among the Celts wore a chain-mail shirt, which they had invented and bequeathed to the Romans with the word for a mailed knight, a *cataphract*. They were a formidable threat in the Po Valley.

Already engaged in a hit-and-run war against the Romans, the Celts flocked to join the Carthaginian host. At the Ticinus river, the legions of Cornelius Scipio were routed by Hannibal's Numidian cavalry attacking their rear, while the vanguard was cut apart by the Celtic horse. The Roman remnants joined up with a relieving force from Sicily, and with 40,000 men, the two consular armies moved on the enemy, but they were drawn from their camp and ambushed and surrounded. Only half of the Legionaries survived. And the Celts were loosed to forage and burn, as much as they would before a decisive battle.

That conflict would begin at Cannae in 216 BC at the rising of the sun. The Roman commander, Gaius Varro, had 80,000 footsoldiers and 6,000 horse, while the Celtic warriors made up half of Hannibal's 40,000 spearmen and 10,000 horse. Between the horns of two wings of flanking cavalry, the Carthaginian general placed his infantry under orders to fall back as the Roman legions pressed forward. Onto the sides of this extended salient of the enemy, the Celtic and Numidian mounted troops closed the jaws of the trap. Some 50,000 Romans lost their lives in the slaughter, while Hannibal's casualties were one-tenth of that number. After the exploits of Alexander the Great, Cannae was the greatest strategic cavalry victory of its age.

Hannibal dithered and did not march on Rome, and he and his allies were eventually dispersed. The Celtic horse, however, had proved so valiant in the field, that the Romans began to engage them as mounted squadrons to supplement the legions. Although many auxiliaries were raised from Germanic cavalry in Europe and from client kings in Syria and Asia Minor, the historian Strabo preferred the Celts, 'for they are better as cavalry than as infantry, and the best of the Roman Cavalry is recruited from among them'. By the middle of the 2nd century AC, some 200,000 auxiliaries were serving in the armed forces, of which a quarter were mounted.[*] Increasingly, these foreign troops became absorbed in the structure and society of imperial Rome. And significantly, the Celtic horse goddess Epona was now worshipped among the imperial deities.

The strategical importance of light cavalry had been shown by the Parthian defeat of the wealthy consul Crassus in 53 BC in northern Mesopotamia. Under their Kings Mithradates the First and Second, these semi-nomads had seized an empire, which stretched from the Euphrates to the Indus rivers. Renowned for his mailed cavalry or cataphracts, and his horse archers and Nisean horses with a baggage train of 1,000 camels carrying spare arrows, the Parthian emperor Suren ambushed Crassus at Carrhae, now called Harran, and destroyed the whole Roman force. Suren himself was assassinated for appearing to be too powerful after this victory.

The final success of the light chariot and horse was the campaign of the tribal leader Cassivellaunus in 54 BC, on the invasion of Britain by Julius Caesar. As the stirrup was not yet invented, the Roman heavy cavalry in support of the legions was cumbersome. Although Cassivellaunus failed in one attempt on a Roman column, with 4,000 chariots he harried the enemy, advancing north of the Thames River. He was a master of guerrilla tactics and a scorched earth policy. Although Caesar captured the capital and the cattle of the British chief, he had to accept a truce in order to secure his own retreat across the Channel to Gaul.

The revolt of Boudicca of the Iceni in 59 AC heralded the swansong of the chariot with its two ponies and driver and javelin-thrower, but without scythes on its resilient wheels. The Britannic heroine was adept at sacking Colchester and London and Verulamium, but her hordes of missile-carriers broke on the iron walls of the Roman shields and spears and swords, and they melted away into their tribal lands, which were laid waste. Had she adopted the hit-and-run strategy of Cassivellaunus, she might have extinguished foreign rule. But from her, the Romans learned that they needed their own mobile squadrons to put down rebellions and contain sudden enemy incursions and raids.

In the north of Britain in Kintyre, there was already the tribe of the Epidii, 'the horse folk'. When Agricola advanced into the central Highlands, he met in the barbarian chieftain Galgacus a tactician as astute as himself. Retiring and firing the ground in order to deprive the Roman legions and auxiliaries of supplies, Galgacus gave battle on Mons Graupius. The strategy of the Picts was described by Tacitus – the footsoldiers on the hill slopes, their cavalry and chariots on the wings. Julius Caesar had praised the British charioteers for breaking the Roman ranks, then leaving warriors behind to fight on foot. They combined the steadiness of infantry with the mobility of cavalry. But rough ground slowed the wheels of these fighting platforms, and in the shock of close encounter, the Roman short sword proved more effective than the Pictish broadsword. Scattered combats prolonged the battle, until Galgacus withdrew with most of his horde, laying waste to the countryside, so that Agricola was forced to retreat himself to winter quarters. The Highlands remained wild and free.

Although the Romans had defeated the Greeks, they surrendered their education to their slaves. 'When in Rome', the saying went, 'do as the Greeks do.' Zeus became Jupiter and was called the Stone. The strongest oath was *Per Jovem Lapidem,* 'By Jupiter and the Stone'. Both Poseidon and Neptune were worshipped as a square stone, while Hermes and Mercury were represented by a plain standing-stone or a head placed on a square column.

The first oriental divinity accepted in Rome was consulted by the Senate in 205 BC and thought to have won the Second Punic War against Carthage. The Sibylline oracle had declared that Hannibal would be forced out of Italy, if the Mother of the Gods, the Greek Rhea, could be sent from Phrygia to Rome. One more black meteoric stone representing the female principle of creation was delivered by King Attalos of Pergamon and installed in Rhea's temple on the Palatine.

The teachings of Zoroaster and the worship of fire and the sun were now to emigrate from Asia as far west as Britain. The *auxilia* of the steppes were transferred many thousands of miles, so that such mercenaries did not have to fight against their own kinsmen. Their Asian sun-god was called Mithras; his cult derived from India and the Persian Mazdaists, who saw the world as a battleground between the forces of light and good and the powers of darkness and evil. Mithras was identified with the bringer of light to humanity, the mediator in the cosmic struggle. The Greeks called him *Helios* and the Latins, *Sol Invictus,* 'The Invincible Sun'.

The widespread Mithraic chapels of the Roman Empire were often built underground or in caves with the signs of the zodiac, set on mosaic floors. Part of the service was a communion with a consecrated cup and a loaf, symbols of the holy supper which Mithras had taken with the sun after his time on earth. The Christians claimed that the followers of Mithras had stolen their Eucharist, although the reverse might have been true.

We discovered an unknown cult temple in a cave beneath the ruins of a house in Jayce after the war in Bosnia. In the carving, the god can be seen at the ritual sacrifice of a bull with a sun disc behind his loose tunic. A dog swallows the blood of the beast as a symbol of the immortality of the soul. The reptile of resurrection, because it sloughs its skin from a renewed body, the Serpent of Wisdom is shown, turning about the sword-arm of this divine killer.

Mithras was depicted, wearing a Dacian conical helmet with ear-pieces. This confirmed the passage of the light cavalry, who had once fought Alexander the Great, from the steppes through the Balkans as far as Hadrian's Wall in Roman Britain. Indeed, about 175 AC, over 5,000 Sarmatian horsemen reached that frontier, converted to animal god worship. Four Mithras altars and two legionary standards bearing the heads of bulls are still preserved in the museum at Maryport in Cumbria. Rudyard Kipling himself wrote a hymn to the beliefs of the 30th Legion, quartered on the Wall.

> Mithras, the God of the Sunset, low on the Western main –
> Thou descending immortal, immortal to rise again!
> Now when the watch is ended, now when the wine is drawn,
> Mithras, also a soldier, keep us pure till the dawn!
>
> Mithras, God of the Midnight, here where the great bull dies,
> Look on thy children in darkness. Oh take our sacrifice!
> Many roads thou hast fashioned – all of them lead to the Light:
> Mithras, also a soldier, teach us to die aright!

In pagan and Celtic Britain, two major cults were those of the severed head and the horned god. Along with the serpent and the stag, the bull and the ram were the divine symbols. Bulls' heads were also linked with hawks or eagles. The greatest of the supernatural bulls, the Donn of Cuálnge in Ulster, had fifty youths playing on its back or leaping over it as in ancient Crete. An effort to rustle the mighty beast resulted in an Irish civil war.

Iron was the most precious metal of its age, for that mineral made the weapons, by which one tribe destroyed another. Once tempered, the metal was fiercer and harder than the bronze weapons of Homer's heroes. In early Irish history, the Firbolg, who first invaded that island, were miners, who used bronze and iron in their weapons. Pushed out by other invaders from northern Europe, the Tuatha de Damaans, they passed over as Scotti to Dalriada or Argyll and the Borders. There they encountered the Picts, who claimed descent from the Scythians and the Thracians. These cavalry tribes had already been strung along Hadrian's Wall by the Romans, and there they joined units of the Tungri and the Batavians. As the historian Tacitus noted, they were so expert in swimming with weapons and horses that they could cross the Rhine, let alone the Humber or the Tweed. 'There is no strength in the Roman armies, but it is of foreign strangers.'

The Greek Herodotus noted of the mounted Scythians that they were tattooed or painted with woad as were the original Picts, who met the Roman legions. They also cast slender javelins as well as swinging broadswords and heavy rounded spears, the forerunners of the fearsome bills of Border war. They became worshippers of the eastern sun-god Mithras. His weapons in the Zend Avesta were the gold club, the bow and quiver and arrows, and the axe, which slew the sacrificial bull that Zoroaster had called the principle of life in man. In northern Britain, the dog below the Mithraic altar also represented Cu'chulain, the great Irish hero; it was the hound of heaven, and the guide of souls across the divide between earth and sky.

In his account of Agricola on his British campaign, Tacitus alluded to battlefield tactics on the Borders. He claimed that three Batavian and two Tungrian cohorts dismounted and fought the enemy with their round shields, 'for the enormous native swords, blunt at the point, are unfit for close grappling and engaging in a confined space'. The bosses of the iron shields mangled the bare faces of the foe, who broke and ran. In the poem of *Beowulf*, a shield was known as a *hilde-bord*, round and small with hollow metal bosses, tapering to a point or knob, while in Gaelic, a *bord* also signified a shield.

With their iron weapons, the Picts and the Scots were prone to fighting and raiding sheep and cattle. The northern tribes justified their forays by continuing to worship the bull as a god, as can be seen on the seven carved stones retrieved from the ancient fort at Burghead in Morayshire.* When the Mithras cult arrived with the legions at Hadrian's Wall, where a whole temple to the Sungod is still preserved at Housesteads, they found previous worshippers of divine beasts, ready to oppose them. And the Sarmatians, indeed, began to settle near Ribchester and Carlisle, taking their tactics into the inheritance of future Border generations.

In the original Temple of Solomon, twelve bronze bulls had supported a huge basin, full of the waters of life, while live bulls were also sacrificed as burnt offerings to Jehovah. That seminal belief would persist into the visions of the Apocalypse in the Christian Bible, with a bull-headed angel and demon in the *Book of Revelation,* an Apis after the Cross. Even at the time of the Crucifixion, the old animal sacred killings persisted in the Jewish faith. On Yom Kippur, the Day of Atonement, the High Priest entered the Holy of Holies in Herod's vast Temple, which enclosed the smaller one of Zerubbabel on Temple Mount in Jerusalem. He sacrificed a bull in the ancient ritual way as an offering to cleanse the sins of Israel. Then he uttered the Tetragrammaton, the hidden four letters of the name of God, and the people prostrated themselves. Afterwards, two goats were chosen for a holy role. One 'scapegoat' was loosed into the desert to die, while the other was slaughtered to purge the errors of the nation. To this day, Jewish and Muslim people purify their meat by slitting the throats of animals and draining the blood.

Until in the Second Rome of Byzantium, the Emperors Constantine and Justinian imposed a Canon of what should be in the Bible and what not, there was a struggle for centuries over the many texts of the time and their meanings. There was even a revival of paganism under Julian the Apostate, when the Temple of Apollo at Claros was deluged with bull's gore in old ceremonies, only to be cast down afterwards by later imperial decree. The followers of Mithras were wiped out in their own blood.

The carved head of a horned bull-god or Ba'al outside the 15th-century St Clair chapel at Rosslyn, wrongly ascribed to the Muslim devil Baphomet, would demonstrate the persistence of the Mithras cult along the Scottish Borders. From the time of Hadrian's Wall for 1,500 years, the cult of the bull has lingered in cattle-owning societies. During the Roman Empire, the veneration of Apis flourished in southern Gaul, where the initiates were thrown into ditches filled with bovine blood, as a baptism into the immortal life. And gladiators, now called matadors, still fight the mighty beasts in Spain and Provence. The Ba'al at Rosslyn pointed back to millennia of heresy and probably indicated a labyrinth within the chapel, where the Minotaur was replaced by Lucifer and slain in the Mass of the Armed Man.

Early Roman historians had noted that the Germanic horses were inferior in quality, probably due to poor grazing. The tribes across the Rhine estimated their wealth in cattle, and they were prone to raiding for the black beasts and slaves and jewellery under temporary war chiefs, elected by an assembly of warriors in a sacred wood. The leader supplied the weapons, fire-hardened wooden lances and javelins and some swords and axes, for iron was scarce. Often, the cavalry was reduced to throwing stones at the enemy. Although Varus lost three legions to a German ambush, the barbarians were contained in their forests for three centuries by bribes as well as force.

Three waves of horsemen from the steppes and Asia, however, would overwhelm the western Roman empire and split it from the Byzantine east. In an effort to hold together the vast imperial domains, the Emperor Valerian led expeditions against the Goths around the Black Sea, and then against the Sassanid King of Kings, Sapor I, who had struck out from Persia as far as Syria. Although the Roman ally, Septimius Odaenathus with his Queen Zenobia, held Palmyra against the invaders, Valerian was captured in 260 and used as Sapor's footstool at royal feasts. Zenobia then had her husband killed and led her cavalry south to take all Egypt. She was seized in a Roman counterattack and taken back in triumph, but her life was spared. Two recent mosaics uncovered at Palmyra show mythological mounted heroes dispatching with spear and arrow, a chimera and a tiger.

Now the Goths attacked from the plains above the Black Sea, only to be struck in the back by the Huns from the original Mongolian peoples around Lake Baikal. These Mongolian nomads cleft apart their rivals into the Visigoths, who were to establish their rule in Gaul and Spain, also the Ostrogoths, who after 489 would carve out a kingdom in Italy itself. They were only mounted lancers and casters of javelins; they did not have the lethal power of the Hunnish bow; and so they were beaten. The Huns were led by the fearsome Attila, who established a large fief above the Danube, but who was defeated by Flavius Aëtius, allied now to the Visigoths, in 451 at the decisive Battle of the Catalaunian Plains. From this victory, also from Attila's brief invasion of Italy, the Byzantines would learn of the advantages of swift cavalry movements, and they would retake Italy in the middle of the 6th century from the Visigoths, who could not give up their cattle-raiding, even when they were occupying other agricultural countries.

Back in Britain, a legendary cavalry hero arose to combat the immigrant Angles and Saxons and Irish armies. Charging against the invaders in the south, King Arthur won the great battle of Mount Badon. The later of his twelve battles were fought in the Cheviot hills north of Hadrian's Wall. In the *Annales Cambriae*, he was claimed to have brought Christianity to the north about 573 at the battle of Arthuret, later the site of a Templar commandery. The brief ancient chronicler of that fabled cavalry commander, the Welsh monk Nennius, made Arthur unite the Clyde kingdom of Dyfnwal in the early 6th century with the command of Camelot over the West Country and Wales, where he was known as Emrys and given a Celtic ancestry. His defeat came at Camlann, 'in which Arthur and Medraut [Mordred] perished. And there was a plague in Britain and Ireland'. And drawing on the lost work of the Greek historian Olympiodorus, Zosimos recorded that during the reign of the usurper Constantine, the Britons seceded from the Roman Empire, and took up arms to free themselves from the attacks of the barbarians.

Their tactics were commemorated in the Welsh poem, 'The Elegy for Geraint', a prince of Dumnonia or Devon.

> In Llongborth, I saw the clash of swords,
> Men in terror, bloody heads . . .
>
> In Llongborth, I saw spurs
> And men who did not flinch from spears . . .
>
> In Llongborth, I saw Arthur's
> Heroes, who cut with steel . . .
>
> Under the thigh of Geraint swift chargers,
> Long their legs, wheat their fodder,
> Red, swooping like milk-white eagles . . .

There had already been British revolts against the Caesars led by the cavalry of Maximus and Constantinus, whose conquests in Gaul foretold the legend of King Arthur's victories on the Continent. In 429, Germanus, later called Saint Germain in his bishopric at Auxerre, was sent on the first of two visits to Wales to suppress the Pelagian heresy, which was backed by the paramount ruler Vortigern. Faced with an incursion by the Irish and the Pictish Scots, Germanus used his military knowledge to destroy the invaders near Mold in Flint by a charge of warriors shouting 'Alleluia!' After this victory, Germanus was called Harmon in Wales. He set a precedent for later claims that King Arthur won a battle bearing the image of Jesus Christ or the Virgin Mary on his shield.

Yet Germanus failed to root out Vortigern's resistance to the rule of Rome. The Welsh king invited the raiding Saxons to act as his defenders against the Irish, who had already established a beachhead in Wales, and against the Picts in the north. He ceded land and tribute to the Saxons, who were later followed from the Continent by other tribes of Angles and Jutes. The new settlers turned on the natives and destroyed the late Roman urban civilisation of the south-east of England. Gildas also wrote in *The Loss and Conquest of Britain* of 'the general destruction of everything good and the general growth of everything evil throughout the land . . . the barbarians drive us to the sea, the sea throws us back on the barbarians, and so two modes of death await us, we are either slain or drowned'.

The twelve battles, in which Arthur was the victor, can only be surmised as being somewhere on the mainland of Britain. They have variously been sited in Lincolnshire, Northumberland, Cheshire, Strathclyde, Somerset, Wiltshire, Berkshire and East Anglia. Certainly, a defence against the Anglo-Saxon incursion would have involved fighting on a shifting frontier drawn from Devon along the Welsh borders to the Firth of Forth, while the Irish pushing into Pembroke and Argyll implied separate battles on the western shores. These were cavalry actions against foot-soldiers, for Arthur probably took over late Roman tactics. And he was successful, for in the late 6th century *Gododdin*, Arthur was said to be supreme at slaughter and glutting black ravens.

Keeping a force of hundreds of knights in the field involved sophisticated planning and a wandering court. Recent excavations at Cadbury castle and other Iron Age hill forts have shown that Celtic warlords returned to these ancient strongholds behind their ditches and earth walls, adding stone and wooden ramparts along with gate towers and halls. Fodder for the horses was easily found on the hill slopes, although not for long. Surprise attack was unlikely over open ground.

The feudal system was not yet in place, as in the later Grail romances. So the court could not be supported by the local country people for more than a month. King Arthur and his fighters had to ride from place to place to maintain themselves. Even in the late Middle Ages, the royal court was a moveable feast. In Arthur's day, Camelot was on the hoof all over Britain. That palace of later dreams went to where the next campaign was.

The probable sites of Arthur's travelling Camelot were these: the Roman city of Colchester, or Camelodunum, where he would have fought the Saxons in East Anglia; Cadbury Castle, here he might resist any advance into the West Country, with Tintagel as a last bastion; Carleon-on-Usk, where he would have struck against the Irish colony in South Wales; Dinas Bran, near Llangollen, which was called after the Celtic god of the speaking head and was given the name of the

Grail Castle Corbenic in medieval times; Carlisle, where he would have contained the Danish invaders; and Arthur's Seat near Bewcastle and in Edinburgh, where he would have opposed the Picts from the north, and from the west the Irish, then called the Scotti. The necessity of feeding the cavalry would have kept Arthur in the saddle, as it did the original Celts of the Russian steppes, who had fought another legendary hero, Alexander the Great.

Tactics insist on movement. That was why the ancient chronicles and Grail romances altered places and names so frequently. And as these sagas and accounts were usually sung or spoken by many voices before they were set down in writing, the variations in spelling and in translation eddied as banners in the wind. What is certain is that the truth of Arthur was taken up by the Celtic bards to create the legend of a conquering hero, who would reflect his fame on to his people.

Already by the 7th century, four British royal families had given a son the name of Arthur. He became the Matter of Britain, as opposed to the Matter of France, which glorified Charlemagne, the supreme Emperor. And there was also the Matter of the classical age of Homer and Virgil, the heroes of Troy and Rome, and of Alexander the Great. These bardic tales would provide the synthesis of the European romances of the Middle Ages, where the Eastern traditions met the British, French and German to create the stories of knights on horseback, seeking conquests and glory, and occasionally the divine.

North of Hadrian's Wall, the cavalry strategy of the Roman auxiliaries and King Arthur had already affected the methods of fighting by the local tribes. Writing in the middle of the 6th century, the British monk Gildas had condemned 'the foul hordes of Scots and Picts . . . two exceedingly savage overseas nations, like dark throngs of worms who squirm out of narrow cracks in the rocks [to rend] their foe like lambs by the butcher'. The Romans had connected the Picts with the Celtic Scythians, who had encountered Alexander the Great, while the Scots derived from Hibernia or north-eastern Ireland. They could muster an army of some 2,000 men, while the Pictish warbands could command much the same number. They were accomplished metal workers, although iron was in short supply; their sculpted stones showed anvils and hammers and tongs. They were aided by the Celtic missionaries. Adomnán, the biographer of St Columba, referred to making blades for weapons. 'Skilled monks softened the metal of that dagger in a hot fire, and distributed it by welding it onto all the iron tools of the monastery.'

The northern British raiders were usually on foot, but also mounted on the ponies, spreading up the grasslands from Hadrian's Wall. As well as short swords and small round or square wooden shields with thrusting iron bosses, the warriors were equipped with lances and javelins and spears; a bronze apple butt at the end of the shaft was used as a club. They also carried primitive crossbows or curved bows along with slingshots and stones, battle-axes and dirks. Only the nobles wore mail armour, while the lesser fighters were clad in byrnies or leather jerkins and occasional helmets. The Aberlemno carved stone showed mounted Picts engaged in battle, while the Welsh epic *Gododdin* confirmed a Pictish mounted mercenary prince on the Catreath raid. Certainly, these Border pony-riders were the ancestors of the later Reivers, although their lack of saddles and stirrups made them inefficient as war machines. Unlike the Scythians, indeed, the archers on Sueno's Pictish Stone are shown as dismounted, while they target a group of six horsemen in flight. The war chariot, however, was still in use, although it was ineffective against the early shield wall.

According to the first British historian of importance, the Venerable Bede, Pictish seafarers had sailed from Scythia in a few longships before arriving in Ireland and on the Borders. Before the advent of the Vikings, their fleets of up to one hundred and fifty ships dominated the sea coasts as far as Orkney and the Western Isles. Seven-bench rowing and sailing ships could hold a crew of forty-five men on incessant piratical expeditions. As with the land forces, the chosen plunder was in precious or other metals, slaves and cattle and sheep. The reiving tradition was the dominant male way of life, while the women tended the shifting farms and villages at home. Yet in the east would rise another mounted and seaborne culture, which would dominate an environment, almost the size of a continent.

CHAPTER TWO

Islam and Norman

The fresh nomad conquerors to create an empire were the tribes of the desert. For the Arabs, the horse proved mightier than the camel. From the earliest rock art of the Sahara and from the Greek historian Herodotus, we know that cattle and the horse-drawn war chariots preceded the coming of the dromedary. Indeed, there are engravings of mounted throwers of javelins and of ox-carts, before the Bedouin brought the swift camel to the western wastes of Africa. That beast was quicker and better scudding over the dunes, but as a war platform in close combat, it was inferior to the horse, and more suited to serve as a baggage carrier for infantry and weapons.

The rise of the Arab empire in the 7th century across western Asia and the coasts of the Mediterranean was a classic example of sparse nomad tribes, which became in a brief period a sophisticated culture, based on old and new cities. The success of Islam lay in its primal purity and its plain and simple rules, which appealed to those who lived close to survival between the stars and the sand. Without falling into the causalities of an Aristotle or a Montesquieu and claiming that countries derive their governments from their climates, we may argue that the conflicts between the people of the forest and of the plain, the people of the interior and of the coast, the people of the city and of the desert have much to do with environment as well as economics.

Six centuries may divide the Arab historian Ibn Khaldun from the French historian Braudel, but both would agree on the reason for the success of the Muslim faith. Islam was 'the desert, the emptiness, the ascetic rigour, the inherent mysticism, the devotion to the implacable sun, unifying principle on which myths are founded, and the thousand consequences of this human vacuum. In the same way, Mediterranean civilisation grew up under the determining influence of the emptiness of the sea; one zone peopled by ships and boats, the other by caravans and nomad tribes. Islam, like the sea and like the desert, implies movement.'

A place influences its people, new or old. The invader becomes the settler and finally the native. Cultures derive from their countries. At bottom, as Braudel wrote, a civilisation is attached to a distinct geographical area, and this is itself one of the indispensable elements of its composition. Another element of a civilisation is its exclusion from power and influence of those peoples who do not share its language, beliefs and boundaries. The prophet Muhammad had founded Islam by a unique art of exclusion and aggression, more sweeping than any Chinese contempt of the barbarian or Christian condemnation of the pagan. When he formed his first religious community or *umma* at Medina after his withdrawal from Mecca, he divided humanity into the *Dar al-Islam* and the *Dar al-Harb*. Those who did not dwell in the Abode of Islam – and these only numbered a few hundred at the time – dwelt in the Abode of War. This commandment was not a matter of stating that those who were not for Islam were against Islam; it was a declaration of holy war against all unbelievers. Muhammad's attacking faith inspired a divided group of tribes, the Arabs, into acquiring a Mediterranean empire in less than a century. As Ibn Khaldun noted, a Christian then could not even float a plank in that sea.

During the 'Dark Ages' of Europe, when the invading forest and plains tribes lost the urban habits of the Roman Empire and when the farms of the colonists reverted back to the woodlands, Arab civilisation reached its height. Ibn Khaldun may have imitated Tacitus in extolling the warlike and savage virtues of the wandering Bedouin and Berbers in contrast to the urban vices and luxuries of the ruling Arab families, who were slowly weakened until they 'fell into a long sleep in the shadow of glory and peace'. Yet the fact was that the extraordinary achievements of the Arabs in medicine, chemistry, physics, botany, astronomy, mathematics and, above all, in clinical observation could only have been fostered by these enlightened urban centres and courts. The Christian counter-attack on Islam, which would be called the Crusades, was a barbaric assault on a cultured people, who both beat off and instructed their attackers. Without Arab science as the intermediary between Greek method and Renaissance enquiry, the technological explosion of Europe would have been impossible.

Two traditions of horsemanship were developing within the Arab world and Africa as well as in eastern and western Europe.* As the wise writer on *Man and Culture* noted of the early times of equine societies:

The horse was a different thing to the wild nomad, on the one hand, and the Egyptian [or the civilised man], on the other. To the Egyptian he was a mere fighting machine and so but a military incident in Egyptian life, but to the nomad, the horse was as much a part of individual life as his master's boots. From what glimpses we have of the ancient nomad life it seems that everybody rode at all times, in fact lived on horseback. Hence, for the nomad to fight as cavalry was the natural or only way, for the truth of the matter is that his whole life was adjusted to the horse rather than to fighting. When he moved about, he rode; when he indulged in sport, he also rode; and when he met with dangers, the chances are that he was mounted.*

In the 8th century in Spain, the light cavalry of Islam had struck from North Africa and defeated the heavy cavalry of the Visigoths, who dominated the Iberian Peninsula. The northern armoured horsemen depended on the spear and the javelin, while the Saracens as angry hornets stung them with arrows, fired from the saddle. Breaking through the Pyrenees, the Islamic armies descended on the Gallic plains, where a decisive battle heralded the past and the future. Usually in a pitched battle, the Greek phalanx and the Roman legion, and the later Saxon shield-wall and the Scots schiltron, human redoubts bristling with pikes and spears, pricked and battered the charge of barbarian light cavalry into destruction. And so it was again at Poitiers in 732, when the standing knights of the Franks overwhelmed the riders of the scimitar and the curved bow. Such weapons and Parthian tactics had previously destroyed the Roman legions in the near East, but now Charles Martel with his Austrasians announced the future supremacy of heavy armoured men, the tanks of their time. The mobile cavalry of the Saracens charged the massed Frankish ranks and were slaughtered. As one chronicler related:

> The men of the north stood motionless as a wall; they were like a belt of ice frozen together, and not to be dissolved, as they slew the Arabs with the sword. The Austrasians, vast of limb and iron of hand, hewed on bravely in the thick of the fight; it was they who found and cut down the Saracen King.

As the Byzantines had done, Charlemagne's forces and the later Franks would use both the heavy-armoured knight, and also lighter-armed mounted archers as skirmishers.* In a summons to arms, the Holy

Roman Emperor demanded a muster of the knights from Saxony, 'so that each horseman shall have a shield, lance, sword and dagger, bow and quivers with arrows'. These requirements may well have been a counter-measure against the steppe bowmen on their ponies, the Avars, who were piercing the eastern imperial frontiers, and following the example of the Hunnish forays into Europe.

The Franks would develop into the mailed knights of European expansion. Yet another sea-borne and horseless race would carve out a brief ascendancy of armour and the broadsword. The raids of the Vikings on Ireland and Scotland, England and France devastated the defenceless cultures, which fell before their axe and blade and fire. Britain was totally unprepared for the assault, for the country had no competitive navy. The great monasteries of Iona and Jarrow and Lindisfarne had been built on islands or by the mouths of rivers, as had other rich towns. The plunder was enormous, the defences negligible against the crews of the dragon ships. Then the invaders began to settle in the middle of England, in what would become known as the Danelaw.

They met the first English King of power and presence, Alfred of Wessex. After initial defeats, he and his thanes fell back on the Somerset marshes, merely harassing the advancing mailed infantry, as Cassivellaunus had harried the legions of Julius Caesar. Using some cavalry and his foot-soldiers, Alfred beat the Danes in a series of battles, forcing them back towards East Anglia. He was also credited with forming an embryonic Royal Navy, as well as creating through wise administration an entity that might be called the English nation. He was the Charlemagne of a third of an offshore European island.

The Vikings were not only pushing down to Normandy and into the Mediterranean through the Straits of Gibraltar, but also down the great western rivers of the steppes, the Vistula and the Volga. These northern raiders and traders had reached the Black Sea and Byzantium. They were assaulted on their ships by mounted tribal archers, deluging them with a hail of arrows, although intermarriage also took place in the settlements along their portage. The Vikings were fatalistic about their endings, as could be seen in the burial ceremonies of the Scythians and the Rus along the Volga river. At the barrow of Kostromskaya, twenty-two slain horses faced away from the interior burial chamber with its arrow and spear heads; armour and pots and grindstones surrounded the skeleton.

Human sacrifice was an element in the Viking expansion through Russia to the Mediterranean. In the first half of the 10th century, the traveller Ibn Fadlan described the Scandinavian Rus as sacrificing men and women and cattle to their gods. If a poor man died, he was burned in a small boat. If a chief died, everybody became drugged or drunk. After heaping a huge ship funeral pyre with the bodies of animals, the kinsmen raped a slave girl with the words, 'Tell your master that I have done the duty of love and friendship.' Then she was strangled and stabbed by an old woman, representing the Angel of Death, to be the companion of the chief in the afterlife. One of the kinsmen told Ibn Fadlan that the Arabs were fools. 'You take the dear people you honour and put them in the ground for the insects and the worms. We burn our man in a moment, so he can enter Paradise at once.'

This Nordic way of war was preserved in poetry and song. Even the Roman historian Tacitus wrote of the ancient songs of the Germanic tribes, their only historical tradition. In *Beowulf*, naturally, we learn of the armour and swords and fighting prowess of the Danes, as Homer had recorded the war materials and tactics of the Greeks and the Trojans. When Beowulf's men grounded before the hall of Hrothgar to fight against the monster Grendel, their weapons were marked by the poet:

> Their shirts of mail-gleam,
> Hard-linked by hand; the shining iron
> Ringing in sheathing. So they came to the hall
> In their grim-grey warmongering
> From the sea's roistering, stacking the wall
> With wide oak shields, hardened by firing.
> Then they fell on the trestles, the armour
> Clashing with broadswords. Their spears
> Of ash were left tapering in a stand,
> The soldiers as iron as their arms. Then a Dane
> Asked the men, 'Where do you come from?
> Whence these painted shields and shirts of link-mail,
> These helmets with cheek-guards, and these javelins?'

Later, after King Athelstan invaded Scotland in 934 in one of many successive Border wars, the first of the ballads of these conflicts was written in Anglo-Saxon, *The Battle of Brunanburh*. It was again a tribute to tactics and weapons:

> In this year king Athelstan, lord of warriors,
> Ring-giver of men, with his brother prince Edmund,

> Won undying glory with the edges of swords,
> In warfare around Brunanburh.
> With their hammered blades, the sons of Edward
> Clove the shield-wall and hacked the linden bucklers,
> As was instinctive in them, from their ancestry,
> To defend their land, their treasure and their homes,
> In frequent battle against each enemy.

At a sea-battle won by Erik Bloodaxe, then the ruler of York, the poet Egil Skalla-Grímsson, gave a magnificent description of combat by missiles:

> Darts splintered and points bit;
> Bow-strings sped arrows from the bow.
> The flying javelin hit, peace was broken;
> The elm-bow was spanned, the wolf rejoiced at it,
> The leaders of the host defied death,
> The yew-bow twanged when swords were drawn.
> The prince bent the yew, wound-bees flew,
> Erik offered corpses to the wolves from his sea-fight.

Such later heroes as Haraldr Sigurøarson, the later King Hardrada III of Norway, voyaged through Poland and Russia, and he composed a poem on his sailing in to Byzantium:

> The cool wind drove swiftly
> The black prow of the ship
> The iron-clad vessels
> Held up their masts in splendour
> The great king saw the metal roofs
> Of the city gleaming ahead . . .

With his men, Haraldr was taken into the service of the Emperor Michael IV to command the Varangian Guard. He was sent to Palestine, and he helped to take back Jerusalem into the Christian faith. Before the Knights Templars, his saga stated that he 'made an offering at the grave of Our Lord, and to the Holy Cross, and to other holy relics in Jerusalem, of so much money in gold and jewels that it is hard to compute the amount; he also put the entire way to Jerusalem at peace, slaying robbers and other evil folk'.

Haraldr's major campaigns were against fellow Vikings, the Normans who had conquered Sicily and Southern Italy. On one campaign, he wrote back to his queen:

> The ship was filled with blood
> By the cape where blood blew;
> The ships ran to the shore,
> The Lord fought nobly . . .
> The bodies of the dead let the blood
> Pour onto the planks of the keel.

After imprisonment on a charge of fraud, Haraldr broke back to Norway, where he became King Hardrada III, before invading Northumbria in 1066. There he was confronted with his host at Stamford Bridge by the English King Harold with his mailed infantry of the axe and the broadsword and the spear. The Norse King had drawn his men up in a bristling shieldburg. Although English cavalry attacks did not break the metal ring, the flight of many arrows did. Provoked, the huge Hardrada led an attack on the English spearmen and almost hacked his way through the lines before being killed by a shaft through the throat – an uncanny prophecy of King Harold's own tactics and death against the Normans. And so Hardrada achieved what his mounted rival had promised: 'seven feet of English ground, or as much more, as he may be taller than other men'.

With more forced marches, King Harold returned to the southern coast to confront at Hastings another sea assault from William, Duke of Normandy. Now he adopted Viking tactics. Between two tracts of sea marshes, he blocked the Norman advance on London with a wall of the long yellow and red shields of his house carls, wearing helmets and hauberks, and armed with battle-axes and maces. Behind them were thousands of levies, carrying bills and scythes and clubs. There were few bowmen or horsemen.

William led off with an attack by his archers whom the *Chansons de geste* said were responsible for the victory; but the shield wall held firm. A second assault by his men-at-arms with their spears was repulsed by thrown axes and javelins and stones. This was followed by repeated cavalry charges with lances, but these also failed. For the great battle-axes of the thanes could cut off a leg or a head of an armoured knight at a stroke, as can be seen on the Bayeux Tapestry, woven and thick with lopped limbs.

Either by a stratagem or the need to regroup, the Norman horsemen withdrew. The shield wall broke ranks in a rush after the defeated foe. But when the pursuers were killed, more Norman charges uphill were unsuccessful, except on a wavering left flank. Turning to meet this weakness, King Harold was killed in a cloud of arrows, fired high over the shield wall, or in a last stand around his raised ensign, The Fighting Man. The following massacre of his forces in retreat showed the superiority of heavy cavalry in most of the routs of the Middle Ages.

William, Duke of Normandy, thus became King of England. With his professional mailed knights and a system of fortifications and the feudal system, he would establish a successful European strategy for warfare and government, which would endure until the coming of cannon and gunpowder. The broadswords and the axes and the foot soldiers would win few victories against the armed men on their chargers, backed by spearmen and the terrible archers of the longbow, which could pierce chain mail a hundred yards away, without mercy or redress.

The tribes, from where the horse culture had begun 3,000 years before this battle, would now have a terrible and invigorating effect on the arable and urban civilisations of Asia and eastern Europe. First called Tartars, and later Mongols and Turks, these associated tribes and clans were not entirely nomadic cattle and sheep herders. From the cities of central Asia, they needed to acquire metalwork and weapons, linen clothes and carpets and embroideries and household ware. In return, they exchanged horses and furs and slaves, beef and mutton. They had established markets before their great raids upon the west. The opportunity of the Mongolian tribes in their escape from a survival economy lay in the decline of feudal China and the corruption of the urban Near East. Only by conquest could they escape from their destiny, which was summed up in the proverb, 'the steppe is wide and heaven is far'.

The Franciscan monk, John of Plano Carpini, described the resources of the Mongol cavalryman. The crown of his helmet with earflaps was made of metal. His armour was several plates of overlapping leather, while he carried a light and heavier bow with three quivers and two different sorts of arrow, one of them for close combat. His lance was long, his sabre slightly curved, while an axe and a lasso completed his armament. He was his own repairer, with a sharpening stone and kettle and file. His rations were dried meat and curdled milk and a leather waterbag and a sack. In crossing rivers, the inflated sack supported the supplies and weapons, while the rider guided his swimming horse across the torrent.

Tactically, the Mongols advanced in a wide swathe. When the enemy tried a pitched battle, they withdrew. If they stood and seemed to fight, the light cavalry was put on the wings and in the vanguard. The mounted archers pricked the foe with a hail of light arrows, four to a minute, before they peeled away. Then the heavy Mongol horse attacked at full bellow with sabre and lance. If their charge failed, they did not engage in hand-to-hand combat, but they split open their ranks to allow the enemy a way through. The residue of the opponents could be picked off later in the day.

The Mongols were adept at deceit, using dummies on horses to suggest great reserves, and lighting torches at their night camp to treble their apparent numbers. When they took prisoners, these were marched in front of the army to increase the ranks of auxiliaries. At first, the Mongols were incapable of taking walled cities, but they learned, in their conquest of Chinese and Arab civilisations, the use of battering-rams and catapults and mines. They were capable of infinite adaption and recruitment through fear. For the whole population of Mongolia in the 13th century was hardly half a million people, and yet they managed to occupy most of Asia as far as the Vistula river at the end of the steppes.

While the assault of Europe on Islam in the Crusades was defeated, Ibn Khaldun was proven correct. The Arabs were 'all softened, even the cutting edge of their swords'. Civilisation is too often the pander of its own downfall. If the early Islamic conquerors were fierce and ruthless in their nomadic assaults across the deserts of the Near East and North Africa, the later Arab rulers were to be destroyed by the savage hordes of the Turks and the Mongols. It is interesting that, at one point, the Arabs actually defeated the T'ang Empire at the Talas river and forever prevented the expansion of China, while converting Central Asia to Islam. Yet they had no forests as the North Europeans had to defend them from the Mongol horsemen, when these came across the plains and over the mountains to reduce many of the cities of Asia to dust and total massacre. Genghis Khan, indeed, so hated urban culture that he had to be dissuaded from returning the whole of northern China to pasture for his war horses. Even Ibn Khaldun would not have praised such warrior virtue.

Except for the Turks, who were to defeat the Byzantines and form an enduring empire in Eastern Europe and Asia Minor and Egypt, the Mongol horse under their conquerors Genghis Khan and Tamerlane and Khubilai Khan would lose China and Central Asia. At the end of the day, a nomadic and herding assault culture would be penetrated by the subtle skills of the city civilisations, which they overwhelmed, but which assimilated them and tamed the whirlwind. The Alexandrian poet Cavafy best put the fear and the stimulus, which a decaying urban culture perceived in 'Expecting the Barbarians':

What are we waiting for, assembled in the public square?

The barbarians are to arrive today.

. . .Because night is here but the barbarians have not come,
Some people arrived from the frontiers,
and they said there are no longer any barbarians.

And now what shall become of us without any barbarians?
Those people were a kind of solution.

CHAPTER THREE

Crusade and Cossack

Most unfortunately, one of the Reivers' Trails would point towards Jerusalem. For the medieval crusader, plunder was the reward of his faith. As the result of his endeavours, he wished to own and loot all he could in the name of God. And for militant Christianity, the prologue was fought in Spain, where victory would lead to the expulsion of Islam from European soil. The *reconquista* by the Iberian northern kingdoms began before the crusading movement, and was mightily helped by it. The idea of a continual holy war promoted by the Papacy, the Frankish knights and the Cluniac monks provided spirit and recruits for the cause. Many crusades passed through the Spanish peninsula on their way to Palestine and never reached their goal, fighting their Muslim adversaries on the way and remaining to occupy the hard-won lands.

Both the Knights Templars and the Hospitallers were originally welcomed as ascetic warriors against the Moors, but these Military Orders were largely replaced by home-grown varieties. For the emphasis of the primary Orders was still on the Holy Land. Spain was a place to stop off, not to defend. The Knights of Calatrava took over that abandoned frontier fortress from the Templars. They were originally Cistercian monks, who had put on the sword. By the 13th century, they had become the effective standing army of the kingdom of Castile.

The other leading Spanish Order was the Knights of Santiago, formed to protect the pilgrims on their way to pray at the shrine of Saint James at Compostela. Their duty, according to the Archbishop of Toledo, was the sword of defence. 'The sword reddens with the blood of Arabs, and faith burns bright with the love of their mind.' Their rule was adopted from the Templars, but they were allowed to marry and have families and personal possessions, although these were surrendered to the Order on the death of each knight. They transcended the borders of Spain, reaching France, Italy, Hungary and Palestine.

The frontier war with Islam in Spain led to a continuous crusade. A class of popular knights emerged, any Christian who had enough money to buy weapons and a horse. They were known as *caballeros villanos*, and these medieval cowboys often reached a noble status by their deeds. A successful mounted warrior could aspire to high estate. The Spanish frontier was an early version of the American frontier, with the Moors playing the role of the Plains tribes. It produced the virtues of an independent raiding society, which built communities and cities behind its forays and its new castles.

The conquest of the interior of Spain, which effectively excluded the Muslims to the kingdom of Granada in the south, was a looting expedition and a migration, helped by ethnic clearance. 'Waves of friars, contemplatives, military monks, canons, parish priests, and nuns, transported like a numerous garrison into this borderland, gave tangible shape to the Christian self-image, making it a living thing.' The Word of Christ was imprinted upon the land through its new settlers, although tolerance was ordered by a royal edict. 'We decree that Moors shall live among the Christians in the same way that . . . Jews shall do, by observing their own law and not insulting ours.'

Versions of the epic medieval *Song of Roland* were already being sung at the time of the First Crusade towards Jerusalem, and these gave the best contemporary insight into the barbaric and fearful and proud temperament of the European knight. Recalling a defeat by Charlemagne in his campaign against the Ummayads in Spain, the destruction of Roland's rear guard at Roncesvalles in a Basque ambush was translated into a heroic slaughter of the Muslim hordes and the martyr's sacrifice of a hero through betrayal. This legendary epic was shot through with the silk and blood of the period. It was a declaration of a holy war against Islam, in which chivalry was restricted to the knights on both sides, while there was no mercy for the rest of humanity. Those who died in Charlemagne's cause would enter the gates of Paradise, as the sanguinary Archbishop Turpin promised. 'Infidels are wrong and Christians are in the right,' Count Roland proclaimed. 'I will set no bad example.' Killing a few hundred Muslims with his sword Durandal, Roland thought a good example, even though he condemned himself and his 20,000 men to death by refusing to summon help from Charlemagne with his horn.

Without faith, the First Crusade of 1097 would never have reached the Holy Land or taken Jerusalem. The multitudinous rabble of Peter the Hermit was totally destroyed; but the three following professional forces of Frankish knights fared better in classic encounters of the heavy-armoured horsemen against Balkan and steppe light cavalry. In Bulgaria, the Norman Prince Bohemond of Taranto swam across the icy river Vardar with 2,000 warriors to surprise and defeat the mounted archers of the Mongolian Patzinak mercenaries in the service of the Byzantine imperial army At the succeeding battle of Dorylaeum, the Christian vanguard was entrapped by circling Turkish bowmen, but an advancing column led to an assault, which put the enemy to flight. Failing to use guerrilla tactics to hinder the march of the crusaders through the mountains of Asia Minor, the Turks fell back on their great citadel city at Antioch, which was besieged in winter. There, seven hundred crusading knights at the charge surprised and defeated a relieving army, caught in narrow ground between lake and river. Antioch later fell, and it was successfully defended, after the discovery of the Holy Lance, said to be the one which had pierced the side of Christ on the Cross.

On their chosen battlefield, the Frankish cavalry were irresistible, set against the mounted archers and lancers of the Muslim forces, although these were later recruited as mercenaries by the crusaders under the name of Turcopoles. The knights wore a conical steel helmet with a chain-mail tunic over a quilted shirt, padded breeches and a long shield. Their weapons were the lance, the two-edged broadsword and the mace. On the march, they rode an old horse or a mule, keeping their huge warhorses ready for the shock of the fray. Their infantrymen were a protective cordon, wearing quilted chestpieces and armed with spears and battle-axes and crossbows. They faced an elusive enemy, who wanted to overwhelm with a rain of arrows before closing in for the kill by scimitar or yataghan. The quarry was the horse, for without that mount, nobody could assault or escape.

The seizing of Jerusalem and its recapture after a battle by Saladin ninety years later were set-pieces in the endless wars between static conflicts, which gave the Franks the advantage, and continual harassment, which favoured the light and mobile Muslim forces. The garrison of Jerusalem was encircled by the crusaders, who were provoked by the minarets, which signalled the Muslim occupation of the Holy City. The infidel was translated into the devil, because he was polluting the holy places with pagan temples and presence. No more than the Muslims could have tolerated a cathedral beside the Ka'aba at Mecca could the Crusaders accept the sight of the Dome of the Rock crowning Jerusalem. A sudden fervour and fanaticism inspired the Christian host to an extraordinary assault on a complacent enemy, which had not yet seen that it was engaged in a *jihad*, not of its choosing.

The siege of the Holy City lasted for forty days, the period that Christ had spent in the wilderness. The Crusaders followed the example of the Israelites before the walls of Jericho. The army went in procession seven times around Jerusalem. The soldiers walked with bare feet and sang hymns. They halted at the holy places outside the city where Peter the Hermit and the other priests preached the deliverance of the Church of the Holy Sepulchre. Two siege towers had been prepared to back the sermons. The Christians launched themselves against the fortifications and were repulsed. Holy rituals and observances were not enough to win Jerusalem. Its walls had not tumbled down like those of Jericho at the blast of the psalms and the trumpets.

Stupidly, the Sudanese and Egyptian garrison had answered the Christian ceremonies with boorish insults, desecrating crosses stolen from churches and shouting obscenities against the infidels outside. This inflamed the fervour of the Crusaders. As William of Tyre wrote: 'Their hearts swelled with desire to avenge this shame done to Jesus Christ.' They advanced their wooden siege towers, lined with flayed hides soaked in vinegar to protect them from the defensive mixture of oil and sulphur called Greek fire, which had been prepared by the Fatimid commander Iftikhar. Reinforcements from Egypt were on their way. The Crusaders had to take the city or be destroyed, as at Antioch. In the words of the Arab historian Ibn al-Athir:

> Of the two siege towers constructed by the Franj, one was on the side of Mount Zion to the south, while the other was to the north. The Muslims succeeded in burning the first one, killing all those who were inside. But they had only just finished destroying it when a messenger came asking for help. The city had been breached on the opposite side. In truth, it was taken from the north, one Friday morning, seven days before the end of Sha'ban [in July, 1099].

Iftikhar with his picked troops had established his command post in the octagonal Tower of David, the hinge of the fortifications. The Christians led by Godfrey de Bouillon had crossed from their mobile tower near Herod's Gate. Flemish and Walloon soldiers occupied the northern walls, and then poured into the interior of the city, driving back the demoralised defenders before them. The Muslims fell back towards the al-Aqsa mosque, which they trusted for protection from this barbarous onslaught. And now in the south, the troops of the Count of Flanders and the Duke of Normandy, of Tancred and of Baldwin, broke through and continued the massacre. Iftikhar saw that the Holy City was lost. He surrendered to Raymond, Count of Toulouse, in return for a safe conduct for him and his men. 'The Franj kept their word,' Ibn al-Athir noted with surprise, 'and let them leave by night for the port of Ascalon, where they set up camp.'

Such wise mercy was the prelude to an orgy of destruction that shamed Christendom and led to a *jihad* against the crusaders as well as confirming the pogroms of the pilgrims against the Jews in Germany. There was a slaughter of the Muslims, who had taken refuge in the al-Aqsa mosque, 'more than seventy thousand of them', according to Ibn al-Qalanisi, although he exaggerated the numbers of the victims. And all the Jews, who crowded into their synagogue, were burned alive. William of Tyre did show disquiet, writing that 'the city offered such a spectacle of the massacre of enemies, such a deluge of bloodshed, that the victors themselves could not help but be struck with horror and disgust'.

In spite of religious fervour and rapacity which inspired the Crusaders, divine greed could not sustain them in the Holy Land. There were too few of them on the ground, while many of these few could not tolerate eastern conditions. They existed, anyway, on the disunity and the tolerance of the Muslims. When Saladin brought his peoples together and recaptured Jerusalem, the sacred purpose of the Crusades was over. Some thousand mounted Franks with 5,000 auxiliaries had held four principalities in the Near East for a century or so. They were out of place, unable to colonise. The Muslims were in their homelands. 'The weather was natural to them,' Richard of Devizes noted, 'the place was their native country. Labour was their health, frugality was their medicine.'

If the Crusaders taught the Arabs the shock of a heavy cavalry charge, the great Kurdish commander known as Saladin proved time and again the value of mounted archers and lancers, harrying the slow marching Christian columns, as falcons swooping on their prey. Although the invaders had their light cavalry of the Turcopoles, who were the skirmishers, they were vastly outnumbered by Saladin's army, moving at speed over desert and rocky ground. The Muslim lancers in black rode ahead, flanked by scouts searching out an ambush, while the train of camels was in the rear.

Spearmen, javelin-throwers and axemen would be carried two at a time, one on each side of a camel in panniers, in addition to baggage. Some just ran to keep up with the horses and now and again were allowed to beg a lift, one foot in the stirrup. Others rode tandem. March discipline was maintained by the beating of drums, and drums gave the signal for breaking camp. This was in the very early morning to avoid the heat which could be intolerable, particularly if the early summer wind – the *khamseen* – was blowing, when dust turned the sun to orange and the way ahead was obscured.

In his conflicts with the Crusaders, Saladin used the false retreat, with his centre taking flight before the charge of the armoured Christian knights, who were then enveloped by the left and right wings of the Muslim horse. Closing on the surrounded heavy Frankish cavalry, the result of the battle lay in combat at close quarters, a stabbing and hacking of lance and sword, axe and club. The advantage of the Saracens was in their mounted archers, while the Italian crossbowmen were flat-footed, incapable of scattering before an assault. Even if his ranks were broken, Saladin was a master of the rally and the quick counter-attack. And in 1187, at the Horns of Hattin, he destroyed the whole Christian army by driving it onto waterless ground, surrounding it and peppering the thirsty infidel men and horses with clouds of arrows. Two desperate charges by the Military Orders nearly reached the Sultan's tent, but they were overthrown. As the chronicler Imad al-Din noted, the mailed Frankish knight was invulnerable, but he fell with his horse. 'Although they numbered thousands, there were no mounts in the booty.' The dying horses were all brought down with their masters, still alive on their backs.

The chivalry of the armoured knight was a recognition of the value of the horse in war. Encased in mail and mounted on his charger, one knight could overwhelm a hundred foot-soldiers. A cult of the tamed beast arose, which was echoed in God's words to Job:

> The glory of his snorting is terrible.
> He paweth in the valley, and rejoiceth in his strength:
> He goeth out to meet the armed men.
> He mocketh at fear, and is not dismayed;
> Neither turneth he back from the sword.
> The quiver rattleth against him,
> The flashing spear and the javelin.
> He swalloweth the ground with fierceness and rage . . .

The recapture of Jerusalem by Saladin had confined most of the Christian forces in a coastal strip about Acre. Then an unlikely salvation emerged from the east, the Mongol hordes. And indeed, the fortunes and faiths of western Asia would be at hazard in the most crucial cavalry battle since the time of Alexander. Fighting in 1260 at Ain Jalud, the Pools of Goliath, the Mameluk Sultan Qutuz of Egypt inflicted the first defeat on an invading Mongol army, in this case commanded by three Christian leaders, the general Kitbuqa, the Frankish Count Bohemund of Tripoli, and the Armenian King. Sparing only the allied Christians, the Mongols had slaughtered nearly a million of the population of Baghdad: this massacre seemed to fulfil the prophecy of the *Book of Revelation*: 'Babylon is fallen, is fallen!' The same fate had met Aleppo in Syria, where the King of Armenia had set fire to the grand mosque. Unfortunately, the bulk of the Mongol horse under Hulagu had been withdrawn towards the Caucasus in a succession struggle, so that the depleted Mongol and Christian cavalry met the Egyptian army in equal numbers in the crucial battle.

The Muslim tactics were superb. A vanguard, under the command of the next Sultan Baibars, was the decoy. At the charge of the enemy, Baibars turned and fled. The Mongols and Christians found themselves trapped in a horseshoe of hills. Down the slopes poured the Mameluk cavalry, which destroyed the foe. Kitbuqa was captured and beheaded. This was the prelude to the destruction of the kingdom of Jerusalem at Acre by Baibars, and the ending of Christian power in the Near East. Below the Caucasus, the Mongols were to adopt Islam as their religion. The destiny of western Asia had been decided.

The legacy of the Mongols was the destruction of the cultural unity of Islam after its four centuries of dominance. That fresh urban civilisation had been the most enlightened of its time, but it would now retreat under the Mameluks and later the Seljuk Turks into a narrow and rigid interpretation of the Koran, which would result in the teaching schools of the *madrassas* dedicated to a pedantic and narrow vision of society, a continuing struggle between the faithful and the infidel. And in eastern Europe, the raiders of the Golden Horde had also devastated Orthodox Christian Russia, which would take more centuries to recover and resist the influence of Islam, pushing across the Black and Caspian seas into the Balkans and up to the steppes.

In 1396, a last crusade was mounted in order to save Byzantium from Bayezid, who had proclaimed himself the Sultan of Rome. He had recruited regiments of *spahis*, horsed archers, who were also equipped with a steel helmet and a mail shirt, a shield, a lance and a yataghan; many of them were Christian mercenaries from Serbia. Against him were arraigned a motley collection of west European knights and 60,000 Hungarian light cavalry or spearmen. The two armies met outside the Bulgarian city of Nicopolis. The Sultan Bayezid put his auxiliary light horse and javelin men in front of lines of pointed stakes, protecting his foot of archers and axe-wielders. The Frankish knight scattered the feeble Turkish vanguard, but were stopped by the stakes. They dismounted to attack the bowmen, who also fled up the hill. Now 40,000 hidden *spahis* appeared over the crest and cut down the unhorsed knights. A counter-charge by the Hungarians failed, and a general massacre ensued. As at Hattin and Ain Jalut, the charge of the knights was enveloped and wholly destroyed. And the Balkans were lost to the Islamic advance.

After the fall of Byzantium in 1453, the legendary Cossacks found their role as the defenders of Christendom. Emerging from the heterogeneous nomads left behind by the Mongols on the borderlands, the Cossacks retaliated against the Muslim raiders from the east and the south as the guardians of the frontier. There were striking parallels between these horsemen of the steppes and the later American pioneers. As a historian wrote of these mounted clans:

> The venturers who sought fortune, freedom from poverty or from religious and political oppression in 17th century western Europe fled to the Americas. Those of eastern Europe fled to the borderland of Tartary to become Cossacks. Nor do the similarities end there. If the American frontier encouraged democracy, so did the Russian. If the American frontiersman disliked taxation and the restraints of law and order, so did the Cossack . . . Examination of the institutions of more developed Cossack communities reveals the village ataman in the role of sheriff, and the Cossack elder representing the judge. We find Cossack cattle-rustlers, Cossack ranch-owners feuding with Cossack farmers, and Cossack posses chasing Cossack 'badmen'. High-spirited, coarse-humoured and frequently drunk, brigand, hunter and brawler, this wild dog of the prairies was in many ways closer to the popular idea of the cowboy than was the cowboy himself.

Unlike the American westerners, the Cossacks became rebels and revolutionaries, as well as police enforcers for the state and pathfinders over three hundred years through Siberia to the Pacific Ocean. The

Russians had always thought of the steppe as their land. In the 18th century, the period of great expansion southwards and to the east, the polymath Vasily Tatischev would come up with the concept of the Ural range as the frontier between Europe and Asia. To him, the Slavs had always occupied the grasslands above the Black and the Caspian Seas and even the Crimea, the most recent imperial acquisition. The idea that the remnants of the Mongolian and Scythian tribes, who had brought the horse culture to Europe, had already colonised the lands to the east of Moscow did not trouble the Tsars, any more than the appropriation of the Wild West disturbed the American Presidents. Once the Tartar strongholds at Kazan and Astrakhan had fallen in the 17th century, the sparsely populated land was for the taking, until the Russians would meet the stiffer resistance from the mounted tribesmen of the Caucasian mountains.

The original Cossack communities were spread around the Don and Volga rivers. In their piratical raids by sea against the Turkish coastal towns, the Cossacks were even praised as if they were 'noble knights' of the Military Orders, since 'their principal duty [was] the conduct of continuous war against the infidels'. On land, a German observer noted of them that 'from their earliest youth they were . . . accustomed to all kinds of difficult equipment, using firearms and lances and shooting well from long bows'. They were inseparable from their unshod hardy small horses, described by Purchas in *His Pilgrimes* as 'neat, excellent, stomackfull, swift and indifferent good and commodious to undergoe great labours'.

Tactically, the Cossacks were also pioneers in the later strategies of the American pioneers and the Boer trekkers. On the march, a cavalry column would be flanked by baggage carts. If the enemy threatened, the two files of waggons would form a point, sealed at the back in a triangle, joined by chains. From this improvised defence, the *tabor*, later used in the corral and *laager* systems, the Cossacks would pick off the circling enemy, discharging a hailstorm of arrows. Then they would burst out with pike and sabre in a furious sortie. Their cavalry formation was the *lava*, a horned line, long enough to outflank the wings of the foe. Three *lavas* would attack, one after the other, sweeping away from strong points and striking through weaknesses, as billows against a dyke.

Under their wily leaders, Bogdan Khmelnitski and Pugachev and Mazeppa, whom Byron would falsely turn into a romantic hero, the Cossacks three times established an independent homeland. Pugachev even threatened Moscow with his wayward frontiersmen, appealing to a rural utopia. In a manifesto, he granted the peasants the right to practise freely the old Orthodox faith, to pay no taxes, to liquidate the aristocratic landowners, and 'to be Cossacks for ever [in] peace and tranquillity and a quiet life'. Eventually routed by the guns of the professional Tsarist army, he was captured and caged like an animal, condemned to death by the Kremlin court of Catherine the Great, then beheaded with his quarters exhibited on the city gates.

From this time forth, the Don Cossacks would become the spearheads of the Russian military machine, as the defeated Scots Highlanders would be recruited as the assault forces of the British Empire. Within three generations, the change from the liberty of the steppes to army discipline would be accomplished. A Cossack Major Igurov, a veteran of the 1812 war against Napoleon, would appear in the report of a Russian staff officer:

> The grandfather is a representative of the blunt old spirit of the sons of the steppe that Peter the Great began to bridle with his iron hand. This was a difficult task at that time; but now a check is kept on everything so that the chastising hand of our emperor can smite the Cossacks with the speed of lightning. The Major himself is the type of a transitional generation. He would by no means relish the old equality and anarchy of the steppes. He has seen and tasted the beauties and delights of Western Europe in the Napoleonic Wars. Yet he has one foot in the past and sighs and longs for the freedom of the good old days. His son is quite a creature of modern times, coming from the cadet school with the vices and the advantages of large cities, elegant in his manners, superficial and empty in mind and heart. The Cossacks now answer the purpose of trained elephants to tame the wild ones, so that the warlike hordes of the Siberian steppes are taught to obey the command from the banks of the Neva.

So most of the Cossacks would be incorporated into a Tsarist tyranny before the heyday of the Wild West in America. They would form two-fifths of Russia's cavalry arm, and they would distinguish themselves in combat against the Swedes and the Turks, and particularly in the Napoleonic struggle. They were the best military scouts in Europe, admirable in penetration and ambush, expert snipers and piercers with their lances. They could even lassoo a prisoner and drag him back for interrogation behind the tails of their horses. These last wild crusaders of the open plains were only equalled by the Reivers of the Borders between England and Scotland, another people, whose survival depended on raiding, and who were devastated by serial wars.

CHAPTER FOUR

The Creation of the Reivers

In his 'Essay on Border Antiquities', Sir Walter Scott explained why there were so few antiquities to be found on the Borders. There were two reasons; the scorch-and-burn tactics of the Scots leaders, when faced with an English invasion; and the later reforming zeal of the Covenanters, who considered a carved Catholic abbey as a monument to ostentation, if not Satan. The guerrilla strategy adapted by the Scots may have been necessary, but it 'was destructive to property, and tended to retard civilisation'. They destroyed the resources of their own country to deny these to the invaders, and 'they viewed with great indifference the enemy complete the work of destruction'. They hid their cattle in mountain and forest and bog, waited for the English to retreat, and then 'retaliated upon the enemy's country the horrors which were exercised in their own'.

When John de Vienne and French auxiliaries came to the aid of the Scottish army in 1384, they were astonished at the campaign. Their allies would not fight in open combat. They destroyed, as the chronicler Froissart wrote, 'all as they went, and burned towns, villages and manors, causing all the men, women and children to retreat with their cattle into the wild'. While the English army ravaged north, finding little to sustain them, the Scots laid waste in the rear to Cumbria and Northumbria, doing more damage in the bishoprics of Durham and Carlisle than all the towns of Scotland were worth.

Loaded with plunder, the allied forces returned north of the Border to find another wasteland, 'but the people did set but little thereby, and said how with three or four poles they would soon set up their houses again, and that they had saved much of their cattle in the woods'. So it was written in the *Scotichronicon*:

> On foot should be all Scottish war;
> Let wood for walls be bow and spear,
> By hill and moss themselves to guard,

> That enemies do not press them hard.
> In strait places so keep all store,
> And burn the plain land them before;
> Then shall they pass away in haste,
> When they find naething but waste.

In his estimation of the Borderers, Sir Walter Scott was particularly influenced by the work of John Leslie, the Catholic Bishop of Ross, which was translated from the Latin text. Leslie harked back to the clan system, which still ruled on that frontier. The chieftain asked no rent of his people, but only battle service; in return, they shared in the herds and flocks on their land. They hardly cultivated the soil, even if it was fertile, for fear the crops would be destroyed by raiders. They lived chiefly on flesh, milk, and boiled barley. Their residences consisted of makeshift huts and cottages, while the chiefs constructed for themselves, as at Aikwood, 'pyramidical kind of towers, which they call *peels*, made entirely of stone'.

These *peel* or *pele* towers and bastle houses were the last defences of the lairds of the frontier. Four-storey square stone towers, their levels connected only by ladders and trapdoors or a turnpike stair allowing the use of a sword-arm, were surrounded by a barmkin, an enclosure within a palisade of oak beams and clay mortar. Under assault, the sheep and cattle were driven into the barmkin, and the milking cows and horses inside the *pele* ground floor, accessible only through a grated iron grille and a studded oak door. Slits and loopholes in the thick masonry allowed the air to get in and missiles to be shot out. For Walter Scott: 'Smailholme, or Sandiknow Tower, is one of the most perfect specimens of these species of habitation, which was usually situated on the brow of a rock, or the brink of a torrent; and, like the cast of the chief, had adjacent huts for the reception of those who were called upon to act in its defence.'* The bastle houses evolved from timber and turf dwellings, rather similar to the later prairie cabins of the North American pioneers, into fortified farmhouses with a basement for livestock and an upper storey with a fireplace for living quarters. Barricaded within thick stone walls, a family had a chance of short survival during the incessant Border wars, should the enemy move on, for easier pickings.

In his infancy, Walter Scott had clapped his hands at lightning striking near to Smailholme Tower, and in his 'Border Minstrelsy', he told of the baron of the keep, who killed the lover of his wife, though his victim returned to haunt her on 'The Eve of St John'. The killer wore the equipment of the period:

> Yet his plate-jack was braced, and his helmet was laced,
>   And his vaunt-brace of proof he wore;
> At his saddle-gerthe was a good steel sperthe [battle-axe],
>   Full ten pound weight and more.

> Yet was his helmet hack'd and hew'd,
>   His acton pierced and tore;
> His axe and his dagger with blood embrued,–
>   But it was not English gore.

It was the blood of the baron's victim, a dead man returning to admonish the avenging husband and the faithless wife, come from their trysting-place, a crag above Smailholme called the Watchfold, the site of a warning beacon:

> Who spilleth life, shall forfeit life:
>   So bid thy lord believe:
> That lawless love is guilt above,
>   This awful sign receive.

The existence of the Borderers lay in their knowledge of the ground, particularly the Marches, where the enemy was enticed, only 'to give way, and in a moment to swallow him up into the deep abyss'. Their unshod ponies were agile and light enough to evade the morasses, which engulfed any pursuit by heavy cavalry. Such frontier clans were nearly all mounted on small and sturdy ponies, called 'galloways' or 'bog trotters'. These beasts could also look after themselves, 'being never tied up or dressed, but are turned after the day's march to pasture on the heath, or in the field'.

As Leslie observed, if the Borderers 'be possessed of nimble horses, and have sufficient wherewith to ornament their own persons and those of their wives, they are by no means anxious about other pieces of household furniture'. Curiously, however, while they lived by looting near and far, they tried to avoid the shedding of blood. 'For they have a persuasion that all property is common by the law of nature, and is therefore liable to be appropriated by them in their necessity, but that murder and other injuries are prohibited by the Divine Law.'

The exception to the rule of plunder without slaughter was the blood-feud or clan revenge. There were ambushes and executions without ending from generation to generation. One murder had to be repaid by another killing, interminably. Despite their lawlessness, the Bishop of Ross noted a devotion to music and the old faith, even after the Reformation. The conservative Borderers had not, 'with such ready frenzy as many others of the country, joined the heretical secession from the common faith of the holy church'.

> They take great pleasure in their own music, and in their rhythmical songs, which they compose upon the exploits of their ancestors, or in their own ingenious stratagems in plundering, or their artificial defences when taken. Besides, they think the art of plundering so very lawful, that they never say over their prayers more fervently, or have more devout recurrence to the beads of their rosaries, than when they have made an expedition, as they frequently do, of forty or fifty miles, for the sake of booty.

The patterns and customs of Border warfare derived from their Gaelic roots. Often the Highlanders raided the Lowlanders, who then had to steal back their cattle from the English on the Marches. The mountain men were organised for combat. Even their deer drive, or *tainchel*, was a military operation, involving flanking movements in the manner of the Mongols; the encircled game was driven into the arrows and spears of the chieftains. As Bartholomew wrote in the middle of the 13th century of the Highlanders: 'The men are lygthe of harte, fiers and couragious on theyr enmyes. They love nyghe as well death as thraldome, and they account it for slouth to die in bed, and a great worshyppe and virtue to deye in a felde fyghtynge agynst enmyes.'

Unfortunately, the blood-feud was more urgent among the northern clans than their loyalty to the Crown. For many centuries, the Kings of Scotland could hardly count on the support of the Gaelic warlords. In his *Basilikon Doron* of 1597, King James the Sixth would still be lamenting the feckless and arrogant conceit of the Highland code of honour, which allowed the chiefs –

> To thrall by oppression the meaner sort that dwelleth neere them to their service . . .

> To maintaine their servants and defenders in any wrong although they be not answerable to the laws . . .

> To take up a plaine feide against their neighbour and without respect
> to God, King or Commonweale to bang it out bravelie, he and all his
> kinne against him and all his.

With all the feuding and the raiding, the problem for the clan chiefs
was the maintenance of enough armed men to protect themselves
and their cattle. As an observer noted, 'The Scots, living then in factions, used to keepe many followers and so consumed their revenew
of victuals, living in some want of money.' And so, a continuing supply shortage ensured more seizures from the neighbours. As early as
the 11th century, indeed, the dynasties of Scotland and England had
begun to point the daggers of future Border warfare. With the help
of Edward the Confessor, Malcolm Canmore had killed the usurper
Macbeth, who had murdered his father, King Duncan the First, as
Shakespeare was to note. And at the Battle of Hastings, William the
Conqueror of England had killed King Harold and asserted Norman
rule over the invaded country. That rule was enforced by the feudal
system, based on the mailed knight and the fortress castle. Harold's
heir, Edgar Atheling, shipped north with his sister Margaret, who was
married by King Malcolm the Third, thus giving their children a claim
to the English throne. This first attempt to unite the two Crowns and
erase the shifting borderline was ended by the invasion of William the
First by land and sea. Malcolm paid homage and remained quiescent
for nine years, until raiding south through Cumbria and Northumbria,
and so engulfing all those lands. The treaty of Falkirk of 1080 tempo-
rarily confirmed the *status quo*, with William's son building the first of
the Norman strongholds at Newcastle on the Tyne river. Another Scots
raid led to the construction of a second castle at Carlisle; these two
strongpoints on the Irish and North Seas would be the *foci* of Norman
northern strategy. When, on a last sortie, Malcolm was killed near
Alnwick, the site of another formidable castle, the Norman dominance
of the frontier territories seemed secure.

Successive Scots kings were vassals of England, until the reign of
David the First, the youngest child of the first Canmore monarch.
He married into the Norman aristocracy and became a great landowner in the Midlands, the Earl of Huntingdon, as well as 'prince
of the Cumbrian region'. He began to recruit hundreds of Norman
lords to defend his possessions, in particular Robert de Brus, who
was given the barony of Annandale, and Walter Fitzalan, the ances-
tor of the Stewarts. He also favoured the creation of a civil service,

staffed by monks, especially the Benedictines at Kelso Abbey, and the Augustinians at Inchcolm and Holyrood, and the Cistercians at Melrose and Newbattle. Taking advantage of the civil war after the death of King Henry the First, David and his Scots army marauded south, even capturing both Carlisle and Newcastle. His advance, however, was halted in 1138, at the Battle of the Standard, where the Yorkshire archers first proved the ability of arrows to stop the charge of light-armed pikemen. The poetic words of the chronicler Ailred described the storm of missiles:

> The southern flies swarmed forth from the caves of their quivers, and flew like closest rain; and irksomely attacking the opponents' breasts, faces and eyes, very greatly impeded their attack. Like a hedgehog with quills, so you would see a Galway man bristling all around with arrows, and none the less brandishing his sword and in blind madness rushing now to smite a foe, now to lash the air with useless strokes.

Despite this defeat, David the First did create a stable situation on the Borders, financed by trade from royal burghs and the minting of the first Scots coins, dug from the Alston silver mines in Cumbria. His death soon led to the long reign of William the First, who began his rule by losing Northumbria at the beginning of a fresh English dominance of the frontier. Taken prison during the siege of Alnwick castle, he was humiliated by King Henry the Second and made to become his vassal. All his efforts to regain control of Northumbria proved abortive, for there was no weaponry strong enough to batter down the formidable castles rising on the coastline at Bamburgh and Warkworth.* His heir, Alexander the Second, did achieve the long-dreamt alliance with France in the last years of King John of England. For once, the Scots king penetrated as far as Dover to link with the French Dauphin Louis, hoping to take over the throne in London. The English nobles, however, rallied round the young King Henry the Third, and Alexander was excommunicated by a hostile Papal legate and forced to make peace. Without an heir until a late marriage, Alexander made one significant decision, electing his cousin Robert de Brus or Bruce as his heir presumptive.

The declining years of the Canmore dynasty ended in 1290 with the watery grave of the child Margaret, 'The Fair Maid of Norway'. King Edward the First of England had intended to unite the two countries by marrying her to his son Edward, but her death threw the Scots succession to the dogs of conflict, provoking a Border war that would last sporadically for three hundred and fifty years. The previous raids and counter-raids were but squalls before the tempest. The massive English interventions on the side of one claimant or another would lead to Scottish independence, but at a terrible price to town and village, beast and man.

The two rival claimants were the Brus or Bruces of Annandale and the Balliols, the Lords of Galloway. Thwarted in his plans to incorporate Scotland by marriage, King Edward arrived with an army on the Borders to judge the issue. He awarded the Crown to the weak John Balliol, who began a reign of disaster. When an Anglo-French war and a Welsh rebellion removed English pressure, the dissident Scots nobles elected a Council to make common cause with France. And so in 1296, King Edward began the devastation of Scotland that would never be forgotten. He sacked Berwick, the centre of Scots trade with Flanders and the Baltic; all its citizens were massacred and massive fortifications built; it would become the great English redoubt and port of the north. With ferocity, Edward subjugated the troops and castles of Scotland and forced the abdication of John Balliol, 'Toom Tabard' or 'Empty Coat'. As a symbol of total power the Coronation Stone was removed from the abbey church of Scone and hauled to Westminster Abbey.

The following year, the revolt led by Andrew Moray and the outlaw William Wallace cut in two an English army, caught halfway at Stirling Bridge. Compelled into the offensive, King Edward made his headquarters at York, where his seat of government remained for six years. Instead of adopting the ancient tactics of wasting the land in a subtle retreat, Wallace decided to stand his ground at Falkirk.* In two hours, the English cavalry outflanked and converged on the rear of the hedgehog Scots schiltrons of pikemen, already assailed by the new armour-piercing arrows, shot by Welsh archers, and the bolts of Gascon crossbowmen. They were broken and crushed by the troops of the self-styled 'Hammer of the Scots', who failed to track down the skirmishers of Robert the Bruce. Chosen as one of the two 'Guardians of Scotland' with John 'the Red' Comyn, he directed resistance in the south-west Borders. But two years later, King Edward struck at Dumfries and Galloway, seizing the imposing castle of Caerlaverock, and achieving nothing, with the rebels melting into the hills.* Ironically, he returned to Sweetheart Abbey, deriving its name from the woman who endowed it, Devorgilla; she had buried there the embalmed heart of the husband, the father of John Balliol, whom the English king had enthroned and deposed.*

Betrayed by his fellow Guardian John Comyn, Bruce arranged to meet him for a parley in front of the high altar of the church of the Grey Friars in Dumfries. There, Bruce stabbed his rival for the Scots throne. Leaving the church, he met his brother-in-law, Christopher Seton, who cut down Comyn's uncle and asked if Bruce's victim was dead. In a notorious phrase, another follower, Roger Kilpatrick, said he would 'mak siccar' and returned to make sure that the murder of the bleeding Comyn was completed.

If Bruce had not committed a ritual slaying, he had killed in a holy place. He would be excommunicated by the Pope, an act that allowed any nation to mount a crusade against him. He had to seize the initiative. Capturing Dumfries and Lochmaben castle, which commanded the western approaches to Scotland, Bruce had himself shriven by the Bishop of St Andrews and crowned at Scone in front of three bishops and four earls. Provoked into his final act of cleansing, King Edward the First vowed to avenge the sacrilegious killing; he would never again bear arms against a Christian, but only against the Saracens. In a surprise dusk assault outside Perth at Methven, Bruce's small force was cut to pieces. Its leader was nearly killed, but Bruce was saved again by Christopher Seton, who struck down the king's captor, only to be taken later himself and barbarously executed.

In a way, this defeat made Bruce a master of guerrilla warfare. Necessity was the mother of his strategy. Retiring to the wooded and wild hill country, ambush and stealth, strike and surprise, feint and retreat were his ambassadors. Foiled only by fortresses, he would learn to destroy them in order to deny them to the enemy; his supporter, James Douglas, burned down his own hereditary castle; it could later be rebuilt. And Bruce's increasing resistance brought about the death of his old foe. The ailing King Edward the First died at the frontier village of Burgh-on-Sands, where the fortified Church of St Michael was built on the site of a Roman fort on Hadrian's Wall.* Both were secure places against raiders from across the Solway Firth, beside which the memorial pillar to the 'Hammer of the Scots' still stands, surrounded by grazing black cattle on the drained marshland.

Given three years of respite from war by the new King Edward the Second, Bruce concentrated on crushing his own dissidents, particularly the Earl of Buchan and his English allies. Scattering his enemies, Bruce scorched the earth in a harrowing or *herschip* of Buchan's lands, so devastating that they did not recover for another fifty years. This was followed by the subjugation of tricky Galloway. The Scots King could afford no opponents, ready to put a dirk in his back, before the inevitable onslaught from the south across the borderline.

Rearmament was the main consideration. Although manners may make man, weapons make an army. Rome had first produced a unit of professional armourers, the *fabriciae*. They travelled with the legions all over the Mediterranean coasts and northern Europe. By the 3rd century, many of them were based in arms factories in cities, from where they provided the sinews of the empire. And when St Bernard of Clairvaux created the Knights Templars as the armed fist of the church in order to defend his Cistercians in their monasteries, set often so close to the military commanderies, he did not forget that a trade in weapons might benefit both Holy Orders. The industrial technology of the white monks matched their agricultural expertise. To their fired pottery kilns, they added water-powered trip-hammers over the forges at the abbey of Fontenay. Clairvaux itself was situated in the heart of the best deposits of iron ore in France. Before 1330, the monks already owned a dozen factories, which produced ingots for sale to armourers and masons. They were the leading iron and steel producers in the Champagne region, and also significant in Cumbria and the Borders, with rich metal and coal resources.

The use of water power was the Cistercian contribution to an industrial revolution in the weapons trade. Powered by rivers and burns, stamping mills were built to break up the iron ore, while water-driven bellows could produce a draught that raised the temperature of the furnaces to 1,500 degrees Centigrade. This heat allowed the furnaces to produce molten iron, ready for casting. In the 14th century, the first blast furnace was already in operation, although the blacksmith with his forge was still the usual metal-worker. Spanish steel had to be imported to Britain for the creation of the best sword blades, also at Portchester, 'for the hardening of the axes and other tools of the masons'.

The Knights Templars were known as those 'of the trowel and the sword'. In Palestine, they were totally dependent for their weapons and castle-building upon Semitic and Arabic craftsmen. The laymen of the Military Orders were recruited from local skilled workers. And at the time, the Saracen sword was superior to the Frankish broadsword. After their expulsion from the Holy Land, the Templars would have taken their armourers with them, as the Roman Legions once had. These craftsmen would become known as Romanies or Egyptians or gypsies. They were accustomed to a vagrant life with a cart and a forge, camp-followers at the back of an army. Without them, the military could not sustain a campaign. The path of those Templars who fled to Scotland was recorded in gravestones near Loch Awe in Argyll, which charted a way from the Western Isles to Lothian. In Muckairn churchyard, there was a tomb with a piece of the staff of a cross, on which a sword was incised. At Taynuilt, a gravestone was carved with a crusading sword, surrounded by leaping thistles and dogs and a hare, while another showed a battle-axe and a Lombard sword.

A welter of resources in Cumbria also reveal that the many Templar commanderies there were weapon factories as well as cattle and sheep farms. In fact, the look of the local Herdwick flocks resemble those from Mesopotamia, a breed perhaps imported by the crusaders. Along the Solway Coast, iron ore is still washed upon the beaches, while old mines pepper the interior, as do ancient smelting works. A whole medieval foundry has been restored in the Duddon Valley. For the techniques for smelting iron were simple and effective. River water was poured down a perforated pipe, which allowed oxygen to enter with the wind. The deluge fell into a covered pit with a funnel for the steam to blow out. In the pit was red-hot charcoal and the crushed and washed mineral ore. The iron melted and flowed out of a small drain, which the Catalans called the tail of the fox.

Certainly in his conflicts, Robert the Bruce had need of the refugee Knights Templars and their armourers, excommunicated as all of them were. He had enough galleys and cogs to penetrate the attempted English embargo, prohibiting trade with Ireland. The Scots secured weapons and armour and supplies through the Western Isles, also from the Baltic, in exchange for wool and timber and hides. Now well-equipped, Bruce easily repulsed probing raids from the south, doing more damage by his swift counter-attacks into Northumbria, where he levied huge taxes on the towns and monasteries to spare them from his wrath, so beginning a system of Border 'blackmail', which the later reivers were to adopt. The word for this new form of Danegeld derived from the old Anglo-Norse *mal* or 'tribute', while 'black' signified that the extortion could be paid by *reditus negri*, such as grain or meat, rather than the 'white rent' of silver.

Two *ultimata* forced the intervention of King Edward the Second, for he had to overthrow Robert the Bruce. In November 1313, the Scots king threatened to disinherit all his opponents within his country, unless they paid allegiance to him within one year. And the brilliant cavalry commander, Edward Bruce, also the king's brother, had agreed on the surrender of the last English bastion, Stirling Castle, if it were not relieved by next year's Midsummer's Day. In a pre-emptive strike, Robert and Edward Bruce ravaged the southern Borders, even sacking Durham and Hartlepool, and taking an immense amount of stores and weapons and horses and prisoners for ransom. The royal exchequer was filled by blackmail, extracted from the towns and abbeys of Cumbria and Northumbria, all trembling in fear of what would happen, if they did not pay. Within three years of raiding, Bruce collected the huge sum of £40,000 in tribute. Later he swelled his coffers with the capture of the rich port of Perth, which he razed to the ground, along with the other great castles of Caerlaveroch and Dumfries. He now applied his policies of levelling all the strongholds as far as Lothian, where Crichton and Roxburgh and even Edinburgh castle were laid low.* Only Hume castle was spared, expected to hold out on its hill, overlooking the rich grain plain of the Merse, its crops now put to the torch.*

An invasion had to be. In 1314, the young Edward the Second marched north with some 25,000 men, but he lost up to half his forces to disease and dysentery and lack of supplies, for nothing had been left on the landscape for his foraging parties. Of his heavy-armoured knights, 2,000 of them would reach the field of Bannockburn, and the same numbers of his expert Welsh longbowmen. Opposing him outside Stirling were some 5,000 pikemen with small contingents of archers and light horsemen. After preliminary skirmishes, in which Bruce himself on a pony shattered the head of a Norman English knight on his charger, the Scots advanced from the forests in four schiltrons. The contemporary chronicler Geoffrey Baker of Swinbroke revealed the course of the combat:

> The Scots chose a fine position, and dug ditches three feet deep and three wide along the whole of their front from right to left, covering them over with intertwined branches, that is to say, hurdles, screened by grass, across which indeed infantry might pass if they knew the trick, but which could not bear the weight of cavalry. None of the Scots were allowed to mount their horses, and arrayed in brigades as usual, they stood in a closely formed line behind the aforesaid cannily, I will not say deceitfully, constructed ditch.
>
> As the English moved from the west, the rising sun shone on their gilded shields and helmets. Such a general as Alexander would have preferred to try conclusions on some other ground or other day, or at least could have waited till midday when the sun would have been on their right. But the impetuous and headstrong obstinacy of the English preferred death to delay.

In the front line were the cavalry with their heavy chargers, unaware of the concealed ditch; in the second were the infantry, including the archers who were kept ready for the enemy's flight; in the rear the King, with the bishops and other clerics . . .

The front line of cavalry charged, and as the horses' legs were caught in the ditch through the hurdles, down fell the men and died before the enemy could strike; and at their fall on came the enemy, slaughtering and taking prisoners, and sparing only the rich for ransom . . .

Many were killed by the archers of their own army, who were not placed in a suitable position, but stood behind the men-at-arms whereas at the present day the custom is to post them on the flanks. When they saw the Scots charging fiercely on the horsemen who had fallen at the ditch, some of them shot their arrows high in the air to fall feebly on the enemy's helmets, some shot ahead and hit a few Scots in the chest, and many English in the back.

Over two days and a night, these tactics were repeated, cavalry charges against ranks of spears. As the Lanercost chronicler stated: 'The two hosts came together, and the great steeds of the knights dashed into the Scottish pikes as into a thick wood; there arose a huge and horrible noise from rending lances and dying horses, and they stood locked together for a space.' The spearmen in thick leather coats and iron caps aimed at the chargers. Once the knights were dismounted, they were easily dispatched by short sword and dirk and dagger.

A dangerous flanking attack by the lethal Welsh longbowmen threatened the Scots position. As John Barbour recorded, 'The arrows flew so thickly there, that those who saw them could well have said that they made a horrible shower, for wherever they fell, I promise you, they left tokens behind them that needed medicine. The English archers loosed so fast that if their shooting had persisted, it would have gone hard for the Scotsmen.' Now Bruce ordered his Marshal, Sir Robert Keith, to charge with his 500 light horsemen from the Borders on the unsupported enemy archers. And so, 'the men of all his company rode quickly against them, and came upon them at a flank; he rode among them so forcefully, spearing them so relentlessly, knocking them down and slaying them in such numbers without mercy, that one and all they scattered; from that time on none gathered to try such shooting.'

An intervention then occurred of legend and dispute. A new Scots force appeared and charged, making a fearsome noise. The English retreat turned into a rout. These people were said to be yeomen and camp-followers, banging their pots and pans, and assisted by some of the refugee Templars in Scotland, fighting for its tortured and excommunicated leader. Yet no army can win a victory without its weaponry. This last body available to Robert the Bruce consisted of his armourers. Some of them had been brought over by the Templars from the Near East. Many of them, however, were blacksmiths, taking to wagons with their anvils and ladles and hammers and charcoal to maintain the axes and bills and swords of the host. Robert the Bruce was not only a brilliant general, but a superb forager and quartermaster, as much concerned with his repair and supply systems as with the combat ahead.

King Edward the Second just escaped the battlefield, although the flower of his nobility was lost or captured. The surviving English barons continued to harry their monarch because of his royal favourites, who were imprisoned or executed. Taking advantage of his enemy's weakness, Bruce continued on his Border raids, training an army, which became expert in pillage and extortion; he was particularly adamant in appropriating the iron ore of Furness for his weaponry. Under the command of his brother Edward, Bruce even opened up a Second Front across the sea in Ireland. Although the office of High King was briefly won over there, the long campaign was to founder.

The great success of Bruce was the capture of Berwick and its trading port. Instead of destroying its walls, he strengthened them, for the city was vital to the Scots economy. Continuing sorties and dismantling castles as far as South Yorkshire, Bruce continued to victual and pay his forces by blackmail and plunder. 'They made men and women captive,' the *Lanercost Chronicle* stated, 'forcing the poor folk to drive countless cattle before them, carrying the beasts off to Scotland without any opposition.'

On a grand scale, the style of the future Reivers was being set, with almost annual excursions for loot by expeditions south of the Border. On one occasion at the 'Chapter of Mitton', 300 priests were left dead, after the Archbishop of York had mustered a scratch array to take on the seasoned marauders. They had been driven into Swale water by a sudden attack of the Border *hobylers* or 'prickers', who had fired the horse fodder in their camp: 'and the smoke thereof was so huge that the Englischemen might not see the Skottes.' Eighty-four towns and villages were also burned on this foray, a brilliant attack in the rear, which succeeded in raising the siege of Berwick, then being invested by the English in an attempt at recapture.

The Scots king was still under the interdiction of the Pope with his coronation unrecognised. He had, however, secured the allegiance of his own countrymen. At Arbroath in 1320, a famous Declaration of Independence was signed by eight earls and thirty-one barons for delivery to the Holy Father, then based at Avignon. After a brief history of the conversion of the Scots to Christianity, followed by a comparison of Robert the Bruce to Joshua and Judas Maccabeus for delivering his people from the hand of their enemies, the document declared of the king:

> To him we are obliged and resolved to adhere in all things, both upon his right and his own merit, as being the person who has restored the people's safety, in defence of their liberties . . . As long as one hundred of us remain alive, we will never consent to serve under the dominion of the English. Not for glory, not for riches, not for honour, do we fight and contend, but for freedom alone, which no honest man will lose but with his life.

The Pope proved obdurate, asking for more crusades against the excommunicated king. In response, two years on, King Edward the Second led a large army to the sack of Lothian. In his brutal strategy, Bruce had already forestalled the invasion by striking 80 miles into England and burning both Lancaster and Preston, before retiring with his spoils and leaving only scorched earth behind him. The enemy army, however, was supplied by sea and had no trouble in reaching Edinburgh. There Holyrood Abbey was burned down, but hunger and an invisible foe forced a retreat, which also resulted in the firing of Dryburgh and Melrose Abbeys in revenge for the stripped soil. This desecration of the holy places of Scotland would set a precedent for the spoiling of the nation's soaring medieval heritage, the twenty-six abbeys and cathedrals of royal or noble foundation, all of which, bar one at Glasgow, would be ruined by war or Reformation.

Eventually, the Pope gave up his *anathemas*, while Bruce achieved his dream of a defensive alliance with France. The murder by red-hot poker of the imprisoned Edward the Second led, however, to a counterattack in 1327 by the new young King Edward the Third, bringing with him the future destroyer of cavalry and castle, the primitive gunpowder cannon. Again, the host crossed burned and desolate moors in pursuit of vanishing men on horseback. In the words of Jehan Le Bel:

> The Scots are exceedingly hardy through their constant wearing of arms and experience in combat. When they enter England they will in a single

day and night cover twenty-four miles; for they ride on sturdy horses and bring no waggons with them. They carry no provisions of bread and wine; for their abstemiousness is such that they will live for a long time on stewed meat and drink river water ... When they have eaten the stewed meat they place [an iron] plate on the fire and when the plate is hot they spread on it a little paste made of oatmeal and water and make a thick cake in the manner of a biscuit which they eat to comfort their stomachs. So it is no wonder that they can travel farther in a day than other soldiers ... They enter into England, and burn and devastate the country, and find so many cattle that they are a loss what to do with them all.

Outmanoeuvred by his elusive enemy through burn and bog, Edward the Third had to retire to York and disband his army. To fight the Bruce was to lunge at ghosts. After another harrying of Northumbria, the Scots King declared that he was ready to annex the borderlands. He was already ailing, but his threats and tactics achieved the improbable, the recognition of his sovereignty by England and the Pope. His four-year-old son David was married to the six-year-old sister of the English king in the hope of a Union of the Crowns to come. And then, indeed, Robert the Bruce did give up his own ghost. He required his close companions to carry his embalmed heart for burial in Jerusalem, on a little crusade, which he had never achieved. A casket was made of silver and enamel, and Sir James Douglas, the supreme Scots commander of the light horse, put it on a chain about his neck for the journey to the east. Only the English archers had bothered Douglas on his many campaigns, and when he captured them, he had their right hand cut off or their right eye put out, not wishing to be pricked again 'on account of their bows and arrows'.

On this long last requiem, Douglas was joined by six *lairds* loyal to Bruce; the chief of these were Sir William Keith and Sir William St Clair, who had fought at Bannockburn. On their way to the Holy Land, the Scots knights sailed up the Guadalquiver river to land at Seville, where they were met by Alfonso the Eleventh, the King of Castle and Leon. He pressed them into his crusade against the Moors at the battle of Zebas de Ardeles. Leading the cavalry vanguard, Douglas was outwitted by the tactics, which he had so often used himself. The Saracen light horse feigned a flight, but when Douglas and his knights charged against them, they encircled their pursuers in a ring of several hundred lances. Aytoun's ballad on 'The Heart of Bruce' told the rest of the tale, after Douglas had refused to escape, once William St Clair was struck down:

But thicker, thicker, grew the swarm,
    And sharper shot the rain,
And the horses reared amid the press,
    But they would not charge again.

'Now Jesu help thee,' said Lord James.
    'Thou kind and true Saint Clair!
An' if I may not bring thee off
    I'll die beside thee there!'

Then in his stirrups up he stood
    So lion-like and bold.
And held the precious heart aloft
    All in its case of gold.

He slung it from him, far ahead,
    And never spake he more.
But – 'Pass thee, first, thou dauntless heart,
    As thou wert wont of yore!' . . .

'We'll bear them back unto our ship.
    We'll bear them o'er the sea.
And lay them in the hallowed earth
    Within our own countrie.'

Because of a broken arm, Sir Robert Keith had been unable to fight. He had the body of his Douglas cousin and that of Sir William St Clair boiled, so that the skulls and bones of these two knights could be removed. Carried back to Scotland, the embalmed heart of James Douglas still lies beneath the floor of his family chapel beside his gigantic effigy, while the Templar tombstone of William St Clair, small enough to cover a skull and crossed bones, can still be seen in the family church at Rosslyn. As for the Heart of Bruce, that was dedicated to Melrose Abbey, which was already being rebuilt in greater splendour, because of the King's benefactions. Yet the harrowing, which had brought about the independence of Scotland, would now be let loose, as from Pandora's Box, in the ills and despairs of more than three hundred years of Border warfare, often without any redeeming quality of hope.

CHAPTER FIVE

Harry and Burn

For 350 years, from the 14th century until the English Civil War, light cavalry raids penetrated the shifting frontier. In their arms and their tactics, these Borderers or Steel Bonnets hailed back to the Roman soldiers on Hadrian's Wall and the legends of King Arthur. On their sturdy fell ponies, cross-bred from stock as far away as Hungary, Poland and Spain, the Borderers used a strategy that derived from the steppes and the desert. The Parthians had defeated the Roman legions by raiding their flanks and using bows from the saddle and picking off the enemy without a charge. The Dacians, Sarmatians and Scythians had been brought over to harass the attacks of the Picts and the Scots from the north. Now once again, mobile horsemen would be able to defeat their enemies by continual harassment.

For the frontier was the breeding-ground of the Reivers. Across a lawless line, chieftains amassed wealth by stealing cattle and sheep. As well as the meat to eat, wool meant riches, once woven into cloth. As in Thomas Love Peacock's 'The War-Song of Dinas Vawr':

> The mountain sheep are sweeter,
> But the valley sheep are fatter;
> We therefore deemed it meeter
> To carry off the latter.
> We made an expedition;
> We met a host and quelled it;
> We forced a strong position,
> And killed the men who held it . . .
>
> We there, in strife bewild'ring,
> Spilt blood enough to swim in;
> We orphaned many children,
> And widowed many women.
> The eagles and the ravens

We glutted with our foemen;
The heroes and the cravens,
The spearmen and the bowmen.

As models for the men of the Marches, further tactics and weapons were being brought back by returning Crusaders, who had been beset in Asia Minor by mounted light horsemen and Turcopoles. The Borderer now fought under an iron helmet, which first looked like a pudding-bowl, hammered into shape by a local blacksmith. Over his chest, he wore a jack, a white quilted coat of stout leather, studded with metal plates. On his lower limbs were britches and leather boots. He carried a curved bow or a short-range cross-bow and a long lance, which could be thrown as a javelin. He had a small round shield and a slicing sword and a dagger or dirk. His supporting infantry had the long bill, which combined a cleaver with a pike, and also the Jedburgh Axe with its round cutting edge.

All these weapons may still be seen carved on medieval grave-stones, mainly of Templar origin, in Cumbria, and in Argyll and Fife and Lothian. The likelihood is that some of the proscribed Knights Templars in their many commanderies on this frontier region continue to prosper from their cattle and sheep herds, but now as local war leaders. Again, the symbol of the shears, used by laymen Templars, often appeared on their tombstones along with their swords. The Military Knights, excommunicated after 1307, merged into the warlords of this frontier, part of which was called 'The Debateable Land'.

Up to 30,000 horsemen could be raised in small bands from a total Border population of five times that number. Outside the forti-fied houses and small keeps and towers of the warlords, the clans of the Marches lived almost as the tribes of the Great American Plains in their teepees. Makeshift crofts and shepherds' shelters sufficed, for all expected a destruction from the next party, raiding their cat-tle and sheep. To the antiquarian, Camden, these Reivers were 'rank robbers . . . as it were the ancient nomads, a martial kind of men who, from the month of April until August, lie out scattering and summer-ing, with their cattle in little cottages here and there, which they called sheils and sheilings.' For them, survival was a series of continual skir-mishes over the centuries, which would end in a triumph against a whole Scottish army.

As Robert the Bruce had pointed out, the woods and hills of their country were the safest bulwarks of the Borderers, and the Douglases had a maxim: 'Better to hear the lark sing than the mouse cheep.' And, as Sir Walter Scott noted: 'Their morality was of a singular kind. The rapine, by which they subsisted, they accounted lawful and honourable . . . Robbery assumed the appearance of fair reprisal.' The Scots and the English Wardens of the East and the Middle and West Marches had too few forces to contain the Reivers; only 200 spearmen and the same number of archers for each official district. Except in exceptional times of a royal edict against them, the Border clans were a law unto themselves in shifting alliances and looting expeditions that went on, hugger-mugger and tit-for-tat, as far as memory stretched. And particularly in the matter of pursuit over the frontier, a new custom was introduced, the *hot trod*. This gave the victims of theft the right to pursue thieves in the recovery of their property and deal with them summarily. The robbers might be lanced or hanged, or kept for ransom, or occasionally for the King's justice. Indeed, a treaty in 1563 between England and Scotland declared in favour of 'lawfull Trodd with Horn and Hound, with Hue and Cry and all other accustomed manner of fresh pursuit'.

Of the Border ditties, 'The Fray of Support' seemed to Walter Scott 'by far the most uncouth and savage. It is usually chaunted in a sort of wild recitative, except the burden, which swells into a long and varied howl, not unlike to a view hollo'. It was 'used to carry a burning wisp of straw at a spear head, and to raise a cry, similar to the Indian war-whoop'. According the Articles of the Wardens of the English Marches, 'all, on this cry being raised, were obliged to follow the fray, or chase, under pain of death'. However that might be, the ballad promised a loud pursuit:

> Ha, lads! shout a' a' a' a' a',
> My gear's a' ta'en.

> Captain Musgrave, and a' his band,
> Are comin' down by the Siller-strand,
> And the muckle toun-bell o' Carlisle is rung:
> My gear was a' weel won,
> And before it's carried o'er the Border, mony a man's gae doun.
>> Fy, lads! Shout a' a' a' a' a',
>> My gear's a' gane.

> Sae, whether they be Elliots or Armstrangs,
> Or rough-riding Scotts, or rude Johnstones,

Or whether they be frae the Tarras or Ewesdale,
They maun turn and fight, or try the deeps o' Liddel.
　　Fy, lads! Shout a' a' a' a' a',
　　My gear's a' ta'en.

With his usual clarity, Walter Scott noted that, unless they were needed in war, the men of the Borders were 'a kind of outcasts'. They had little faith in their monarchs, and they pillaged each other as if they were attacking a foreign country. In his *Britannia*, Camden best described why they were so adroit as cattle-stealers:

> They sally out of their own Borders, in the night, in troops, through unfrequented byways, and many intricate windings. All the daytime, they refresh themselves and their horses in lurking holes they had pitched upon before, till they arrive in the dark at those places they have a design upon. As soon as they have seized upon the booty, they, in like manner, return home in the night, through blind ways, and fetching many a compass. The more skilful any captain is to pass through those wild deserts, crooked turnings, and deep precipices, in the thickest mists and darkness, his reputation is the greater, and he is looked upon as a man of an excellent head. And they are so very cunning, that they seldom have their booty taken from them, unless sometimes, when, by the help of bloodhounds following them exactly upon the track, they may chance to fall into the hands of their adversaries. When being taken, they have so much persuasive eloquence, and so many smooth insinuating words at command, that if they do not move their judges, nay, and even their adversaries (notwithstanding the severity of their natures) to have mercy, yet they incite them to admiration and compassion.

These very qualities might make them invaluable in time of war, in service as scouts and foragers and raiders behind the lines. The only problem, however, was that both the English and the Scots Marchmen were closer to each other than to either country. This arose from the payment of blackmail, which a Scots Reiver might take from an English drover, thus putting the herdsman under his sworn protection. The Grahams, indeed, collected that protection money on the porch of Arthuret church, a vantage point for overlooking their pursuers. Intermarriage also linked some of the clans, while it was noticed in battle, with the Borderers ranged on either side, that they would wear handkerchiefs with embroidered letters, so that they could recognise their common ground. They pretended to fight each other, yelling and missing; in the chronicler Patten's opinion, their chasing was 'like the running at base in an uplandish town, where the match is made, for a quart of good ale'. In battle, too, the prickers badly demeaned themselves, 'more intending the taking of prisoners, than the surety of victory; for while other men fought, they fell to their prey; that as there were but few of them brought home his prisoner, so were there many that had six or seven'.

Yet many of the Reivers were notorious killers. If they shied off from doing away with each other, it was often from fear of starting a blood-feud, which would involve serial revenge, almost without ending. In their raiding, they preferred plunder and ransom to bloodshed. For who could sell dead meat? As with later gangsters running protection rackets, death was the penalty only for those who betrayed them or threatened their livelihood. Their brutal mercy was a means of their survival.

Unfortunately for Scotland, with the death of Robert the Bruce, his heir David was only five years old, and the royal advisers had little use for their relentless, although unreliable, Border scavengers. And they were needed. For King Edward the Third soon took the opportunity to try and put back on the Scots throne the exiled collaborator, Edward Balliol. In three battles, the brilliant guerrilla strategy, taught by the Bruce brothers, would be wasted, but not the earth. Hardly supported by cavalry or archers, the schiltron would fall before the longbow, the ultimate weapon in a series of English victories on the Borders and in the Hundred Years War in France.

At Dupplin Moor, a small English force was deployed in an arc, rather as the curved longhorns of Spanish cattle. Armed with long captured pikes, the men-at-arms blocked a defile with the bowmen posted ahead on rising ground. In the words of the *Bridlington Chronicle*, 'the archers were disposed so they could attack the columns of the enemy from the flanks'. Led by the Regent, the Earl of Mar, and the illegitimate Robert Bruce, the Scots advanced in two divisions, forming a wedge on a narrow front. But, as the *Lanercost Chronicle* observed, 'they were chiefly defeated by the English archers, who so blinded and wounded the faces of the first division of the Scots by an incessant discharge of arrows that they could not support each other'.

Stopped by the pike wall of the enemy and skewered at the side, the frontal Scots charge foundered in a wall of the heaving wounded and slain. On a collision course, the second division flooded into the backs of their own men. Again the *Bridlington Chronicle* was clear on the reasons for the disaster. 'The forward troops of the enemy were heavily wounded by the arrows and driven to close up to the main force; jammed together in a small space, one was crushed by another. Suffocated by each other, and beaten by that rather than by blows of swords, they fell in a remarkable way in a great heap. Pressed together in this way, and squeezed against each other as if by ropes, they perished miserably.'

When the Scots rear broke and fled, the English surrounded the bloody hillock of the fallen and killed them with spearthrust and arrowpoint. Robert Bruce and three Earls were butchered including the Regent, along with more than 2,000 men. The English losses were minimal, with not a single archer laid low. The Scots had been punished for their overconfidence and their abandonment of a hit-and-run strategy. 'Wise men should dread their enemies,' Andrew de Wyntoun commented. 'For downgrading them and excessive pride often leads to defeat.'

Edward Balliol was now inaugurated as the King of the Scots, and most of the rebel nobles attended his coronation, which might have become a *coup d'état* or a regal excuse for a mass execution. All who attended 'were armed save for their helmets, since the people and their nobles inclined to Balliol more from fear than from love'. Such opposition soon forced Balliol to free south again. He relinquished the sovereignty of his kingdom to Edward the Third, who sent him back with an army to besiege the lost city of Berwick, the pearl of the Baltic and Flanders trade. The agreement of its defenders to surrender in mid-July, unless they were relieved, reversed the previous situation, when the Scots were investing Stirling before the Battle of Bannockburn. Now they would have to attack an English defensive position, if they wished to break through to their beleaguered city.

In the field himself, Edward the Third took up a strong blocking line on Halidon Hill in front of the Tweed river. He repeated the tactics of Dupplin Moor, with his dismounted armoured men in the centre and flanking archers on either wing on the contour of the hill. Marching from Duns, the Scots attacked in three or four divisions. Unfortunately, again in a reversal of Bannockburn, they found themselves crossing a narrow marsh and assaulting upslope, where, as the wise Wyntoun noted, 'a single man might defeat three; but that they could not see beforehand', for they had no scouts to reconnoitre the ground. And as in their previous disaster, they suffered from the bowmen on the English flanks, who 'shot arrows as thickly as the rays in sunlight, hitting the Scots in such a way that they struck them down in their thousands; and they began to flee from the English in order to save their lives'.

The English now mounted their horses for a dreadful pursuit, killing with iron maces their foemen, even when they tried to rally. There was no Scots light horse to halt the rout nor to disperse the English archers in conflict, as Sir Robert Keith had done at Bannockburn. And thirteen years later in 1346 at the battle of Neville's Cross, it was proven that the heirs of the Bruces would not learn. Edward the Third had just won his shattering victory at Crécy against the French chivalry and was besieging Calais. So the young King David the Second with his army sacked the priories of Hexham and Lanercost, crossed the Tyne river, and extorted blackmail from Durham to spare its religious foundations. Opposing them were the northern levies, led by the Archbishop of York and the two great houses of Neville and Percy. For once, the Scots were using 500 prickers as foragers under the command of Sir William Douglas, the 'knight of Liddesdale', who had already seized back from the Nevilles the crucial Border fortress of Hermitage castle.* Trying to avoid past errors, King David drew up his forces in three divisions across the road to Newcastle, while the English matched his strategy on a ridge in front of Neville's Cross, a quarter of a mile away.

The English were particularly strong in their numbers of mounted bowmen, with about 1,000 from Lancashire and 3,000 Yorkshire archers on horseback. The English commanders used this firepower to dislodge the Scots, always too ready to charge, from their hillside. Five hundred archers ran on in advance and peppered the Scots with missiles. As Wyntoun wrote: 'The English archers came so near that shoot among them well might they.' The Earl of Menteith now asked for a repetition of Keith's charge at Bruce's signal victory:

> Then good Sir John de Graham did say
> To the King, 'Get me no more
> Than a hundred horse with me to go,
> And all yon archers scatter shall I;
> So shall we fight more securely.'

Fatally, the King refused this request in pursuit of a greater glory. Ordering the advance of the schiltrons without gathering intelligence, he met the usual obstacles to a frontal assault, gulleys and ditches and fences. Sending his right wing forward under the command of Douglas and the Earl of Moray, David the Second followed with his centre of dismounted knights, better armoured by their French allies, so that they could withstand a rain of arrows. Fierce fighting twice forced the retreat of the English bowmen, who now shot over the heads of the mailed Scots forward ranks at the quilted jacks of the rearguard. This third schiltron was under the command of the king's nephew, Robert Stewart, and they took to their heels rather than back up the press around their struggling monarch, still flying the royal ensign. In Wyntoun's dry words:

> For when the fleears two miles and more
> Were fled, the banners were still standing,
> Face to face still fighting . . .

Surrounded, the king's schiltron fought until he was captured and spirited away to imprisonment in the sea-castle of Bamburgh, before being delivered to Edward the Third, now returning from France. The conflict at Neville's Cross had been a close combat; but once more, the refusal to use light horse and the skill of the English archer had led to the downfall of the Scots slow advance. Far off, the monks of Durham had watched the struggle from their tall cathedral tower; freed from blackmail, they tolled the bells in peals of victory; for another 300 years, these would ring in joyful anniversaries.

The kingdom could not pay the 100,000 marks demanded for the ransom of David the Second, while the English were more preoccupied with battles over the Channel than on the Borders, which were so thoroughly devastated. Yet worse was to come, the grim reaper of pestilence. The Black Death winnowed the population by one-third and nobbled most attempts at warfare. The English had occupied the Tweed basin and the Selkirk forest and the shire about Peebles, and at the treaty of Berwick of 1357, these seizures were confirmed. Yet by continual raiding, the Scots nobles were gradually reclaiming their borderlands, led by the Douglases and the Humes. Robert Stewart then took the throne in 1371 and signed a new alliance with France. In spite of English incursions as far as Edinburgh, which the magnanimous John of Gaunt refused to sack, Robert the Second resumed his Border invasions, while refusing to fight pitched battles. Although reinforced by French knights under John de Vienne, the commanders of the Scots forces preferred to skirmish and harry. To counter these intrusions, the new English King Richard the Second marched north in 1385 with a large army, bent on destruction. But the Scots earls had rediscovered their old tactics, and the earth was scorched as far as the Firth of Forth. Richard burned down the great abbeys of Dryburgh and Melrose and reclaimed Teviotdale and the Tweed basin, while fortifying Roxburgh Castle as another bastion on the Borders, which were meant to remain in English hands.

That was a wishful hope. After three years, the Scots under James, the Earl of Douglas, led an expedition to harrow Northumbria as far as Newcastle. Returning with a vast amount of cattle and booty, Douglas was caught at Otterburn by a surprise attack on his camp at dusk by Lord Henry Percy, called 'Hotspur' for his reckless courage. The Scots had already reconnoitred the ground, and with a quick rally, they counter-charged the enemy in the flank. The English archers were unsighted at night and out of rank. In the *mélée*, Douglas was killed, although not by Hotspur himself, who was captured with his brother, while his forces were decimated.

The ballad of the battle was confused with another encounter between Douglas and Percy, 'The Hunting of the Cheviot'; referring to that poem, Dr Johnson said that he would rather have been the author of Chevy Chase than all his other works. Both poems dealt with a Scottish raid down south, either for hunting or looting, and the fatal encounter between James Douglas and Henry Percy:

> Our English archers bent their bowes;
>   their harts were good and trew;
> Att the first flight of arrows sent,
>   full foure score Scotts they slew . . .

> O Christ! it was great greeve to see
>   how eche man chose his spere,
> And how the blood out of their brests
>   did gush like water clere.

> At last these two stout erles did meet,
>   like captains of great might;
> like lyons woode they laid on lode;
>   that made a cruell fight . . .

> With that there came an arrow keene,
>   out of an English bow,

Which stroke Erle Douglas on the brest
a deepe and deadly blow . . .

Then leaving life, Erle Percy tooke
the dead man by the hand;
Who said, 'Earle Douglas, for thy life,
wold I had lost my land! . . .

Of fifteen hundred Englishmen
went home but fifty-three;
The rest in Chevy Chase were slaine,
under the greenwoode tree.

Fourteen years on, the released Lord Henry Percy had his revenge at Homildon Hill, where the Scots army was drawn up defensively, after another reprisal sortie into Northumbria. The impetuous Hotspur wished to charge uphill at the enemy, but he was 'reined back', as the *Scotichronicon* related, and told that 'he should not move, but should send archers who could easily penetrate the Scots as targets for their arrows and defeat and capture them'. And so the English bowmen took to another hill, separated from Homildon by a ravine, and mowed down the foe as grasses at long range. The volleys of return arrows failed to reach the English archers, who shot at will into the enemy ranks. A cavalry counter-charge led by Archibald, the Earl of Douglas, made the opposing bowmen fall back, 'but still shooting, so vigorously, so resolutely, so effectively that they pierced the armour, perforated the helmets, pitted the swords, split the lances and pierced all the equipment with ease'. The Earl of Douglas was struck in five places. 'The rest of the Scots who had not descended the hill turned tail, and fled from the flight of arrows. But flight did not avail them, so that the Scots were forced to give themselves up, for fear of the death-dealing shafts.'

No English ballads of chivalry could wash down with rosewater the future conduct of Border wars. By ruthlessness and ravages, the Black Douglases extended their authority over Ettrick and Selkirk Forests as well as Eskdale and Lauderdale and Teviotdale. They were over-mighty subjects and the rulers of their lands, especially when the child heir of the weak and dying Stewart King Robert the Third was sent to France for safe keeping under the protection of the Lord High Admiral William, the Second Earl of Orkney. For that young life would not have been spared, any more than those of the Princes in the Tower were to be by their uncle, Richard the Third of England. If the boy Prince James were also to die young, the throne of Scotland would pass to the king's brother Robert, the Duke of Albany, who was already the Regent of the realm.

Whether or not information was passed on to the English, Prince James and Earl William were captured. This was the Earl's second imprisonment, for the English had already taken him at Homildon Hill, before releasing him. As the St Clair chronicler Father Hay recorded, the Earl and the royal child had cast themselves 'to the sea's mercie; but when they had sailed a little space, Prince James not being able to abide the smell of the waters, desired to be att land, where when they were come (for they landed att his request upon the coast of England) upon their journey to the King [of France] they were taken and imprisoned'.

While the pair were held in England, the Duke of Albany acted as king of the realm. In a letter of 1410 to the gaoler Henry the Fourth, Albany referred to the English king's subjects in Scotland. He shrewdly allied himself with the powerful Earls of Douglas, the major power on the south-western Borders. When the grown Stewart King James the First was finally released in 1423, he found that the interregnum under the Albany clan had beggared Scotland. Yet he was determined to rearm his country, also to live in some style, maintaining an extravagant court.

All arms manufacture depended on the royal control of the organisations of the weapon-makers. The Scots kings chose the three St Clair Earls of Orkney and Rosslyn to serve as the Grand Masters of their Crafts and Guilds as well as their Lord High Admirals, in charge of rebuilding the national fleet. Both sides on the Borders took great care of the weapons trade. As Bartholomew wrote in late medieval times 'without iron the commonalty be not sure against enemies. Well-nigh no handiwork is wrought without iron: no field is cared without iron'.

Metal-workers were highly valued and given the freedom of cities, particularly in York during the period of the Scottish conflicts. In 1295, a special smith's lodge was created to build a galley for the King of England. The leading smiths and cutlers and blade-makers and armourers were the cream of their trade. Although iron ingots had to be imported from Sweden and smelting works were small-scale, the guilds of iron-workers in York 'dight no swerds but workmanlike' and 'skabberds but of good stuff'. In that city, plate armour was manufactured and refurbished, while women were used in making chain-mail from iron wire and sewing it onto the leather jerkins used in Border warfare.

The makers of the supreme weapon of the period, the longbow, were also organised in the three guilds and crafts: the bower, the stringmaker and the fletcher. Because of the Border wars, King Edward the Third took over the responsibility for supplies of his armies. For instance, in 1436, the sheriffs of Yorkshire were given the order to have plucked 100,000 goose-wing feathers and to find 'sufficient workers and put them to work on the said arrows'.

The bowers were the cream of their crafts. Because English yew was considered too grainy, Baltic yew with its greater give was imported. Within one century, over a hundred bowers were made free in the city of York alone. The prosperous fletchers made cross-bow bolts as well as arrows, and so they had to employ smiths for the spare parts. The arrow shafts were made from aspen and oak, ash and birch. In their carpenters' guilds, they were joined by the turners and joiners, patenfers and coopers or barrel-makers. This last craft for conveying drink was also vital for military operations. For an army marched, not only on its stomach, but in its throat.

The rearmament begun by James the First was continued by his son and heir, James the Second, when he succeeded to the throne. He managed to deal with the current Black Douglas as Robert the Bruce had done away with the Red Comyn; he stabbed his rival with a dirk in a parley. He was so enthralled by artillery that he brought from Flanders the greatest cannon in Britain, Mons Meg. And in 1456, his Council or early parliament insisted that it was 'speedful that the king make request to certain of the great barons of the land that are of any might to make carts of war, and in each cart two guns, and each of them to have two chambers, with the rest of the gear that pertains thereto, and a cunning man to shoot them'. While quartered with his Queen at Hume Castle four years later, the King was killed at a siege of Roxburgh castle. One of his own cannon 'brak in the fyring'. He was only thirty years old, and left another boy heir to the throne, although he did fulfil a prophecy that the castle would be won from the English only by a dead monarch. And the fortress did surrender in the end, only to be razed to rubble.

When, in 1488, James the Fourth ascended the throne, he would vie with the new Tudor Crown as the creator of a powerful national navy to rule the seas. In 1511, when he lost two ships in a firefight with the Lords Howard, the *Lion* and the *Jenny Pirwin*, he demanded their return, only to be told that they were pirates. And both by land and sea, cannon were the new weapons. Those who made and serviced and moved them demanded payment in coin. Early trials of carting cannon were made at Stirling before going to Edinburgh castle, which also manufactured powder and shot. The costs of maintenance and movement were high. In a raiding expedition of 1497, the Scots King had to engage nearly 400 road-builders, quarrymen and masons to smooth the way for the gun-carts, and also more than 100 drivers and 30 smiths and armourers.

Before his reign, the Scottish navy had merely consisted of armed cogs or merchantmen. The first new warship was the *Margaret*, which boasted 21 guns. Yet the pride of the new fleet was the great *Michael*, which rivalled Mons Meg as the largest weapon in existence. Some 80 yards long, she sported six cannon on either side with three basilisks at stern and prow, and 300 smaller guns, 'falcons, slangs, pestilent serpentines, and double dogs, with hackbutts and culverines'. She also needed 300 sailors and 120 gunners for her use, while she carried 1,000 men-at-arms. Unfortunately, *Michael* hardly saw action and was sold to King Louis XII of France: she rotted away in the harbour of Brest.

This vast exercise in shipbuilding was under the supervision of the Lord High Admiral, Earl William St Clair, also the lawgiver to the Guilds, as recorded in his 'Lawis and Costumis of Ye Schippis' from the Rosslyn Library. He was made Chancellor and Lord Chamberlain to supervise these works. Some of the artillery was supplied from family sources. Lord Henry St Clair served the King as 'Master of all our Machines and Artyllerie' and sold to his royal leader eight great 'serpentynis' for £100, which would be paid to his widow after both of their deaths at Flodden field.

King James had long been accused of putting his bravery above his command. 'He is courageous even more than a king should be,' the Spanish ambassador Don Pedro de Ayala said. 'He is not a good captain because he begins to fight before he has given his orders.' Such impetuosity was bolstered by the introduction into the Scots army of Highlanders, riding bareback on small ponies with their feet dangling on the ground. Dismounted for action, their equipment was simple.

From the mid-leg to the foot they go uncovered: their dress is, for an overgarment, a loose plaid and a shirt saffron dyed. They are armed with a bow and arrows, a broadsword and a small halbert. They always carry in their belt a stout dagger, single-edged but the sharpest. In time of war they cover the whole body with a coat of mail, made of iron rings, and in it they fight. The common-folk among the wild Scots go out to battle with the whole body clad in a linen garment, sewn together in patchwork, well daubed with wax or pitch, and with an overcoat of deerskin.

Leading the Scots line as skirmishers, these Gaelic troops were to draw first blood at Flodden. As the Scottish chronicler Piscottie observed, 'the Earl of Huntley's Highland men with their bows and two-handed swords fought so manfully that they defeated the Englishmen'.

The battle had begun in 1513 with a flanking movement by the English forces under the Earl of Surrey, and an artillery duel. With their superior cannon placed high on Branxton Hill, the Scottish gunners could not lower their muzzles enough to strafe the English ranks, while the enemy bombards made hay among the schiltrons. Broken into disorder, the advancing men with pikes came into contact with the dismounted English Borderers with their eight-foot shafts and battle-axes. As the Bishop of Durham later wrote: 'Our bills quit them very well . . . for they shortly disappointed the Scots of their long spears wherein was their greatest trust.' However well the Scots then fought with their swords, large and strong men had to fall 'when four or five bills struck on them at once'.

Weapons and tactics remained the masters of battles. King James the Fourth had been supplied by the King of France with 400 muskets, 600 handguns, and 6,000 each of pikes, spears and maces. Sergeants had been sent over to instruct raw troops in the use of these three arms. Moreover, two cannon and forty cartloads of gunpowder had been contributed to add to the fifteen Scottish big brass guns, some made by the Master Gunner, Robert, Lord Borthwick. A mobile workshop of armourers accompanied the cannon train, which had a complement of smiths with cranes and tools, anvils, iron ingots and coals.

During the opening barrage, many of the Border light horse under Lord Dacre fled the field, terrified by the noise. This loss to the Earl of Surrey's side was compensated, when Dacre still held onto some 2,000 of the cavalry behind the divisions of the two main bodies, flanked by two wings. This force came mainly from Cumbria and Westmoreland and was true to Dacre, who was the Warden of the English Middle and West Marches. They rescued Lord Edmund Howard, when he was surrounded alongside his billmen, and they saw off the prickers of Lord Hume; but then they deserted the field to rob the slain and to steal horses. Hume or Home's dallying from the main fight was either due to the notorious reluctance of Borderers to fight each other to the death, or to a refusal to commit himself too much, even when his King was beset. 'We have fought our vanguard already and won the same,' he was reported to have said, 'therefore let the rest do their part as well as we.'

King James the Fourth fought in the van with a pike. He was killed, perhaps as King Harold had been at Hastings, by enemy archers. Many of the Scots threw down their useless overlong pikes and took to lead maces or stabbing swords. The arrows won the day against a final charge of the heavy Scots knights, with their leader Bothwell dying, pierced with a grey goose-feathered shaft. The vultures of the English soldiers acquired all the Scots munitions of war, including seventeen cannon and 2,000 pikes, while the sword and body armour of King James were hung with his standard in St Cuthbert's shrine at Durham cathedral, where the Bishop denounced the English Borderers as being 'falser than the Scots and have done more harm at this tyme to our folk, than the Scots did . . . rifling and robbing as well on our side'.

The Scots monarch had married Margaret Tudor, who became the Queen Dowager and the brief Regent of the kingdom, while her brother King Henry the Eighth blew hot and cold over his policy across the Borders. Another Duke of Albany, who had been reared in France and was the heir to the throne if the young James the Fifth were to die, replaced the Tudor widow as the Regent of the nation. When he was old enough to govern, the young king tried to bring some order to the lawless Borders. Before a celebrated sortie in 1529 with 10,000 men, he imprisoned the chiefs of the Reivers, the Earls of Bothwell and the Lords Home and Maxwell and the Scotts of Buccleuch. Now he struck through Ettrick and Ewesdale at Johnie Armstrong of Glenockie, who had spread the terror of his name as far as Newcastle and 'levied blackmail, or 'protection and forbearance money', for many miles around'. Thinking a brief surrender the best policy, Armstrong presented himself with forty of his freebooters, arrayed so finely that they outdid the King's own court. He offered to serve James faithfully, and to bring him any English earl or baron, quick or dead. But the king replied, 'What wants that knave that a king should have,' and ordered the execution of the outlaw and his men. 'It is folly to seek grace at a graceless face,' Armstrong replied, for James had lost a formidable ally in time of war. 'Had I known this, I should have lived upon the Borders in despite of King Harry and you both; for I know King Harry would down-weigh my best horse with gold, to know that I were condemned to die this day.'

His ballad lamented his hanging on the sentence of the King:

> 'Away, away, thou traitor strang!
>   Out o' my sight soon mayst thou be!
> I grantit nevir a traitor's life,
>   And now I'll not begin wi' thee . . .'

> John murdered was att Carlinrigg,
>   And all his gallant companie;
> But Scotland's heart was ne'er sae wae,
>   To see sae mony brave men die –

> Because they saved their countrey deir
>   Frae Englishmen! Nane were sae bauld,
> While Johnie lived on the Border side,
>   Nane of them durst cum neir his hauld.

The Scots king also wanted to bring some order to the Highlands and the Western Isles, and to incorporate their fearsome warriors into his army. With the large and well-armed fleet which he had inherited, he sailed from the Firth of Forth to Orkney, where he met his future favourite, the handsome Oliver Sinclair of Pitcairn, who was made the lessor of Orkney and the Shetlands. On another voyage to the Isles in 1540, James took a fleet of sixteen vessels, including the French warship *Salamander*. The expedition was victualled at Leith and armed from Edinburgh castle. As an English chronicler noted, 'In all Scottlande was not leffte ten peces of ordenance besides that wyche the Kynge dothe take with Hym.' He was well defended, even on his travels.

On the Borders, James the Fifth once again already proceeded to destroy the powerful Douglas family, which had already forfeited most of its estates. The important fortress of Tantallon on the Firth of Forth was now assigned to Oliver Sinclair, who had entered the royal Household, where he became the keeper of the king's purse and his cupbearer and his Ganymede. He was accused of abusing the royal bedchamber and serving as a 'familiar'.

With King Henry the Eighth threatening an invasion, if James did not repudiate the authority of the Pope, and with the reformer John Knox trying to lead the people of Edinburgh in a Protestant revolution, the Scottish King stuck to the Old Alliance with France and the Catholic faith. He married two French ladies with large dowries; the second was Mary of

Guise, who had turned down King Henry's advances, when he was look-ing for his fourth wife. As for Oliver Sinclair, he was denounced by the radical reformer, John Knox, as a 'pensioner of the priests', and he was prominent on a list of heretical nobles. To the English Earl of Hertford, he was 'the most secrete man, leving with the said King of Scottis'.

Various frontier and sea raids were the prelude to a military disaster. The rebellious nobility had turned against their royal master and his upstart favourites, as had happened in England with King Richard the Second and his minions. A large Scottish army under its feudal Lords was assembled in November, 1542, to pre-empt an English attack. Against them stood the old Border warrior, Sir Thomas Wharton, who described his strategy as 'fighting the battle as he saw it, with a reiver's eye and a reiver's tactics'.

A force of some 10,000 men advanced from Scotland, burning their path through Cumbria between the Esk river and the marshland of Solway Moss. A force of 700 enemy prickers and 200 Kendal archers drew them forward by retreating at speed. The Scots found themselves enmeshed and leaderless. In the words of Father Hay, the angry aristocracy could not stomach the elevation of the King's familiar, Oliver Sinclair:

> Oliver thought time to shew his glory, and so incontinent was displayed the King's banner, and he holden up by two spears lift up upon men's shoulders, there, with the sound of trumpet, was declared Generall Lieutenant, and all men commanded to obey him as the King's person, under the highest pains, so soon a great noise and confusion was heard. The enimie, perceaveing the disorder, rushed on, the Scots fled, some passed the water, but escaping that danger, not well acquainted with the ground, fell into the slimy mosse; happy was he that might get a taker. Stout Oliver was without stroke taken, flying full manfully, and so was his glory suddenly turn'd to confusion and shame.

This was the finest and final victory of the Border cavalry. As with the Parthians and the later Apaches, mounted archers with javelins and tomahawks or axes could harass and defeat armoured ranks, which outnumbered them ten times over. If the morale and strategy of the foe failed, as at Solway Moss, the light horse could harry the legions and the schiltrons and the heavy knights into the wet ground. That was the military lesson of this frontier over the 600 years of its fighting times.

'Oh fled Oliver!' King James the Fifth of Scotland cried, when he heard that Sinclair had lost the battle of Solway Moss. 'Is Oliver tane?

Fie fled Oliver! All is lost!' Soon afterwards, he took to his deathbed at the age of thirty, stricken by the 'pest' or cholera. When he heard the news that his wife, Marie of Guise, had borne him a daughter, he said of his kingdom, 'Adieu, fare well, it came with a lass, it will pass with a lass.' The independent kingdom had come to the Stewarts through their marriage with a Bruce princess, and it would pass with James's child, Mary, Queen of Scots. Although the Stewarts would inherit the English throne as well as that of Scotland, the twinning of the Crowns would mean the lessening of Scottish liberty and the eventual fall of the Reivers.

CHAPTER SIX

Ballads of Circumstance

The total destruction of the Borders, which reduced the fertile dales to a smoking wasteland, was the result of cruel diplomacy. After 1544, for four years, an open war broke out between England and Scotland. King Henry the Eighth wanted his heir, Prince Edward, to marry Mary, the child Queen of Scots. Thus the crowns of England and Scotland would be united. When a Scottish Council renewed the Old Alliance with France and defended the Catholic faith, Henry decided on 'a rough wooing'. The instructions of the Privy Council to the English commander, Edward Seymour, Earl of Hertford, were explicit. Over the Borders, he was to pursue a scorched-earth policy.

Put all to fire and sword, burn Edinburgh town, so razed and defaced when you have sacked and gotten what ye can of it as there may remain forever a perpetual memory of the vengeance of God lighted upon them for their falsehood and disloyalty. Do what ye can out of hand and without long tarrying to beat down and overthrow the Castle, sack Holyrood House and burn and subvert it and all the rest, putting man, woman, and child to fire and sword without exception, where any resistance shall be made against you; and this done, pass over to the Fifeland, and extend like extremity and destruction in all towns and villages whereunto ye may reach conveniently, not forgetting among all the rest so to spoil the cardinal's town of St Andrews as the upper stone may be the nether, and not one stick stand by another, sparing no creature alive within the same.

Lord Hertford with his army and fleet landed on the Firth of Forth, while another column struck across the Borders. He slashed and burned Edinburgh and Holyrood, Dunbar and Leith. He was joined by 400 'light horsemen from the Borders by the King Majesty's appointment, who after their coming did such exploits in riding and devastating the country, that within seven miles every way of Edinburgh, they left neither *pele*, village or house standing unburnt, nor stacks of corn; besides great number of cattle, which they brought daily in the army'.

The *peles* were particular targets. Near Dunglas, Lord Home's Thornton Tower and Anderwike were set on opposite crags, 'divided a stone's cast asunder, by a deep gut, wherein ran a little river'. These two strongholds were bombarded by four great canon, their loopholes and small windows covered by English hackbutters or 'hook-gun' marksmen. One *pele* was fired from underneath, the other mined and penetrated and all the defenders put to the sword or hanged. At Smailholm, however, which served as a beacon to warn the Borders of attack, the Pringles survived with great losses, losing 600 cattle and 100 horses, with the same number of prisoners, to raiders from Tynedale and Redesdale.* They were forced to change sides and swear allegiance to King Henry the Eighth. Not that vows among the Reivers were long-lasting. As the ballad went:

> Oaths are but words, and words but wind:
> Too feeble instruments to bind.

By the end of the following year, seven monasteries, including Dryburgh and Kelso and Melrose, had been plundered and torched, along with sixteen forts, five market towns and 243 villages until the very skies ran red.* The only retaliation by the Scots the following year was the rout at Ancrum Moor of another raiding party, which had reached Melrose on a further despoiling and was retiring with its booty. The hero of the occasion was Sir Walter Scott of Buccleuch, who wanted revenge for losing whole herds of cattle and forty kinsmen, while his outworks were burned at Branxholm, and the Moss Tower near Eckford was 'smoked very sore'. He advised the Earl of Angus on traditional Reiver tactics. The English were decoyed into a pell-mell advance by seeing spare horses galloping away on the skyline. They believed the enemy was in full flight, so they thrust uphill to find a phalanx of Scots spearsmen, waiting to counter-attack their disarray. As another Walter Scott, the novelist, recorded of the battle: 'with the setting sun and wind full in their faces, [they] were unable to withstand the resolute and desperate charge of the Scottish lances. No sooner had they begun to waver, than their own allies, the assured Borderers, who had been waiting for the event, threw aside their red crosses, and joining their countrymen, made a most merciless slaughter among the English fugitives.'

One year later, even the turncoat Reivers could do nothing to prevent a Protestant revolt. With the assistance of the Queen Regent, Mary of Guise, Cardinal Beaton had defended the old Catholic faith against the militant Reformers. The rebels murdered the Cardinal in the castle of St Andrews, for he was, in the words of the aggressive minister John Knox, 'an obstinate enemy of Christ Jesus'. Under threat himself, Knox took off to St Andrews, only to be seized in an assault by the French fleet and sent off to row in their galleys. This treatment hardly endeared him to that foreign country.

Although Henry the Eighth now died, Lord Hertford, the new Duke of Somerset, became the Protector of Edward, the nine-year-old King of England, and he pursued the previous royal policy. Invading in September, 1547, he wisely bypassed the fortress of Tantallon, which was defended by the Earl of Angus, who had refused a French garrison, offered by Mary of Guise. Feeding a falcon on his wrist in the royal presence, Angus had said: 'Yea, madam, the castle is yours; God forbid else. But by the might of God, madam! I must be your captain and keeper for you, and I will keep it as well as any you can place there.'

And so he did against Somerset, who had to press forward on the coast route to Edinburgh, in order to stay close to the guns and supplies of his flanking fleet. He found a Scots army twice his size, which was defending Edmonstone Edge, a strong position behind the Esk river near Musselburgh. He encamped at Prestonpans, where he was irritated by the daily skirmishes of Lord Home with his 1,500 prickers and scouts. He loosed most of his own 2,500 demi-lancers and 'Bands of Northern Horsemen' at the Scots Borderers, who were turning downhill in the evening. The retiring horsemen were scattered and fled with heavy losses, while Lord Home himself was wounded and retired to Edinburgh, leaving his army without any cavalry.

Although the Scots were outgunned, the Earl of Argyll had a division of 4,000 Highlanders under his command. They had taken over the role of mounted archers from the Reivers, who were increasingly equipped with the 'dag' or pistol rather than the bow, even though Somerset had noted that the 'Scotishe borderers . . . love no gonnes, nor he will abyde withyn the hearing of the same'. Although usually dismounted in formal battle, the Highlanders of Galloway were a fearful sight:

When they go to War, the Armour wherewith they cover their bodies, is Morion or Bonnet of Iron, and a Habergeon, which comes down almost to their very heels; their weapons against their Enemies are Bows and

Arrows, and they are generally reported good Marks-Men upon all occasions; their Arrows are for the most part barbed or crooked, which once entered within the Body cannot well be drawn out again, unless the Wound be made wider; some of them fight with broad Swords and Axes, and in the room of a Drum make use of a Bagpipe.

Although suffering cross-fire from the ships' cannon offshore, a bombardment which made some of the Highlanders run, the schiltrons crossed the Esk, while Somerset's army was still marching to meet them. His heavy cavalry baulked at a charge on the massed pikes of the enemy, but Somerset had time to form a battle-line and deploy his artillery on the high ground of Pinkie Cleugh. Unwisely, the schiltrons retreated to regroup and were broken by gunfire. An English counter-charge ended in their rout and massacre. As the chronicler William Patten noted, the dead bodies of the Scots lay about as a herd of cattle, grazing on the pasture. Ten thousand died in that pitched battle, which was the beginning of the end of the old ways of war. The musket and the culverin could now deal with massed infantry and a Highland charge. Even the raiding days of the Reivers would be numbered, for gunpowder and the bayonet were mightier than horse fodder and the lance.

The English invaders took the opportunity again to sack Holyrood Abbey, where they only found a lead roof, good for casting balls for their muskets. The destruction was so complete that the most ornate church in Scotland became a stone quarry for looters after the Reformation. The four-year-old Mary, Queen of Scots, was separated from her mother, Mary of Guise, and bundled off to an Augustinian island priory. Then, after the arrival of French troops, she was carried away in a royal galley, pledged to marry the Dauphin, when she came of age.

So the bold Tudor plan of uniting the Crowns of England and Scotland would come to an end for the time being. Protector Somerset considered making a strip of wasteland 12 miles wide through the Debateable Land to separate the two nations, while a proposal would later be put to Queen Elizabeth the First to rebuild Hadrian's Wall, this time to be defended by 'great gonners . . . in an arteficiall fortyficacion, consystinge for the most parte onlye of mayne earthe, raysed with trenche and rampyour, and flaunched with bulwarkes'.

Yet the frontier had been ravaged almost to extinction. As Walter Scott testified: 'the Border counties, exposed from their situation to the incursions of the English, deprived of many of their most gallant chiefs, and harassed by the intestine struggles of the survivors, were reduced to a wilderness, inhabited only by the beasts of the field, and by a few more brutal warriors.' And though 'not more sanguinary than the rest of a barbarous nation, the Borderers never dismissed from their memory a deadly feud, till blood for blood had been exacted, to the uttermost drachm'. And so, the swansong of the Reivers began in a lawless countryside, where looting and revenge were merely honourable reprisals for the long ravishment of beast and field and home.

Stealth was superior to a scaling ladder in taking a Tower on the Borders. When Sir Thomas Carleton from Cumbria reached the Johnstone *pele* of Lochwood, he mixed aggression with surprise. First, he made a night raid on the outer palisade around the barmekin. The cattle and the women there were seized, and men were put at dawn by the bolted main entrance into the stone inner keep. A Reiver, wearing only a shirt, shouted to the lassie inside to open up. As she pulled back the heavy door, the raiders 'brake too soon'. Yet in trying to slam the door shut, she was overwhelmed by the charge of the invaders, and they burst in. Lochwood Tower was taken with no blood spilt at all.

The most extreme of the Border feuds was between the Maxwells and the Johnstones for control of Dumfries and the post of Warden of the Western Marches, which gave some legitimacy to their depredations. Their endless reprisals reduced the whole of the Debateable Land to anarchy. In 1586, the English Warden of the West March, Lord Scrope, complained to Westminster of the situation: 'I look to no justice from the opposite Border as I am told Maxwell has refused the Wardenry and every laird, gentleman and Borderer rides against the other. As the nights grow long and dark, I expect their accustomed insolencies against us will proceed afresh.' A year later, the Border and Highland Reivers were proscribed by Act of Parliament, with all the Lords of Misrule and their clans 'rendered jointly answerable, and liable to be proceeded against, in the way of retaliation, for the delinquencies of each individual'.* The chieftains were to deliver all miscreants to the due process of the law, probably hanging, or else suffer imprisonment and the large fine of £200 in forfeit.

As with mice and cats, however, the question was: Who would bell the Reivers? That was impossible for any state troopers in the eighty years of backstabbing between the Maxwells and the Johnstones; as early as 1528, Lord Dacre had complained that the feud had already turned the Debateable Land into a waste. The leaders of both clans vied for royal favour and the Wardenship of the West Marches was batted between them like a tennis ball. In 1585, their forays burst into open war, with Lord Maxwell and 1700 prickers devastating the Johnstone lands and capturing all their towers and strongholds except for Lochmaben Castle, which also surrendered when the captured Johnstone Warden was threatened with the gallows. In spite of his attack on royal authority, Lord Maxwell's success led to his promotion. His power made him the preferred new Scots Warden of the Western March. Often he had backing among the Armstrongs and the Elliots, the Grahams and Scotts, and his marauding forces far outnumbered the enemy. Lord Scrope considered him the chief congener of 'loose Borderers'. Indeed, one of his occasional allies, the Moffats, cut a rival raiding party to pieces. Their chief hacked off the heads of the dead men and put the trophies in a sack with the remark: 'There you are then, Johnstones, ye can a' greet togither the now.'

Early in 1589, Lord Maxwell and his bastard brother Robert burned down the Johnstone keep of Lochwood, so that the Lady there 'might have a light to put on her hood'. The king demanded retribution; but the Maxwells were too powerful, sacking nearly 400 houses of the rival clan, and carrying off 3,000 head of cattle. Yet, as an ardent Roman Catholic, Lord Maxwell fell into disfavour with the Reformers near to the Crown. Imprisoned in Edinburgh, he contrived an escape into exile, where he plotted to aid the Spanish invasion with its Armada. On his return to his homeland, he was captured by the King's forces and put in gaol again, only to be restored five years later as the lifelong Warden of his region.

A younger Laird, Sir James Johnstone, had inherited on the death of his defeated father. He faced the old fox at a climactic battle at the Dryfe Sands, near Lockerbie. The shifting clans had changed sides, led by Buccleuch and the Scotts. In the opinion of the family historian, these were 'the most renowned freebooters, the fiercest and the bravest warriors, among the Border tribes'. Outnumbered five to one by the 2,000 horse of the foe, Johnstone's men ambushed the Maxwell vanguard and slashed into the main body. Their back-handed sword strokes at the faces of their felled and fleeing victims were known as 'Lockerbie licks'. The dismounted Lord Maxwell was said to have held out his hand for mercy, only to have it severed at the wrist, before he was executed.

His son John vowed vengeance, but was again imprisoned in Edinburgh castle, and escaped once more. He pretended to seek a reconciliation with Sir James Johnstone, at the safe house of a relative by marriage of both the feuding parties. There Maxwell 'shott him behind his back with ane pistoll chairgit with two poysonit bullets, at which shott the said Sir James fell from his horse. Maxwell not being content therewith, raid about him ane lang tyme, and persued him farder, vowing to use him more cruellie and treacherouslie than he had done . . . A fact detested by all honest men, and the gentleman's misfortune severely lamented, for he was a man full of wisdom and courage.'

The killer escaped to France, but returned to Caithness, where he was betrayed by the Earl and put on trial. He was indicted for murder and fire-raising, which involved the forfeiture of his estate, although the lands would be later returned to his brother. Beheaded in 1613, John, Lord Maxwell, ended the 'foul debate' with the Johnstones. In the long course of this feud, Sir Walter Scott noted, 'each family lost two chieftains; one dying of a broken heart, one on the field of battle, one by assassination, and one by the sword of the executioner'.

The legacy of this extraordinary feud was one of the more haunting of the Border ballads, 'Lord Maxwell's Last Goodnight', which inspired the later Scots Lord Byron in the first canto of his *Childe Harold*. After murdering his sworn foe, Lord John had to go into exile:

> 'Adieu! fair Eskdale up and down,
> Where my puir friends do dwell;
> The bangisters will ding them down,
> And will them sair compell.
>
> But I'll avenge their feid mysell,
> When I come o'er the sea;
> Adieu! my ladye, and only joy,
> For I may not stay wi' thee.'
>
> The wind was fair, the ship was clear,
> That good lord went away;
> And most part of his friends were there,
> To give him a fair convey.
>
> They drank the wine, they didna spair,
> Even in that gude lord's sight –
> Sae now he's o'er the floods sae gray,
> And Lord Maxwell has ta'en his Goodnight.

One strange commentary on the Maxwell history is the square stone Tower that stands by Hoddam Castle in Annandale. Above its door are carved the figures of a dove and a serpent with the word REPENTANCE between them, emblems of grace and remorse. Probably built by Sir John, the Master of Maxwell, who was created Lord Herries in 1566, the property was acquired by marriage with the heiress, Agnes Herries. She was the price of sacrificing his kinsmen, who were hostages with the English, and his changing sides to join the Laird of Drumlanrig and his Reivers from Scotland. In the ballad of 'The Lord Herries His Complaint', he sat in the Repentance tower 'mirk was [his] soul, the chief sae sad and sour'. He had cut the throats of his prisoners and thrown them overboard to lighten his ship in a storm.

> To help my boat, I pierced the throat
> Of him whom ane lo'ed dear;
> Nought did I spare his yellow hair,
> And een sae bricht and clear.
>
> She sits her lane, and maketh mane,
> And sings a waefu' sang, –
> 'Scotch reivers hae my darling ta'en;
> 'O Willie tarries lang!'
>
> Alas! twelve precious lives were spilt,
> My worthless spark to save;
> Bet had I fall'n withouten guilt,
> Frae cradle to the grave.

CHAPTER SEVEN

The Prickly Pride

The problem of blood feuds was that murders were long remembered and hardly forgotten. An imperative of nations had always been to assign the struggles of tribes against each other to the rule of law. In more primitive regions, there could be little cohabitation or toleration without the incoming of some civilised values – and even legal verdicts, however much resisted. Otherwise, deportation or confinement were the only remedies for the clashes of the clans.

Against these encroachments of society on the culture of the Borders, stood thousands of years of the arts of survival. Blood called for payment in blood – or in money, for the spilling of it. And if a family had a tradition of living on the raiding of black cattle, how easily might it change its way of life? What were the alternatives offered in the Middle Ages? Feudalism might be creeping across the frontier, but then a Reiver would have to give up his liberty to become a retainer or a serf of the local warlord. The King and his ministers were too far away for any employment or much justice. And the Church had become the major landowner and restraint in the Borderlands. Thus any affray might be named as a sacrilege. The punishment of marauders might lead to a cursing and the loss of the mercy of God, as well as to a verdict of death by the noose or on the scaffold.

So fearful were many of the Borderers of the teachings of the Church that, at the christening of a male child, his right hand was left out of the holy water of the font, so that it was unhallowed, and could strike down any foe in a blood feud. Anathema could be avoided. Such a terror of God did not extend to Lord Borthwick in his castle. Excommunicated by the Bishop of St Andrews in 1547, the Border peer seized the legal papers before they were read out in the local church, ducked the messenger in the mill-dam and forced him to eat the pieces of the torn parchment, soaked in a bowl of wine. Calling himself the Abbot of

Unreason, Borthwick swore that more Church documents 'should a' gang the same gait'.

The vendetta in Northumbria was described in 1549 in *Chorographia*:

> The people of this countrey hath had one barbarous custom among them;
> if any two be displeased, they expect no lawe, but bang it out bravely, one
> and his kindred against the other and his; they will subject themselves to
> no justice, but in an inhumane and barbarous manner fight and kill one
> another. This fighting they call their feides, or deadly feides . . .

Paradoxically, however, the threat of retribution preserved the lives of some of the worst of the Reivers. 'The country dare not kill such thieves for fear of feud,' wrote the English Warden of the East March, Sir Robert Carey. For he who killed or took a Borderer of repute, 'is sure himself, and all his friends (specially those of his name) is like, dearly to buy it, for they will have his life, or 2 or 3 of his nearest kinsmen, in revenge'.

Many of the Border feuds began with an attempt to snatch or to save the monarch. For instance, in 1526, the young King James the Fifth wished to escape from the iron grip of the Earl of Angus, who numbered the Kerr clan among his supporters. The King arranged for Scott of Buccleuch to rescue him with 600 prickers from Liddesdale and Annandale, but after a bloody encounter at Melrose, the Kerr leader was killed by an Elliot, who was joining the Scotts in the attempt. Although there was a truce declared after a 'Romeo and Juliet' marriage between the two families, murder was still in the air. When Buccleuch was later walking through Edinburgh, he was ambushed by a Kerr gang and sliced down with the yell, 'Strike! Ane straik for they father's sake!' The killers were outlawed, and the Scotts retaliated, and the feud sputtered to a finish in time.

Because of national politics, there was even a curious alliance between the royalist Kerrs of the Border castle of Ferniehirst and Buccleuch against the Protestant borough of Jedburgh, which was tearing down its magnificent Abbey. With 3,000 men, the supporters of Mary, Queen of Scots, attacked the city, but were driven off by riders under the command of Lord Ruthven. The Reivers went in to assault Roxburgh with 'fyre, sword, and all kind of creweltie'; but in the way of all Border feuds, Sir Thomas Kerr of Ferniehirst proved so troublesome that he even became the Warden of the Middle March and the Keeper of Liddesdale.

The metamorphosis of Reiver into Sheriff had already been brokered by Buccleuch in the ironic ballad of 'The Outlaw Murray'. King James the Fourth was assured of the support of the Scotts:

> 'The man that wons yon Foreste intill,
>   He lives by reif and felonie!
> Wherefore, brayd on, my sovereign liege!
>   Wi' fire and sword we'll follow thee;
> Or, gif your courtrie lords fa' back,
>   Our Borderers sall the onset gie.'
>
> Then out and spak the nobil King,
>   And round him cast a wilie ee–
> 'Now haud thy tongue, Sir Walter Scott,
>   Nor speik of reif nor felonie:
> For, had every honeste man his awin kye,
>   A right puir clan thy name wad be!'

When the Outlaw Murray came before the King, he begged for mercy; but he declared that he had won Ettrick Forest from the English, and he would always defend it for his royal master against the enemy. And so he was rewarded for his misdeeds.

> The keys o' the castell he gave the King,
>   Wi' the blessing o' his feir ladye;
> He was made sheriffe of Ettricke Foreste,
>   Surely while upward grows the tree;
> And if he was na traitour to the King,
>   Forfaulted he suld nevir be.

There was an intense competition among the Border lairds for the Wardenships of the three Marches, and this struggle for power furthered many of the blood feuds, as between the Maxwells and the Johnstones in the West March. The Middle March was, indeed, usually in the hands of the Lords of Buccleuch or Ferniehirst, although the office fell into the grasp of the Earls of Bothwell. As for the East March, it was normally the terrain of the Earls of Home. When the Duke of Albany, during his Regency over the young King James the Fifth, made a Warden of the French knight, the Sieur de la Bastie, Home of Wedderburn attacked him and cut off his head; its flaxen locks were knitted to the saddlebow of his executioner, then left to wither in the winds on the battlements of Home Castle.

As the Earl of Warwick and the Percys had been the kingmakers of the Wars of the Roses, so the Border clans became key players in the succession struggle in Scotland. After the death of her mother and her young husband, who had become the King of France, Mary Stewart had sailed in 1561 to assume the Crown. She was a tall woman, given to hunting and hawking, archery and even golf. She rode with her troops in male costume, saying that she wished she were a man, so that she could lie out in the fields all night. One of her admirers wrote of her 'goodly personage, alluring grace, a pretty scotch accent, and a searching wit, clouded with mildness'. Her mistakes lay in her choice of her next two husbands, although she did her best to conciliate the Protestant lords and the Kirk ministers, who saw their futures in taking over the estates of the Catholic church, as King Henry the Eighth had done with the English abbeys, and cathedrals and monasteries.

In her preliminary encounters with the formidable John Knox, now returned to Scotland, the Queen displayed her intelligence and belief. Knox claimed that the Kirk with its *Book of Discipline* was the only true faith, and that its followers were subject to its doctrines, preached by the ministers. To this assertion, Mary replied: 'I perceive that my subjects shall obey you, and not me; and shall do what they list and not what I command.' When Knox replied that only the Reformed Church could take her to everlasting glory, she countered with the words, 'I will defend the Kirk of Rome, for I think, it is the true Kirk of God.'

The Queen's second husband, Henry, Lord Darnley, was a Lennox with a Catholic mother. A vain and foolish youth, he trimmed over his religion, attending sermons by John Knox at St Giles, and refusing to join Mary in the nuptial Mass after their wedding. He even conspired against his own wife. He plotted with the Protestant lords in the murder of her confidant and secretary Riccio, also a Dominican friar, kept in Holyrood Palace. He did, however, give her a son, the future James the Sixth of Scotland and First of England, baptised by Catholic ceremonial.

The ambitious and unpopular Earl of Bothwell had been granted the post of the Queen's Lieutenant on the Borders. In pursuit of some of the leading Reivers, he was nearly killed by Little Jock Elliot, who was shot out of his saddle; but before he died of his wounds, he stabbed the Earl three times, thus nearly saving the Scots throne. A ballad celebrated his defiance:

'My name is Little Jock Elliot,
And wha daur meddle wi' me?'

On a royal progress through the East and Middle Marches, Queen Mary was advised of Bothwell's injury. She rode from Jedburgh to visit the sick man, now languishing in the formidable Hermitage Castle among the bloody braes of Liddesdale.* They held a tryst alone for two hours, before the Queen's return to Jedburgh. Bogged in a quagmire or moss on the way, she fell sick and nearly died of fever.

Worse was to happen to her husband. Lord Darnley was garrotted at Kirk o' Field, which was then blown up to hide the evidence. And Mary, Queen of Scots, was abducted by a force led by Bothwell and taken to his other castle at Dunbar. Curiously enough, a victim may fall in love with her kidnapper, and certainly she was to marry her reviled gaoler, thus endangering her throne. Even the Pope now had to cut off all communication with the Catholic Queen 'unless, indeed, in times to come she shall see some better sign of her life and religion'.

The Border chiefs split in their allegiance. The Homes and the Kerrs supported the royal cause, while the Johnstones and the Jardines and the Annandale clans took against her. But when the Queen rode against her rebellious barons at Carberry Hill, she found her army melting away, because of the usual choice of the Borderers to join the side of those who were winning, at least for the time being. Bothwell fled into an obscure exile, while his royal wife was imprisoned in Loch Leven castle, where she was forced to abdicate the throne in favour of her infant son. When she escaped, many of Scots lords from the Western March, led by the Catholic Lord Maxwell, joined her standard. For the struggle was developing into the future religious wars between the Old Faith and the new Reformation. Finally defeated at Langside in 1568, the Queen of Scots fled over the Border to England, hoping for mercy at the hands of Queen Elizabeth the First, but there was no compassion to be had, only twenty years of captivity, before execution by the axe as a danger to the realm.

An extraordinary picture of the chaos on the Borders and the powerlessness of the rulers at Edinburgh was recorded by an English spy, Robert Constable, taken to Ferniehirst, where he found 'many gests of dyvers factions, some outlaws of Ingland, some of Scotland, some neighbors therabout, at cards'. He began by enquiring whether 'there was none of any surname that had me in deadly fude, nor none that knew me'. Reassured, Constable sat down to test the swirling waters.

He discovered that the Scots Regent Murray would not bring to justice the rebel Earls of Westmoreland and Northumberland. He could not 'for his own honor, nor for thonor of his country, deliver the earles, if he had them bothe, unless it were to have there Quene delivered to him, and if he would agree to make that change, the borderers wold stert up in his contrary, and reave both the Quene and the lords from him, for the like shame was never done in Scotland'.

During the various Regencies until the child monarch James the Sixth was of age, the power of the Reformed Church of Scotland grew, while the Border raids did not cease. Although by 1572 the 'Concordat of Leith' allowed Protestant ministers to take over parish churches and lands, when these became vacant, a second *Book of Discipline* within another two years demanded the whole patrimony of the Catholic church, also the right to appoint all of the clergy. Moreover, the *Book* also declared that the Kirk 'has a certain power granted by God', and its only head was Christ, not the King. This had been the claim of Thomas à Becket on behalf of the Pope to King Henry the Second of England before that Archbishop of Canterbury was murdered. John Knox had tried this assertion against the refusal of Mary, Queen of Scots; her son and his Council would also deny this usurpation of royal authority with the axiom, 'No bishop, no king'. In his opinion, King James would declare that the Presbyterianism of his country agreed 'as well with monarchy as God and the Devil'.

On the Borders, the continuing southern raids of the supporters of the Scots Queen, such as Buccleuch, were held to 'use all misordour and crueltie [even] destestabil to all barbars and wild Tartaris', the Mongol horsemen. But counter-attacks by the Earl of Sussex equalled those of Lord Hertford in the ferocity of his devastation. Buccleuch, however, did manage to assault with 200 prickers the nobles' Council, sitting in Stirling; but instead of wiping out the King's barons, his Reivers decided instead to steal all their horses and profit from the raid.

Outside politics, the blood feuds continued in the increasing anarchy of the frontier. In 1582, the old Lord Scrope noted the loose cannon of certain clans, particularly the Grahams, who had killed two Bells and one of their own as a collaborator, and so might precipitate 'the greatest feud ever on those Borders'. He was determined to enforce the law, as far as he could. In the ballad of 'Hughie the Graeme', he was praised for hunting down a horse thief with a posse of ten men.

> Then they hae grippit Hughie the Graeme,
>> And brought him up through Carlisle town;
> The lasses and lads stood on the walls,
>> Crying, 'Hughie the Graeme, thou'se ne'er gae down!'

Refusing bribes from Lord and Lady Hume, Scrope insisted on the execution of his prisoner, who left his favourite weapon to another outlaw, who might become an avenger, but was to meet the same fate, at the hands of his own King.

> 'Here, Johnie Armstrang, take thou my sword,
>> That is made o' the metal sae fine;
> And when thou comest to the English side,
>> Remember the death of Hughie the Graeme.'

The chief problem among the ordinary Reivers was their lack of land. The sons and heirs suffered from the old Celtic custom of *gavelkind*, by which the father's brood each received an equal share of an uneconomic estate. For the Norman barons, however, the law of entail ensured the transfer of whole properties to the eldest chid or to the surviving male relation. Thus, the division of the inheritance ensured the struggle of the younger clansmen for more braes to support their cattle. They would have to seize and hold the new ground, which they could not acquire through birthright.

Equally, the law was the enemy of the Reiver. Outside raiding, his chief income came from smuggling cattle and horses, salt and fish and contraband cloth across the porous Borders. Although the English Warden Lord Wharton tried to block off the whole frontier between the two strongholds of Berwick and Carlisle, his efforts to establish a long palisade or a new Hadrian's Wall was as ineffectual as the Pale in Ireland. His 'setters and searchers, sleuth-hounds and watchers by day and night' could not oversee thirty-nine fords and block narrow passes. All these precautions, as Walter Scott noted, might be carefully enforced, but they could not hinder the evil. 'Indeed, the state of the population on either side of the frontier had become such that, to prevent these constant and reciprocal incursions was absolutely impossible, without a total change in their manners and habits of life.'

Even Dante, in the 'Paradiso' of *The Divine Comedy* had noted the fierce commitment which the Borderers had towards their raiding tradition:

> Then shall the prickly pride which dries the mouth,
> The Scots and Englishmen so bloody madden,
> They'll not abide within their North and South.

Their only restraints were the laws, when these could be enforced. Justice was, however, more often summary, rather than practised in the courts. Archibald, the ninth Earl of Angus, was called the Border Nimrod, whose game was man. He took as much delight in hunting down a thief as a horse.

> The Border marauders had every motive to exert their faculties for the purpose of escape; for, once seized upon, their doom was sharp and short. The mode of punishment was either by hanging, or drowning. The next tree, or the deepest pool of the nearest stream, was indifferently used on these occasions. Many moss-troopers are said to have been drowned in a deep eddy of the Jed near Jedburgh.

And, indeed, the Jedburgh battle-axe signified the quick severing of any neck that stuck out too far.

Drowning was an old method of punishment in Scotland. In his *Border Antiquities*, Walter Scott noted in Galloway that there were deep pits, still called murder-holes, which were full of human bones. To him, this was true interpretation of the Latin law, *fossa et furca*, which had been seen as the right to imprison a thief in a pit or dungeon as well as to hang him. The real meaning was the right of any baron to inflict death either by hanging or drowning, as happened to 'Johnie of Breadislee', who went to a laird's forest 'to hunt the dun deer down.' Successful, he fed his bloody hounds with the liver and lungs of a doe, then fell fast asleep. Surprised by seven Foresters, he slew all but one of them:

> And mony mony were the men
>   At fetching o'er Johnie . . .
> For the highest tree in Merriemass
>   Shall be his morning's fee.

> Now Johnie's gude bend bow is broke,
>   And his gude graie dogs are slain;
> And his body lies ded in Durrisdeer,
>   And his hunting it is done.

The Borderers were not literate. They could barely read or write, and so they knew little of the law outside its barbarous punishments, if they were caught. In the incessant frontier wars, they had to back one or other of the rival Kings of Scotland or England, and they were condemned if they fought on the losing side and did not switch in good enough time. And so, willy-nilly, they were either loyalists or traitors. They were as suspicious of judgement by arcane document, as was Jack Cade and his Kentish rebels, when they took London in Shakespeare's *King Henry the Sixth, Part Two*; and the same remedy would have appealed to the Reivers:

DICK THE BUTCHER: The first thing we do, let's kill all the lawyers.

JACK CADE: Nay, that I mean to do. Is not this a lamentable thing, that of the skin of an innocent lamb should be made parchment? That parchment, being scribbled o'er, should undo a man? Some say the bee stings; but I say, 'tis the bee's wax, for I did but seal once to a thing, and I was never mine own man since. How now! Who's there?

The successor to the Earl of Bothwell, his cousin Francis Stewart, was the son of one of James the Fifth's bastard children. He proved to be the most desperate of the Border warlords during the adolescence of the King, who was subject to the guidance of favourites, such as the Earl of Arran. In 1585, the Earls of Bothwell and Maxwell and Home pillaged Stirling and forced the royal minion to quit the government. Imprisoned for plotting against the crown, Francis Stewart escaped, only twice to assault the King by night at Holyrood and again at Falkland Palace. With his Borderers yelling their war-cry, 'Justice! Justice! A Bothwell! A Bothwell!', his first two attempts failed, but on the third in 1593, he burst into the royal bedchamber with his raised sword. According to Walter Scott, the King said: 'Strike, and end thy work! I will not survive my dishonour.' But Bothwell merely demanded the return of all his forfeited estates, where it was said that 'all Teviotdale ran after him'. After another affray, he was exiled and converted to the Catholic faith in Rome. 'So fell this agitator of domestic broils.'

Even after the execution of Mary, Queen of Scots, the sour divisions between the Catholic and the Protestant creeds continued on the Borders. In general, the East Marches struck with the old faith, the Middle March was split, while the Western March was trawled by Presbyterian missionaries, although these preachers took time to make much of an impression. John Cleland, who had commanded a fanatical regiment of the Cameronians, did claim that, by the end of the 17th century, the Reformation ruled the Reivers, even though they were exhorted against that heresy by a Cavalier:

> If their doctrine there get rooting,
> Then, farewell theift, the best of booting.
> And this ye see is very clear,
> Dayly experience makes it appear;
> For instance, lately on the Borders,
> Where there was nought but theft and murders,
> Rapine, cheating, and resetting,
> Sleight of hand, and fortunes getting,
> Their designation, as ye ken,
> Was all along the *Taking Men.*
> Now, rebels more prevails with words,
> Than drawgoons does with guns and swords,
> So that their bare preaching now
> Makes the rush-bush keep the cow,
> Better than Scots or English kings
> Could do by kilting them with strings.
> Yea, those that were the greatest rogues,
> Follows them over hills and bogues,
> Crying for mercy and for preaching,
> For they'll now hear no others teaching.

That was not yet so, for the conversion of the Borderers limped as a lame horse. Their heritage and traditions were too long in the blood, for them to yield to thunder from a pulpit. In his collection of ballads, which he was often accused of improving to suit early Victorian sensibilities, Walter Scott traced the genre back to Celtic bards and on to Border conditions. 'In frontier regions, where men are continually engaged in active enterprise, betwixt the task of defending themselves and annoying their neighbours, they may be said to live in an atmosphere of danger, the excitation of which is peculiarly favourable to the encouragement of poetry.'

Their music and songs were of a military nature, and these celebrated the valour and success of their predatory expeditions. 'The minstrels praised their chieftains for the very exploits against which the laws of the country denounced a capital doom. An outstanding freebooter was to them a more interesting person than the King of Scotland, exerting his power to punish his depredations; and, when the characters are contrasted, the latter is always represented as a ruthless and sanguinary tyrant.'

Walter Scott divided the Border ballads into three categories, 'Historical' and 'Romantic' and 'Imitations of These Compositions by Modern Authors', rather as Lewis Carroll's Mock Turtle described the arts as 'Drawling, Stretching, and Fainting in Coils'. The historical ballads did describe true events, but with an emphasis on the trio of refrains, which the bagpipes were said to play: the Dance and the Charge and the Lament. One of the more celebrated ones was 'Kinmont Willie', which portrayed Buccleuch and the Scott clan, aiding a break in 1596 by the condemned Willie Armstrong from Carlisle gaol, then under the care of Lord Scrope, the English Warden of the West March. Kinmont Willie had challenged Scrope to keep him until he was condemned to die.*

> My hands are tied, but my tongue is free,
> And whae will dare this deed avow?
> Or answer by the Border law?
> Or answer to the bauld Buccleuch?

To which defiance, Scrope answered:

> Now haud thy tongue, thou rank reiver.
> There's never a Scot sall set thee free;
> Before ye cross my castle gate,
> I trow ye sall tak farewell o' me.

Scrope seemed to have forgotten that Buccleuch was the most powerful laird on the Scottish side of the Border, and that it was a time of truce. The ballad had Buccleuch wishing that there was a war between the two countries, so that he could leave not a stone of Carlisle castle standing.* With forty raiders, the head of the Scott clan 'crossed the Bateable Land' and 'to the English side we held'. Although the Eden river was a torrent, the prickers reached the far bank.

Using scaling ladders and ropes and shears to cut lead, the Reivers smashed through to Kinmont Willie's dungeon and brought him out to a stolen horse with broken ankle-chains; he complained that he had never worn such cumbrous spurs. Pursuing with a thousand men, Lord Scrope pulled up, as the raiders again kicked with their ponies through the turbulent Eden flood. He could not believe his eyes or Buccleuch's daring.

> The water was great and meikle of spait,
>> But the never a horse or man we lost.
> 'He is either himsell a devil frae hell,
>> Or else his mother a witch maun be;
> I wadna have ridden that wan water
>> For a' the gold in Christentie.'

Such stirring stuff was not mirrored in 'Maitland's Complaynt', one of the earlier ballads, which attacked the notorious thieves of Liddesdale for their cruel extortions.

> Of Liddisdail the common theivis,
> Sa pertlie stealis now and reivis,
> That nane may keep
> Horse, ox, nor sheep
> Nor yet dare sleep
> For their mischievis.
>
> They plainly throw the country rydis,
> I trow the meikle devil them gydis.
> Where they foray
> Aye on their way
> There is na stay
> Nor door, them bydis.
>
> They leave richt naught, where'er they gae;
> There can na thing be hid them frae;
> For if men wad
> Their horses hold
> Then wax they bauld
> To burn and slay . . .
>
> By commoun taking of blak-mail,
> They that had flesche, and bread and ale,
> Now are sae wrackit,

Made bair and nakit,
Fane to be slakit
Wi' water gruel.

Some of the Border ballads even grieved for the folly of the blood feuds and the interminable killings of clan on clan, family against family. In 'Graeme and Bewick', the two young men fought with swords for two hours to avenge a slight. Eventually, Graeme gave his dear rival an 'ackward stroke, strucken sickelie', but then he was overcome with remorse.

'Oh I have slain thee, billie Bewick,
    If this be true thou tellest to me;
But I made a vow, ere I came frae hame,
    That aye the next man I wad be.'

He has pitched his sword in a moodie-hill [mole-hill],*
    And he has leap'd twenty lang feet and three,
And on his ain sword's point he lap,
    And dead upon the ground fell he.

The two fathers lamented the sore outcome of the duel.

'Alack! A wae!' auld Bewick cried,
    'Alack! Was I not much to blame?
I'm sure I've lost the liveliest lad
    That e'er was born unto my name.'

'Alack! A wae!' quo' gude Lord Graeme,
    'I'm sure I hae lost the deeper lack!
I durst hae ridden the Border through,
    Had Christie Graeme been at my back . . .

'I've lost my hopes, I've lost my joy,
    I've lost the key but and the lock;
I durst hae ridden the world round,
    Had Christie Graeme been at my back.'

CHAPTER EIGHT

Women of Courage and Circumstance

The horse and cattle herding and hunting clans on the Borders were dominated by men. But in the pursuit of grazing land and power, women were vital. Only they could ensure the bloodline of future prosperity through their heritage and their progeny. There were three ways in the forking paths to advancement. In the royal wars, the Reiver had to choose the winning claimant and fight well enough to merit the grant of a forfeited estate. Secondly, he could marry an heiress without brothers. And thirdly, his wife could breed mighty sons, who could prevail in the incessant raiding; she could also force her laird forward, as Lady Macbeth, to further the ambition of the family. As strong as the *chatelaine* in Umbria, when confronted with the Borgias threatening to cut the throat of her hostage son if she did not surrender, the Scottish widow could lift her skirts and show her all, and then cry out, 'I can get more!'

There is little record of ladies' lives at this time, except in the *Border Ballads*. These were very different from the lays of the Provençal troubadours, although both derived from the Celtic minstrels, commemorated in the early English poem of the Far Traveller by Widsith, who claimed to have sung all over Europe and the Near East. He glorified his peers:

> Thus wandering, the minstrels travel as chance will have it through the lands of many different peoples. Always they are bound to come across, in the north or the south, some person who is touched by their song and is generous with his gifts, who will increase his reputation in front of his henchmen showing his nobility of spirit before worldly things pass away, the light and the life. He who works for his own good name will be rewarded on earth by a strong and steady fame.

In the courts of the South of France, courtly love was mostly celebrated; but in northern Britain, the ballads dealt with superstition and honour and the facts of life. The topics ranged from the Otherworld to revenge, from politics to sorrow, from burial to cattle rustling. And in all these actions, women were the doers of evil as much as good.

The seductive powers of the wandering Harpers were well-known. As Orpheus on his lyre, their plucked strings could change nature. In *Glasgerryon* or *Glenkindie*, the minstrel was irresistible.

> Glenkindie was ance a harper gude,
>   He harped to the king;
> And Glenkindie was ance the best harper
>   That ever harped a string.
>
> He'd harpit a fish out o saut water,
>   Or water out o a stane,
> Or milk out o a maiden's breast,
>   That bairn had never nane.

The King's daughter was so smitten by him that she asked him to share her chamber for the night. He was taken aback, but told his servant about the offer. The lad took his master's place and possessed the princess, but he was discovered in the morning. With the paramount importance of the royal blood, the princess had to kill herself, as she might conceive a brat of a base father.

> 'O then it was your litle foote-page
>   Falsly hath beguiled me.'
> And then shee pulld forth a litle pen-kniffe,
>   That hanged by her knee,
> Says, 'There shall never noe churls blood
>   Spring within my body.'

The minstrel knight Glenkindie decided to slay the false 'lither lad', and then turned the point of his sword upon his own breast, 'the pumill till a stane'. All three died, in case a bastard clotted the king's line.

One of the rare mistakes in Sir Walter Scott's *Border Minstrelsy* was to confuse the troubadours or *joglars* with the gypsies and *jongleurs*, who were said to be great enchanters, and the ancestors of modern jugglers. In 'Johnie Faa', the Countess of Cassillis was bewitched by a form of hypnotism: 'they cast the *glamour* over her.' But with the pagan beliefs persisting on the Borders, tending towards Christianity, the world of fairies and brownies and sin beyond redemption was the stuff of song. In the earliest ballad of Thomas the Rhymer, he saw so beautiful a woman riding by the Eildon Tree, that he confused her with the Virgin Mother of Jesus:

> True Thomas he pu'd off his cap
>> And louted low down on his knee:
> 'Hail to thee Mary, Queen of Heaven!
>> For thy peer on earth could never be.'
>
> 'O no, O no, Thomas,' she said,
>> 'That name does not belong to me;
> I'm but the Queen o' fair Elfland,
>> That am hither come to visit thee.'
>
> 'Harp and carp, Thomas,' she said,
>> 'Harp and carp along wi' me;
> And if ye dare to kiss my lips,
>> Sure of your bodie I will be.'

He did not harp and carp along with her, such was the sexual attraction. And so he was given second sight, the prophetic power claimed by the Celtic bards. Yet in another early ballad, young Tom Lin could be plucked back from the lures of the Fairie Queen by human love. The pregnant Janet snatched him back from the haunted procession and covered him with her green mantle, although he was changed into an adder and a bear and a red-hot iron bar. She held on, until he was again her 'ain true-love' and her 'naked knight'.

> Out the spak the Queen of Fairies,
>> And an angry woman was she:
> 'Shame betide her ill-far'd face,
>> And an ill death may she die,
> For she's taen awae the bonniest knight
>> In a' my companie.'

The most curious of the *Border Ballads* was directed at the warlord, who reduced the people of Liddesdale and Teviotdale to slavery, dragging on sledges the great stone blocks to build Hermitage castle. Lord Soulis was meant to be a warlock. The purpose of his fortress was to defy the King of Scotland, and to establish his own tyranny. By royal order, there was a popular revolt, especially after Soulis had kidnapped his bride May, who was betrothed to the heir of Branxholm Tower. He was imprisoned, but his brother, Bold Walter of Teviot, rode up to Hermitage to have his revenge. Although Soulis resisted arrows and lance and noose, he was bound by 'threefold ropes of sifted sand' and put to the fire:

> On a circle of stones they placed the pot,
> On a circle of stones but barely nine;
> They heated it red and fiery hot,
>   Till the burnish'd brass did glimmer and shine.

> They roll'd him up in a sheet of lead,
> A sheet of lead for a funeral pall;
> They plunged him in the cauldron red,
>   And melted him, lead, and bones, and all.

This tradition of the extinction of Lord Soulis was based upon history, and the nine stone Druid circle still stands by Hermitage. During the reign of James the First or the regency of the Duke of Albany, so horrific had been the acts of the Sheriff Melville of Glenberrie, that the monarch had spoken in the manner of the English King Henry the Second about Thomas à Beckett. Which knight would get rid of that meddlesome priest? In the Scots case, the remark was 'Sorrow gin the sheriff were sodden, and supped in broo!' Melville was decoyed on a hunting expedition to the top of the hill of Garvock, which is still called the Sheriff's Pot. There, he was plunged into a boiling cauldron, and the local barons drank the broth.

Whatever the mystic beliefs and punishments for the building of Hermitage castle, it remained the strategic key to the bloodiest part of the Borders. When the Soulises forfeited the stronghold in 1320, Robert the Bruce conferred it on Sir John Graham. After his death, the fortress went to Sir William Douglas, the 'Knight of Liddesdale', who had astutely wed Graham's sole daughter. So through patronage and marriage, Hermitage was passed on. In 1492, Archibald Douglas, the fifth Earl of Angus, resigned the property into royal hands; it was conferred on Patrick Hepburn, the first Earl of Bothwell. The fourth Earl was visited by Mary, Queen of Scots, at Hermitage, and so her realm fell into ruin. In 1594, the Bothwell heirs again forfeited this bastion of the Borders, and it passed to the most successful Reivers of all, the Scotts of Buccleuch, who would preserve, by royal clout and bloodline, their extensive Border domains until this day.

So in ballad and truth, by patronage and heritage, four of the lead-ing Border clans occupied or lost their territories in Liddesdale. Yet any woman, who dared to taint the honour of the family was doomed. Revenge or death would be the retribution, as would be sung in 'The Braes o Yarrow'. The heroine Sarah chose a servant lad as a lover, instead of one of the nine knights selected by her father. Run through by the sword in the hand of one of her suitors, the young man died on the river banks, to be followed by his betrothed:

> She kissed his cheek, she kaimed his hair,
>   As oft she did before, O;
> She drank the red blood frae him ran,
>   On the dowy houms o Yarrow.

Since the Greek tragedies, one of the more extreme vengeances of the father against his wayward daughter was recorded in the Northumbrian ballad about two families of the shire. Lady Barnard went to Mass and 'she cast an eye on Little Musgrave, as bright as the summer sun'. He was called to her bower, to lie in her arms all night long. Unfortunately, a page told Lord Barnard that a rival was with his wedded wife. Finding them in bed together, the husband stuck to some Border code of chiv-alry:

> 'Arise, arise, thou Little Musgrave,
>   And put thy clothes on;
> It shall n'ere be said in my country
>   I have killed a naked man.

> 'I have two swords in one scabberd,
>   Full deere they cost my purse;
> And thou shalt have the best of them,
>   And I will have the worse.'

> The first stroke that Little Musgrave stroke,
>   He hurt Lord Barnard sore;
> The next stroke that Lord Barnard stroke
>   Little Musgrave n'ere struck more.

Such decency did not extend to any mercy for the dishonoured wife:

> He cut her paps from off her brest;
>   Great pitty it was to see
> That some drops of this ladie's heart's blood
>   Ran trickling downe her knee . . .
>
> 'A grave, a grave,' Lord Barnard cryd,
>   'To put these lovers in;
> By lay my lady on the upper hand,
>   For she came of better kin.'

In 'The Douglas Tragedy,' the fearsome clan mother of seven sons bade them follow a Lord William, who had stolen away with Fair Margaret, their eldest sister, in the night. The eloper killed all off her seven brothers and wounded her father, the Black Douglas. But she stopped the death blow:

> 'O hold your hand, Lord William!' she said,
>   'For your strokes they are wond'rous sair;
> True lovers I can get many a ane,
>   But a father I can never get mair.'

The lovers rode on a milk-white steed to reach a stream, which flowed red with the Lord's blood. He said it was only the shadow of his scarlet cloak, shining in the water. But by the time that the two of them reached his home, he was far gone:

> 'O mak my bed, lady mother,' he says,
>   'O mak it braid and deep!
> And lay Lady Marg'ret close at my back,
>   And the sounder I will sleep.'
>
> Lord William was dead lang ere midnight,
>   Lady Marg'ret lang ere day –
> And all true lovers that go thegither,
>   May they have mair luck than they!
>
> Lord William was buried in St Marie's kirk,
>   Lady Margaret in Marie's quire;
> Out o' the lady's grave grew a bonny red rose,
>   And out o' the knight's a brier.

> But bye and rade the Black Douglas,
> > And wow but he was rough!
> For he pull'd up the bonny brier,
> > And flang'd in St Marie's Loch.

The pride of the Border wives in their men's prowess extended to their success in their cattle reiving. When the Captain's wife in 'Jamie Telfer' heard that her husband had been taken on a raid, she could not tolerate the insult:

> Then word is gane to the Captain's bride,
> > Even in the bower where that she lay,
> That her lord was prisoner in enemy's land,
> > Since into Tividale he had led the way.

> 'I was rather have had a winding-sheet,
> > And helped to put it ower his head,
> Ere he had been disgraced by the Border Scot,
> > Wan he ower Liddel his men did lead!'

The fiercer of the women were even Amazons in the battle-line. Fair Maiden Lilliard had an Edge named after her on Ancram Moor, where she died in the struggle. And the Tudor historian Holinshed reported that at the conflict at Naworth between the Dacres and Lord Hunsdon, there were 'many desperate women, who there gave the adventure of their lives, and fought right stoutly'.

Such strong women from a rather brutal society were capable of their own revenge, because of jealousy. In the ballad of 'Young Hunting', his princely confession led to his own murder. He told his mistress, who had a son by him, that he had another 'sweetheart in Garlick's Wells'. She made him as drunk 'as any wild-wood steer', and took him to bed:

> And she has minded her on a little penknife,
> > That hangs low down by her gare,
> And she has gin him Young Hunting
> > A deep wound and a sare.

Then she dressed him in his boots and his spurs, his sword and his hunting-horn, and she drowned his weighted corpse in 'the deepest pot' in the

Clyde. The King's divers, called 'duckers', could not find the sunken prince, but a bonny bird served as an informer. So the mistress was set in a bonfire, 'to heal the deadly sin':

> O it took upon her cheek, her cheek,
>   An it took upon her chin,
>   An it took on her fair body,
>   She burnt like hoky-gren.

The ballad of 'The Queen's Marie' may have been Presbyterian propaganda against Lord Darnley, the feckless husband of Mary, Queen of Scots. For it alleged an affair between the royal Consort and one of the Maids-of-Honour, 'the four Maries', those Scottish aristocrats who had gone to France with the child Queen, and had returned with her, when she came to the throne. True or false, the fate of Marie Hamilton illustrated the choking end of anyone, who interfered with the succession:

> Marie Hamilton's to the kirk gane
>   Wi' gluves upon her hands;
>   The King thought mair o' Marie Hamilton,
>   Than the Queen and a' her lands.
>
> She hadna been about the King's court
>   A month, but barely one,
>   Till she was beloved by a' the King's court,
>   And the King the only man . . .
>
> The King is to the Abbey gane,
>   To pu' the Abbey tree,
>   To scale the babe frae Marie's heart;
>   But the thing it wadna be.
>
> O she has row'd it in her apron,
>   And set it on the sea, –
>   'Gae sink ye, or swim ye, bonny babe,
>   Ye'se get na mair o' me.'

When the Queen heard of the scandal, Marie Hamilton was summoned to a rich wedding in Edinburgh, where she would be put down.

> When she gaed up the Tolbooth stairs,
>   The corks frae her heels did flee;
> And lang or o'er she cam down again,
>   She was condemn'd to die . . .

> 'O, often have I dress'd my Queen,
>   And put gold upon her hair;
> But now I've gotten for my reward
>   The gallows to be my share.'

At the end of the day, however, the role of many women was birth-ing and mothering and rearing the young and setting out the dead for burial. Even in a male-dominated society, as was exercised by the royal prerogative and the warrior Border lords, the having of heirs and the marriages to heiresses were most important, while the arts of heal-ing wounds and running households were highly prized. If the *Border Ballads* were romanticised, they did declare emotional truths. The most moving of them, 'Lord Randal My Son', has travelled from Italy to Iceland, and still remains a staple of North American folksong. The noble young man was poisoned by eating eels or snakes. The murderer was his sweetheart, who wanted another lover. He returned home to die in his house.

> 'O I fear ye are poison'd, Lord Randal, my son.
> I fear ye are poison'd, my handsome young man.'
> 'O yes, I am poison'd, mother, mak my bed soon,
> For I'm sick at the hart an' I fain would lie doun . . .'

> 'What d'ye leave to your trew-love, Lord Randal, my son?
> What d'ye leave to your trew-love, my handsome young man?'
> 'I leave her hell an' fire, mother, mak my bed soon,
> For I'm sick at the hart an' I fain would lie doun.'

As Harold Pinter has said, all statements are false and true. And as with all wars, the Border conflicts could be interpreted in opposite ways, the noble or the dreadful. Were they heroic struggles for sur-vival with fierce family loyalty until death? Or were they a bloody and freebooting way of life which demanded a merciless end? The two versions of 'The Three Ravens' and 'Twa Corbies' represented both sides of the tossed coin of that existence. In the first version, three black scavengers sit on a tree, wanting to plunge their beaks into the fresh corpse of a Cockburn knight, slain by the King's command as a Reiver and a bandit. The carrion birds cannot peck away, because his hounds are lying at his feet, keeping their master safe, while his hawks are flying so eagerly that the ravens may not reach his body. Then his wife appears, great with child, and grieves over him.

> She lift up his bloudy hed,
> And kist his wounds that were so red.
>
> She got him up upon her backe,
> And carried him to earthen lake.
>
> She buried him before the prime.
> She was dead herself ere even song time.
>
> God send every gentleman,
> Such haukes, such houndes, and such a leman.

The alternative ballad of 'Twa Corbies' will have nothing to do with such romantic realism. A Borderer, walking below a tree, hears one raven ask the other black bird, 'Where sall we gang and dine today?' The slain knight is lying beyond an old clay dyke:

> 'And naebody kens that he lies there,
> But his hawk, his hound, and his lady fair.
>
> 'His hound is to the hunting gane,
> His hawk to fetch the wild-fowl hame,
> His lady's ta'en another mate,
> So we may mak our dinner sweet . . .'

So one of the ravens chooses to gorge on the ribs of the dead man, while the other will peck out his bonny blue eyes. The locks of his golden hair will do to fluff their nests.

> 'Mony a one for him makes mane,
> But nane sall ken whare he is gane;

O'er his white banes, when they are bare,
The wind sall blaw for evermair.'

For women, beyond royal and aristocratic codes of honour, stood the bleak necessities of survival with the family. In their terms, the black cattle and horses were life. Reiving was finding food to eat. And in this necessity, the black farce of existence on the Borders was fully expressed. In 'Dick o' the Cow', the hero, as foolish as Perceval in search of the Grail, kidnapped three steeds from Johnie Armstrong, who had stolen three head of cattle from him. Felled with a plummet by his victim, Armstrong lost his steel cap and jack and two-headed sword, and was ashamed:

'And is thou gane? Now, Dickie, than
The deil gae in thy cumpanie!
For if I should live these hundred years,
I ne'er shall fight wi' a fule after thee.'

Seeing Lord Scrope at Carlisle, Dick was told he was to be hanged. But he pointed to his spoils of war and the custom of pursuit, called *Hot Trod*. He would only 'steal frae a man but whae steal frae me'. So he was sent home with twenty pounds for Armstrong's 'gude horse', and a prime milk cow 'to maintain his wife and children three'.

Among the Reivers, to raid was to allow the family to subsist. Without the beasts, the humans could not live. There is small record of the feelings of the women in the 400 years of roistering in a Debateable Land. If what is left lies in verses and song, that is a little legacy for a proud endurance and a resolute going on.

When I was trudging from Edinburgh to York over the Borders to write a novel *Gog*, I passed by Hermitage Castle and talked to the Warden, who told me that Lady Elliot had just ridden by. She was infuriated at John Arden's play, *Armstrong's Last Goodnight*. She wanted to horsewhip him, declaring: 'No Elliot was ever a whore.' The play itself made the Armstrong reiver Johnny Gilnockie call himself the King of Eskdale. He became the victim of English and Scots politics and of the Reformation. His wife defended him with these words:

The Laird and his people have sufferit mickle wrang frae the English.
Ower generation and generation the English hae warkit destruction frae
Carlisle to the Ettrick Forest and frae the forest to the sea-coast, and

alang the sea-coast intil Forth. The Laird has his purposes – they are strang purposes for defence. He has aye been courageous in their difficult fulfilment.

Yet when the young Scots King James had inveigled Gilnockie into a meeting, apparently to turn him into the royal keeper of the Middle Marches, he and the other Armstrongs were disarmed and denounced and condemned:

Ye are ane strang traitor. The hale of your life ye have set at nocht the laws and commandments of the kingdom: ye have made mock of our person and the Crown and the Throne of Scotland: ye have embroilit and embranglit us with England the common enemy: and by dint of malignant faction ye have a' but split the realm! What in the Name of God gars ye believe I wad pardon ye now? Gilnockie, ye maun be hangit: forthwith, direct, nae process of law: our word in this place is sufficient. Hang him up.

CHAPTER NINE

Kirk and Destruction

At the end of the reign of Queen Elizabeth in 1598, Sir Robert Carey, the Warden of the English Middle March, was enlisted by the heir to the southern throne, the King of Scotland, to restore order in his own country. The outlaw Armstrongs had lost a comrade Reiver and had vowed, 'that before the end of the next winter, they would lay the whole Border waste'. Recruiting 200 horsemen, Carey sallied out against the bandits and built 'a pretty fort, and within it wee all had cabines made to lye in'.

> The chiefe outlawes, at our coming, fled their houses where they dwelt, and betooke themselves to a large and great forest (with all their goodes), which was called the Tarras. It was of that strength, and so surrounded with bogges and marish grounds, and thicke bushes and shrubbes, as they feared not the force nor power of England nor Scotland, so long as they were there. They sent me word, that I was like the first puffe of a haggis, hottest at the first, and bade me stay there as long as the weather would give me leave. They would stay in the Tarras Wood till I was weary of lying in the Waste.

Unfortunately for the Reivers, Carey was sufficiently experienced in their tactics to work out a riposte. He sent most of his forces in three squadrons to seal off the trio of paths of escape on 'the backside of the Tarras, to Scotland-ward'. When the ambushes were safely laid, he attacked from the English edge of the forest, driving the outlaws like game into the snares he had laid. Five of the Armstrong leaders were taken, and for their lives, they agreed to return all their hostages and a stolen castle, while the rest of clan was scattered and dispersed.

Even in his own March, Carey had trouble in a feud between his deputy Warden, Edward Selby, and the Grays of Berwick, over cattle reiving. At a meeting of conciliation, the elderly Sir William Selby alleged that he was set upon and wounded by five or six of the Grays, who counter-claimed that they were the victims of an assault by half-a-dozen of 'the most notorious common fighters and evil disposed in Berwick'. Wisely, Carey ordered house arrest for all the Scots in the town and put armed patriots on the streets, until tempers and sword cuts were healed.

Ever mindful of the need for peace along the frontier, Carey was present at the death of Queen Elizabeth. Knowing of plots about the succession, he rode north, only stopping to change horses. Although thrown by his mount and kicked in the head, he reached Holyrood House on the third night after leaving London. King James the Sixth of Scotland was roused from his bed to learn that he had also become James the First, the ruler of England. Thus, at last, the riven frontier had a single monarch.

The ruler of both realms crossed the Borders and headed south, surrounded by a host of greedy courtiers. He intended to force a form of peace on the Debateable Land, no longer in debate. He even considered calling his combined estate by the names of North and South Britain, while the previous frontier would become the Middle Shires. Certainly, he meant to put an end to the incessant skirmishes and raids of the Reivers and their ilk, who had even held an 'Ill Week' of arson and mayhem, when the royal progress had passed by their territory.

In the limbo of an *interregnum*, the Borderers thought that they had a licence to do what they would. The Grahams and the Armstrongs and the Elliots led a spoiling into Cumbria and rustled 5,000 head of cattle and sheep. Yet the new king knew his unruly subjects far too well. He issued a Proclamation against all rebels and disorderly persons. He ordered 'that no supply be given them, their wives or their bairnes, and that they be prosecuted with fire and sword'. He also required that all who were guilty of the recent foul and insolent outrages should submit within two months to the royal mercy, or else they would be excluded from it for ever.

From Berwick, Sir William Selby was sent with a large force into Liddesdale, where most of the *pele* towers were razed to the ground. The Armstrong holdings were passed over to the Elliots and the Buccleuch family. One of the robber clan, Willie of Westburnflat, was taken from his keep near Hermitage water with nine of his henchmen, and they were brought to Selkirk for trial.

When sentence was pronounced, Willie arose; and, seizing the oaken chair in which he was placed, broke it into pieces by main strength, and offered to his companions, who were involved in the same doom, that, if they would stand behind him, he would fight his way out of Selkirk with these weapons. But they held his hands, and besought him to let them *die like Christians*. They were accordingly executed in form of law.

The verdicts of a harsh justice would begin the end of the traditional Reiver way of existence. As King James the Sixth and First declared, he had 'a special regard to the Marchis and the Bordouris . . . the verie hart of the cuntrey sall not be left in ane uncertaintie'. Within seven years, his nobles and lieutenants had pacified the whole region by the gallows and the sword and fire, by deportation and armed service abroad. The purge was led by Lord Home with a special armed guard; 32 Elliots and Armstrongs and other raiders were hanged, another 150 were outlawed or banished, while 2,000 men under Walter Scott of Buccleuch were directed to cross over to the Low Countries to help the Dutch Reformers fight against Catholic Spain. A diplomatic complaint to King James provoked the answer that he was not 'displeased that this rabble should be taken out of the kingdom. . . ' As Satchells' *History of the Name of Scott* commented:

> It's most clear, a freebooter doth live in hazard's train;
> A freebooter's a cavalier that ventures life for gain;
> But, since King James the Sixth to England went,
> There has been no cause of grief;
> And he that hath transgress'd since then,
> Is no *Freebooter*, but a *Thief*.

A draconian regime was forged. The iron gates of castles and swords were literally to be beaten into ploughshares, all weapons were prohibited and only heavy work-horses might be kept. Paid informers and tracker dogs would betray and pursue fugitives. The chief offenders, the Grahams of Esk, had their lands forfeited, and hundreds of the clan were deported to serve in British garrisons in Dutch ports or to settlements in Roscommon in Ireland. Forbearance was thought to breed greater insolence, and so 'Jeddart justice' was meted out – the verdict was given after the use of the noose. As with the White Queen in *Alice through the Looking Glass*, the punishment came first, the trial next, and 'the crime last of all'. The new overlord of the Border Commission, the Earl of Dunbar, was hailed as another Hercules cleansing the Augean stables, for he had 'purgit the Borders of all the chiefest malefactors, robbers and brigands'.

A way to solve lawlessness at home is to export criminals and out-laws to serve abroad as mercenary soldiers, who can indulge in their killing on foreign soil. An opportunity lay in the Thirty Years' War, which was beginning to rage on the Continent. A Scottish brigade of up to 10,000 men would fight with distinction for both the Swedish and the French Kings, who had long had the protection of the royal *Garde Ecossaise*. The reverse side of this exodus was that many exiled Scotsmen became military experts in warfare and the procurement of weapons. These seasoned warriors would be recalled home with their supplies to fight for both sides, when the Reformers, called the Covenanters, were ready to take on the Stewart monarchs and their detested bishops.

By patient negotiation, King James the First and Sixth had managed to rein in the militant Kirk of Scotland. His triumph was to create with the English bishops a vernacular Bible, which still bears his name and has had an even greater influence on the language than the works of William Shakespeare. This was despite the Moderator of the Kirk of Scotland, who had declared in 1591 against 'the belly-god bishops in England [who] by all moyen and money were seeking conformity of our Kirk with theirs'.

In Scotland, King James had wisely held the line between little rebel-lions by Catholic lords and Protestant mobs in Edinburgh. Yet with the coming of the Scottish Reformation and the Covenant, there would be nothing but strife; for, on the death of the King, his son Charles the First succeeded to the throne of both countries. Unfortunately, Charles did not inherit his father's ambiguity about the Kirk of Scotland, but only his intransigence. On his coronation ceremony in Edinburgh, the five officiating bishops in rich vestments were 'becking and bowing as they passed the embroidered crucifix'. On the following Sunday, two royal chaplains read the English Prayer Book. King Charles refused to address a petition that asked for the Kirk to be granted more of the old church lands, which remained in royal hands. The accommodat-ing Bishop Spottiswoode was then made Lord Chancellor, although no cleric had held that post since the reformation. He would hardly oppose the powerful English Archbishop Laud in supporting the divine right of the King in appointing to high rank such prelates as himself.

To the Presbyters and many of the people, the whole idea of an intermediary higher priesthood was anathema. There should be an individual intercourse between the soul and God. This was the essence of the Protestant attack on Rome. Now shrieking mobs of inspired women, the precursors of the *tricoteuses* knitting under the French guillotine, would rage against this new Popishness. And a Covenant would be pronounced in a fresh Puritan accordance with many Members of Parliament in England. These would demand the cleansing of all Catholic influences, and even the overthrow of the King and his bishops, should they seek to oppose such root-and-branch measures.

The Covenanters had begun to import armaments and experienced commanders from the conflicts of the Thirty Years' War. Although Charles the First strove to maintain his control of the Scots Crafts and Guilds, the weapons-makers of previous Stewart kings, they were split between Protestant and Catholic Lodges with competing interests. The time of troubles had begun, and the warriors and the armourers would be hired to serve on either side. The efforts by King Charles and Archbishop Laud to introduce the English Liturgy with its Catholic overtones and ritual was a spark in a powderkeg. So extreme was the royal insistence that, when the new Liturgy appeared in April, 1637, a proclamation was published, requiring all the King's subjects on pain of rebellion to conform themselves to the fresh form of worship. Riot and revolution would be the consequences of that act.

An Edinburgh mob of women 'of the bangister Amazon kind' went berserk in St Giles during the reading of the 'Popish' book. Stools were thrown at the heads of bishops, while ministers were almost beaten to death. In another riot, Bishop Sydserf of Galloway, 'who was suspected of having a crucifix in his cabinet and another under his dress', was pursued by 300 viragos to the Council House, where some noble Earls hurled him through the doorway and put up a barricade. Such outbreaks led to many of the members of the Privy Council petitioning King Charles to withdraw his Liturgy, otherwise he would need 40,000 soldiers to enforce its use.

There was no royal withdrawal. Given the 'long boggling and irresolution of the King', a Covenant based on the old anti-papal Negative Confession was drawn up. As the historian William Law Mathieson noted:

Nobles and lairds carried the Covenant with them for signature wherever they went; whole congregations swore to maintain it with uplifted hands; and all alike, men, women and mere children, were admitted to the oath. Many subscribed with tears, cursing themselves to all eternity if they should prove unfaithful to their vow; and some even insisted on signing with their blood. The churches of Covenanting ministers were crowded to overflowing; and some female enthusiasts, in order to attest their Protestantism by sitting at communion, are said to have kept their seats from Friday to Sunday.

Such was the frenzy of the time that some feared that a religious civil war was approaching, as had happened in Holland and France with the Huguenots. As Robert Baillie wrote: 'No man may speak anything in publick for the King's part, except he would have himself marked for a sacrifice to be killed one day. I think our people possessed with a bloody devil, far above anything that ever I could have imagined.'

The royal plan of action was a naval blockade to prevent trained soldiers and arms being sent over from Holland, followed by seaborne assaults from Ireland in the west and a landing in the Firth of Forth in the east. The old idea of Hadrian's Wall and the shorter-lived Antonine Wall was revived by Sir William Monson – a fortification stretching from Glasgow to Stirling, excluding the Highlands 'where it is not fit for civil men to live'. With few resources, however, and with many of his own Members of Parliament supporting the Covenanters, King Charles could hardly muster an army or a fleet.

The Covenanters were far more efficient, ordering the lairds of each parish in the shires to make a list of all good men, along with their mounts and arms and ammunition. Committees of war were established by every presbytery, and these were in touch with the Lodges of the armourers, who were threatened with 'Excommunication Without Cooperation'. Officers were appointed from the local gentry, but only as colonels and captains and ensigns. The specialist ranks of lieutenant-colonels and sergeant-majors, lieutenants and sergeants, were reserved for those with combat experience, returning from long service in the Thirty Years' War overseas.

These mercenary veterans were often wayward about their employers. The famous Alexander Leslie, a field-marshal in the Swedish army, considered fighting for King Charles, who meant to send forces to aid his nephew, the Elector Palatine, in Germany. But when this mission fell through, Leslie agreed to joint the Covenanters. Another turncoat had set out for England, but found his ship landing in Scotland, and so signed on for Scottish pay, quoting the dangerous military maxim, which had always well suited the Borderers: 'So we serve our master honnestlie, it is no matter what master we serve.'

The first Bishops' War began with skirmishes in the North-east, where the most powerful royal supporter, the Marquis of Huntley, had his castles and estates. The Covenanters chose as their commander, James Graham, the Marquis of Montrose, who would himself pass over to become the best guerrilla general that the King's side ever had in the Civil War. Raiding parties seized Huntley's arms and ammunition *en route* to Inverness castle, and Montrose with Alexander Leslie occupied Aberdeen. Most of the ill-equipped royal castles fell with hardly a fight, including Edinburgh and Dumbarton and Tantallon by the Firth of Forth. The King now seemed to have little support north of the Borders.

The monarch of both nations, however, did manage to gather some 21,000 men, and he camped at Birks near the Border stronghold of Berwick. Meanwhile, the forces of the Covenanters advanced to Duns Law, a few miles off. Their ranks were depleted by royalist Highlanders attacking in the north; Aberdeen changed hands four times over. Complaints were sent back to Edinburgh that the Scots opposing the King had 'no horsemen at all, ther is no provision of victuals and money'. Yet God would surely grant the Covenanters the victory, and so their morale remained high and enabled them to call the King's bluff by threatening to advance to the Tweed river and 'lay down our leagues within shott of cannon to the King's trenches'. There was even a Presbyterian marching song:

> March! March!
> Why the devil do ye na march?
> Stand to your arms, my lads,
> Fight in good order;
> Front about, ye musketeers all,
> Till ye come to the English Border.
>
> Stand til't, and fight like men,
> True gospel to maintain.
> The Parliament's blythe to see us a'coming.
> When to the Kirk we come,
> We'll purge it ilka room,
> Frae Popish relics, and a' sic innovation,
> That a' the warld may see,
> There's nane in the right but we,
> Of the auld Scottish nation.

A subsequent truce and treaty returned to the King and his supporters all the property and castles seized in Scotland. For his part, Charles agreed to summon a General Assembly and Parliament in Edinburgh; all ecclesiastical matters would be subject to Kirk assemblies, while civil matters would be the terrain of Parliament. He declared that he had only intended to maintain his position, not to invade Scotland or to inflict innovations in religion and laws upon its people. Yet nothing specific was written, which would guarantee the ending of the rule of the bishops and the remission of their estates.

The result was a second inconclusive Bishops' war. Both the Scottish Reformers and the King found it difficult to raise an army. Sent to the Borders in 1640, the Duke of Northumberland wrote back to his royal master. 'Our wants and disorders are so great that I cannot device how we should go on with our designs for this year.' The Short Parliament at Westminster would vote no funds for a Scottish campaign, for many of the members there agreed with the King's adversaries. The Covenanters had done a little better, finding enough money to pay their Low-Country trained commanders, who had returned home at a steep price. They managed to put together a force again at Duns, and, to their surprise, Newcastle surrendered, followed by the garrison of Edinburgh castle. Charles the First capitulated, and the friendly English Parliament voted £300,000 to pay off Covenanting army expenses.

Yet now another religious war saved the Royalist cause. A Catholic rebellion broke out in Ireland, and the Scottish Presbyterians were moved to protect their brethren in Ulster, 'planted by their own nation', and under the threat of massacre. By 1642, 11,000 men had been sent across the Irish Sea; such a policy prevented their return to participate in a Civil War over the Borders. This manoeuvre would also foment three-and-a-half centuries of religious wars across another undeclared frontier of divergent faiths.

At the beginning of the conflict between the English Parliament and King Charles, the Royalists were in the ascendancy. So the Puritan leaders at Westminster negotiated a Solemn League and Covenant, which might bring a Scottish army of 21,000 men to oppose the Cavaliers – their own forces had the nicknames of their helmets and their armour, Roundheads and Ironsides. While the Scots wished to impose their Presbyterian zeal on the whole island, the Parliament in London demurred. 'The English were for a civil League,' a Scot complained, 'we for a religious Covenant'. Reluctantly, the Puritans agreed that the Church of England should be reformed 'according to the word of God', whatever that might be.

Such a phrase would never satisfy the extreme ministers of the Kirk. Their excesses were summed up in the words of Samuel Rutherford: 'Better the King weep for the childish trifle of a prerogative than Popery be erected and three Kingdoms be destroyed.' The unrepentant Scottish lords such as the great Graham, the Marquis of Montrose, and the Setons, were imprisoned and their estates were confiscated. Only with his release did Montrose remember his allegiance to the Stewart Crown, and he was appointed the royal commander in the north of Scotland. For, as he declared, the subject 'is obliged to tolerate the vices of his prince as he does storms and tempests and other natural evils, which are compensated with better times succeeding'.

With the coming of the Civil War, the remnants of the Reivers had revived. Since the Border Commission to expunge them had lapsed in 1625, they went back to their raiding ways. Twelve years later, some thirty of them were hanged. The names of the guilty were the usual suspects, Johnstones and Armstrongs and Elliots, Grahams and a Scott called 'Wat of the Bus'. For their skills, these bandits were now being called up by both sides under the name of 'moss-troopers'. They were still the best of scouts and foragers. Even so, as Satchells had also remarked in his *History of the Name of Scott*:

> Near a Border frontier, is the time of war,
> There's ne'er a man but he's a freebooter.

In battle, however, killing is lawful, while plunder is the supply system for the army. A hostile account condemned the remaining Reivers as 'mosse-troupers, thieves and uthers wicked and lawless men', operating in gangs and terrorising their neighbours by night and day with their serial 'outrages, felonies and nefarious crimes'. One of them was celebrated in the ballad of 'Christie's Will', about a descendant of the executed 'Johnie Armstrong'. After a foray, William Armstrong had been imprisoned for stealing two tethers, which happened to be attached to a pair of 'delicate colts'. He was saved from summary death by the Earl of Traquair, who said:

> 'Good Christie's Will, no, have nae fear!
>   Nae harm, good Will, shall hap to thee:
> I saved thy life at the Jeddart air,
>   At the Jeddart air frae the justice tree.'

.

Now accused himself, the Earl required the Reiver to kidnap the hostile President of the Court of Session, until the verdict was pronounced. So Judge Durie was duly spirited away and put in solitary confinement in a *pele* keep near Moffat on the Borders.

> Willie has hied to the tower of Graeme,
>> He took auld Durie on his back,
> He shot him down to the dungeon deep,
>> Which garr'd his auld banes gie mony a crack.

> For nineteen days, and nineteen nights,
>> Of sun, or moon, or midnight stern,
> Auld Durie never saw a blink,
>> The lodging was sae dark and dern.

When the verdict of the Court was passed in favour of the Earl of Traquair, William Armstrong restored the judge to the spot on Leith Sands, where he had been taken. A second exploit was to carry secret papers from the Earl to King Charles the First, a mission which took 'Christie' Armstrong through Carlisle, where a Parliamentary troop of horse were guarding a bridge over the Eden river. Leaping the parapet on his horse, he plunged into the flood and gained the far bank, cutting off his drenched coat, so that his mount could scramble to safety. Although pursued, he menaced his enemies with his damp pistols and swam the Esk river to reach home ground. With such daring shown by the surviving Reivers, they were in demand from both the Marquis of Montrose and the Covenanters, commanded by Alexander Leslie, the Earl of Leven. And at the crucial battle of Marston Moor in 1644, the Border horse combined with Cromwell's Roundheads in their pudding-basin helmets to rout the Cavaliers on the left flank, before wheeling and destroying the Royalist infantry from the rear.

Montrose had raised some 500 horsemen on the Borders, and another 800 footsoldiers. But the wary lairds refused to join the Royalist cause, the trimming Annandales and Maxwells and Johnstones, while Buccleuch was backing the Covenanters. Now excommunicated by the Kirk, Montrose asked the royal cavalry commander, Prince Rupert of the Rhine, for 'a thousand of your horse, and I will cut my way into the heart of Scotland'. Instead, the Marquis had to relinquish his few mounted Borderers and return to the Highlands to fight alone.

1. Mongol horse-archers in a feigned retreat.

2. From Biblical to American Lodges. Pictures from the Certificate of the Independent Order of odd Fellows, Washington Lodge, No.1, 1869.

3. Carlisle Castle, from where Kinmont Willie was rescued.

4. St Michael's Church at Burgh-by-Sands, situated on Hadrian's Wall, with its fortified tower, built against Reiver attack.

5. Sweetheart Abbey in Dumfries, another religious foundation ruined by the Reformation.

6. Smailholme Tower at sunset.

7. A red sunset over the Borders.

8. Reiver ponies by the ruined castle on Bass Rock.

9. Warkworth Castle, a stronghold of the Percy family in Yorkshire.

10. Hume Castle, the primary Border Keep.

11. Hermitage Castle, the key to the Borders in Liddesdale.

13. Crichton Castle, another Border keep on the moors, built to protect a Collegiate Church.

12. The Statue of William Wallace, overlooking Dryburgh.

14. Caerlaverock Castle.

15. The Battle of Aliwal, 1846. The Charge of the Queen's Own 16th Hussars. Aquatint by J. Harris, 1847.

16. Moroccan Rebels Attack a French Army Convoy. From *Le Petit Journal*, 1903.

17. Pulp Fiction Covers.

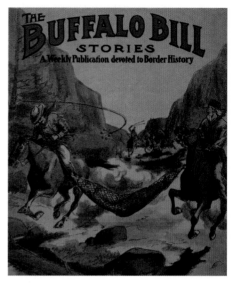

18. Pulp Fiction Covers.

19. The Empress Elisabeth of Austria, jumping on Merry Andrew, painted by John Charlton. Copyright Earl Spencer.

20. These Colonial Troops in the First World War include a Bengal Lancer, a Rider in the Egyptian Camel Corps, and a mounted Spahi from Algeria. Painted for *The Boy's Own Paper* in 1918 by Harry Payne.

1. An Archer on Horseback, *c.* 830. From the *Ultrecht Psalter*.

2. Early English Archers, *c.* 1200. This illustration, and successive ones in this style, are taken from G.A. Hansard, *The Book of Archery*, 1841.

3. Archers shoot at a game bird and a stag. From medieval illustrations.

4. Roman Archers.

5. African Archers.

6. 'A Caboceer of Ashantee equipt for war'. From J. Dupuis, Journal of Residence in Ashantee, 1824.

7. Macedonian and Parthian Horse Archers.

8. The earliest representation of the Knights of the Military Orders in battle against the Muslims. Godfrey de Bouillon leads the Christians. From an engraving of a window in the Church of St. Denys.

9. Muslim Light Cavalry.

10. A woodcut used by Richard Pynson for Chaucer's Yeoman in The Canterbury Tales, 1491.

11. With chain mail stitched over their leather jerkins, the Border light horse use their lances on the Irish cavalry. From Derricke's *The Image of Ireland*, 1581.

12. A Steppe Tartar Cossack scout of the 14th century. He is armed with a lance, a sabre and a bow.

13. A Pindari mounted archer, who worked as a scout and forager for the Marathas in their campaigns in India.

14. Claude Duval robs the Master of the Buck Hounds to King Charles the Second in Windsor Forest.

15. Circassians and a Kalmuk steppe cavalryman. From a 17th-century print.

16. Dick Turpin rides Black Bess, an illustration from Harrison Ainsworth's *Rookwood*.

17. An illustration to the poem of Robert Burns, 'Ballad on the American War'.

18. Colonel Harry Gilmore rides to battle in the American Civil War. From *Four Years in the Saddle*, 1866.

Reaching Perth in disguise, Montrose was joined by 1,200 trained Catholic soldiers, sent over from Ireland; their ranks were swelled by the same number of Highlanders, 'lean, red-shanked mountaineers, plaided, armed with sword and bow, such deadly marksmen that with the latter they could kill a running deer'. A charge broke the 5,000 levies and 700 enemy horse at Tippermuir; the fugitives were massacred. Perth surrendered, and Montrose could arm and supply his ragged army. He advanced on Aberdeen, where the Covenanters were stupid enough to leave the walls and face another charge. 'Thair was littill slauchter in the fight, bot horribill was the slauchter in the flight.' The city was given over to plunder and rape and more murder. The Irish, according to the Royalist Patrick Gordon of Ruthven, killed men with as little worry as they killed a hare or a hen for their supper.

Doubling forward and back through the Highlands, Montrose won three more brilliant victories, while the cause of King Charles the First was destroyed by Cromwell at the battle of Naseby. Robert Baillie asked 'why our forces there have received defeat upon defeat even these five times from a despicable and inconsiderable enemy, while the forces of this nation obtaine victory upon victory by weak meanes against considerable and strong armyes'. So ferocious were the remaining Irish that 6,000 Covenanters were said to have perished at Montrose's sixth victory of Kilsyth near Glasgow. There, for once, the Royalists had a superiority in cavalry, some 600 seasoned troopers, who decimated the opposing forces of Balcarres' horse at Slaughter Howe.

With all Scotland now at his mercy, Montrose was forced to march to the aid of his King, so badly defeated well south of the Border. With his Highlanders melting away to return to their fastnesses, he was forced to recruit a new army. But true to form, the Wardens of the Marches promised much and achieved little more than bold words. The Marquis of Douglas did join with a thousand moss-troopers, but neither the Earls of Home nor Roxburgh, though apparently loyal, came up with reinforcements. 'You little imagine the difficulties my lord marquis hath here to wrestle with,' Sir Ralph Spottiswoode wrote. 'The overcoming of the enemy is the least of them; he hath more to do with his seeming friends.'

Unfortunately, the new Covenanter commander, David Leslie, had raised 5,000 mounted men, and was searching for a confrontation. For once, Montrose was to be surprised at Philiphaugh in a thick morning fog. Leslie's troopers charged through the Royalist camp and set to work with their own fanatical butchery. All the Catholic Irish infantry with their women and children were massacred 'with such savage and inhuman cruelty', Patrick Gordon wrote, 'as neither Turk nor Scythian was ever heard to have done the like'. Montrose himself would escape to Norway and France, but in terms of barbarity, the Presbyterian sword of the Lord and of Gideon was far bloodier than the occasional mercies, which had been doled out by the Scottish nobleman. But then, as John Buchan noted, 'the theocracy knew that it was fighting for its life', and when the ministers were insisting on the execution of those Royalist leaders, who fell into their hands, they declared: 'The work gangs bonnily on.'

A Protestant ballad commemorated David Leslie's tactics at his victory:

> Wi' him three thousand valiant men,
>   A noble sight to see!
> A cloud o' mist them weel concealed,
>   As close as e'er might be.
>
> When they came to the Shaw burn,
>   Said he, 'Sae weel we frame,
> I think it is convenient
>   That we should sing a psalm . . .'[†]
>
> He halv'd his men in equal parts,
>   His purpose to fulfil;
> The one part kept the water side,
>   The other gaed round the hill . . .
>
> And thus, between his armies twa,
>   He made them fast to fa'.
>
> Now, let us a' for Lesly pray,
>   And his brave companie!
> For they hae vanquish'd great Montrose,
>   Our cruel enemie.

Another ballad, however, 'The Gallant Grahams', lauded the support of that clan for the Royalist cause, before they had to flee overseas for their lives and their pay:

---

† *A variant reading of this last line was more likely:*
That we should take a dram.

Five thousand men, in armour strong,
    Did meet the gallant Grahams that day
At Inverlochie, where war began,
    And scarce two thousand men were they.

Gallant Montrose, that chieftain bold,
    Courageous in the best degree,
Did for the king fight well that day;
    The lord preserve his majestie! . . .

Now, fare ye weel, sweet Ennerdale!
    Countrie and kin I quit thee free;
Cheer up your hearts, brave cavaliers,
    For the Grahams are gone to High Germany.

The moss-troopers, who had lately joined the Royalist cause, were not all extinguished. In 1648, some Cavaliers with seventy 'Malignants of Scotland' emulated Buccleuch's raid to rescue Kinmont Willie. They came 'to Carlisle with ladders, scaled the walls, entered the castle, broke open the gaol, released moss-troopers and other prisoners, wounded the gaoler and all marched off together into Scotland'. This last effervescence, however, would be ended when the Covenanters fell out with Oliver Cromwell and his Parliamentarian army. For King Charles had decided to split the ranks of his foes and negotiate with his zealous Scots adversaries. He was assured by David Leslie, now Lord Newark, that his army would protect His Majesty. So Charles surrendered himself to their guardianship, and as Lord Lothian wrote, that action 'filled us with amazement and made us like men that dreame'. Yet Charles would not agree to the establishment of a Presbyterian Kirk in England, and Cromwell threatened invasion if the King were not yielded into English custody. On a payment of £400,000 in two instalments, the Scots sold their monarch, and their army left the soil of their old enemy.

Negotiations continued with the King, who eventually agreed to a separate peace with the Scots, which would confirm the solemn League and Covenant in the English Parliament, although neither he nor his subjects would be forced to subscribe to its terms. In return, Scotland would send an army into England to restore royal authority. Soon the fortress towns of Berwick and Carlisle were seized, and the army was to be swelled to 30,000 men in order to impose the Kirk's commands south of the Border. Half that force advanced towards Preston, where they were routed at nearby Langdale by Cromwell's cavalry, which took some 10,000 prisoners. Since Solway Moss, there had been no greater Scottish disaster.

Cromwell's advance to Edinburgh led to the collapse of the moderate Reformers, who were trying to restore the King in England in order to impose a version of Presbyterianism there. On his return to London, however, Cromwell decided to imitate Queen Elizabeth in dealing with Mary, Queen of Scots, and to have King Charles the First executed. His intrigues in Scotland had made him too great a danger in England. But certain Lords, including the Marquis of Montrose, had gone to Holland to counsel the heir to the throne, who would become Charles the Second; he should go to Ireland and mount an invasion of Scotland. The Covenanters also approached the presumptive King, who was promised support if he would accept their religious dictates. He would not, preferring Montrose's advice, that he would 'signify nothing . . . Trust the justice of your cause to God and better fortunes; and use all active and vigorous ways.'

Faced with another English or a new Royalist invasion, the Kirk was silly enough to purge the army of its best professional soldiers, who were called Malignants. They were replaced by amateur zealots, 'minister's sons, clerks, and such other sanctified creatures, who hardly ever saw or heard of any sword but that of the spirit'. Meanwhile, Montrose was sent to Orkney, where he assembled an army of some 1,200 men. Without waiting for reinforcements, he landed in Caithness and advanced to Carbisdale in Ross, where he was surprised by light cavalry, as at Philiphaugh, and his forces were butchered. He was soon captured, only later to be hanged and quartered. As Archibald Campbell, the Marquis of Argyll, noted, 'the tragic end' of the stoical Montrose showed that he knew 'how to goe out of this world, but nothing at all how to enter in ane other', for he would not pray on the scaffold.

With the defeat of Montrose, Charles the Second appeared to accept the demands of the Covenanters and set sail for Scotland, where he was welcomed with bonfires and dancing and joy. Before he could be crowned, Cromwell crossed the Tweed with some 16,000 men – David Leslie had the same number of troops to oppose him near Musselburgh on the coast not far from Edinburgh. Soon Leslie doubled his forces, while Cromwell's men were suffering from disease and shortage of supplies. In preliminary skirmishing, Robert Montgomerie, leading 800 horsemen, struck at Cromwell's camp, in a successful night raid, which forced the enemy to retreat to Dunbar with the rearguard harassed all the way.

These Border tactics, however, were trumped by Cromwell in the decisive battle. In a dawn attack in a howling storm from their camp at Dunbar, the Roundheads rode down the Scots, still asleep with wet matchlock muskets and unable to find their weapons and horses. One brigade fought to the bitter end, until they were trampled down. The Scottish horse and foot were 'made by the Lord of Hosts as stubble to the swords' of the Ironsides. And as Cromwell rightly predicted: 'Surely it is probable the Kirk have done their do. I believe their King will set upon his own score now.'

Yet the moss-troopers were still in the field, for they were past masters of slipping away from a defeat. 'A party of the Scottish guerrilla', in Walter Scott's words, had taken over the formidable Dirleton Castle, which Cromwell's commanders, General Monck and Lambert, had to reduce. 'He besieged the place, which having surrendered at discretion, the captain of the moss-troopers, one Waite, and two of his followers, were executed by martial law.' More dangerous was the band of 120 Reivers under the command of Captain Augustine from High Germany. They broke through the English forces besieging Edinburgh castle and delivered to the defenders a load of ammunition and pickles for preserving food. Riding back to the Highlands, these guerrillas shadowed the formal coronation of King Charles the Second at Scone abbey church. The moss- troopers mounted a successful raid on Linlithgow, and luring the Presbyterian horse into pursuit, they set about 'cutting and hacking' them back to the town. To outflank the Scots forces, General Lambert crossed the Firth of Forth to North Queensferry, where he took up position at Inverkeithing against an equal number of royal infantry and cavalry. The 200 moss-troopers of Captain Augustine were successful on their first charge with Brechin's horsemen, but they soon broke against a counter-charge by the Roundheads, led by Lambert himself, who survived two pistol balls from *dags* between his breastplate and his leather jerkin.

This was the epitaph of the Reivers, the best light horse of that period in all the world. In their necessary flight abroad, indeed, they were often employed as mercenary scouts in continental wars. As Bishop Leslie had remarked: 'So many of our countrymen have so good success among strange nations, some in the wars, some in professing of sciences, and some in merchandise.' The scatterings of them reverted to banditry, but the game was up. The *Mercurius Politicus* reported in November, 1662, after Charles the Second was restored to the throne: 'The Scotts and moss-troopers have again revived their old custom of robbing and murthering the English, whether soldiers or other, upon all opportunities.' Two officers were waylaid, and five soldiers killed by some mossers, who, after they had given them quarter, tied their hands behind them, and then threw them down a steep hill, or rock. Old habits died hard, but with these bad habits proscribed, the Reivers also died out. Their successors would be the more formal Highwaymen, or Gentlemen of the Road.

CHAPTER TEN

The Social Bandits

As bulldogs without leashes, brigands only flourish in the absence of central authority. Where power is weak, bandits are strong. And if they organise under a warlord, they may become a force in the land, even though the mere followers of a blood-feud or a gang or a clan rather than any cause. In the breakdown of government during internecine struggles and their aftermath, raiders reach their heyday. In the four centuries of the Border wars between England and Scotland, at the close of the Hundred Years War in France and the Thirty Years War in Germany and the American Civil War, there rose the Reivers and the *condottieri*, the robber bands and the rustlers of the Wild West. As the agents of law and order painfully gained control, the freebooters were either recruited, as the Cossacks were, or they were restrained or deported. The frontiers of anarchy slowly, slowly were shackled in their chains.

The medieval mercenary knights and the outlaw bands were not so different in terms of their necessary upkeep. They lived on plunder, and they could be hired for brief expeditions against national enemies. Some of the brigands could become legendary heroes famed in ballad and song, from Robin Hood through Cartouche and Schinderhannes to Jesse James and the Captain Lampião from the Brazilian wastelands. For a poor peasant or serf society, an attacker on the local landowners and sometimes a corrupt church made him appear to be the defender of the oppressed. If he did not rob the rich to give to the poor, the proceeds mostly reached his needy recruits and their families, while his summary justice often satisfied the hope of revenge, felt by the exploited. His defiance of power often appeared as the righting of wrongs, and his inevitable death a kind of social martyrdom.

The later rebels, who sometimes became the leaders of their countries, discovered that no guerrilla campaign could succeed without peasant support in the countryside. The outlaws also depended on their popular backing, and so they had to behave moderately well towards the folk on their home ground. They were, indeed, often the victims of an injustice, protesting against seized cattle or, in the case of Pancho Villa, defending his sister's honour against a Mexican rancher. They could protect peasant communities against predators, as in Kurosawa's epic film, *The Seven Samurai*. And yet, they were on hire as killers and expropriators of land, as in so many of the Western films about the conflicts of the cattle ranchers against sheep-herders and dirt farmers.

At the end of the English Civil War, the myth of the gentleman bandit – or of Robin Hood as the Earl of Huntingdon – reached its apogee. Condemned by Cromwell's Commonwealth, with their estates forfeited, some Royalist cavalry officers did take to the road. Prince Rupert of the Rhine himself became a pirate commander, while the Cavalier highwayman Captain Reynolds, gave these last words on the gallows: 'God bless King Charles, *Vive le Roi!* And even with the Restoration of King Charles the Second, the mounted robbers kept their reputation for good manners as well as discriminating theft, particularly in the case of the dandy Claude Duval, the paragon of his period. 'Highwaymen, in general, are from a superior class,' wrote the French observer, Ferri de St Constant. 'They pride themselves on their education and good demeanour; they are called Gentleman of the Road.' In the *Mémoires*, which appeared in 1670 after Duval's execution, he was said to be buried in a church in Covent Garden under a marble stone with this epitaph:

> Here lies Du Vall, reader, if male thou art,
> Look to thy purse; if female, to thy heart.
> Much havoc hath he made of both; for all
> Men he made stand, and women he made fall.*

By the 18th century, the brutality of the highway robbers overcame their curiosity value. As casual risks, insisting on a toll, many of them could still be seen as collectors, who would only seek passage money. As the Swiss traveller César de Saussure testified, some of the marauders 'take only a part of what they find; but all these robbers ill-treat only those who try to defend themselves'. Resistance meant murder. Others, such as the well-spoken son of Quaker parents, Jacob Halsey, could rape most gallantly, with the words, 'My pretty lamb, I must dismount thy alluring body, to the end I may come into thee.' With his gang, a deserter from the Coldstream Guards, Patrick O'Bryan, raped and stabbed a Trowbridge lady, murdered her father and mother, stole £2,500 in gold and silver, and burned down the country house, roasting within all the poor servants. Even the notorious Dick Turpin was guilty with the Essex gang of brutality and murder; he never rode to York on Black Bess; that was the shotsilk spun by later romancers.

After the victory of Culloden, the fear of another Jacobite rebellion made the Georgian governments fearful of any homegrown outlaw band. Within two decades after 1749, 250 highwaymen were hanged at Tyburn alone, and their corpses set in iron corsets to hang on gibbets as examples along the trails which they had plundered. A police force, the Bow Street Runners, was started in London to supplement the rural sheriffs and watchmen and thief-takers, such as the notorious Jonathan Wild, who was also a fence for stolen goods. Although he nearly had his throat cut by a prisoner he had denounced called Blueskin, Wild was eventually condemned for living on the proceeds of the criminals he had caught. He had apprehended an ineffectual highwayman on Hampstead Heath, the brilliant escapologist Jack Sheppard, whose flights from heavy irons and a chain fixed to a staple set in the floor of his cell in Newgate prison made him the Houdini of that time.* Street ballads and 'Penny Dreadfuls' and even the major plays of John Gay and Bertholt Brecht would turn these desperados into the victims of circumstance rather than the accomplices of crime. In his ironic *Jonathan Wild*, Henry Fielding made his 'Great Man' give some directions about his success:

Never to do more mischief to another than was necessary to the effecting his purpose . . .

To forgive no enemy; but to be cautious and often dilitory in revenge . . .

To foment eternal jealousies in his gang, one of another . . .

That many men were undone by not going deep enough in roguery . . .

That all men were knaves or fools, and much the greater number a composition of both.

In England, the petty highwaymen would be defeated by the new means of transport. For the stagecoach would be doomed by the canal barge and the railway carriage. And while the American cowboy would switch from robbing the horse-drawn mail to the goods pulled behind steam engines, the English crook would retire from the roads and take decades to imitate the example of the first American two-reel western movie, *The Great Train Robbery*. Only in the wild nomad country would the old traditions and satisfactions of the raiding society continue. For the horse culture and the outlaws would survive just so long as urban civilisation held a loose rein on the far frontier. These conditions allowed some powers to the born-again serfs of the Hungarian borderlands, the *Haiduks*, a Magyar word of Mongolian origin, meaning 'cattle-drovers'. As on the Spanish frontier against the Moors, these bands of raiders were earthy crusaders, opposing the Turkish occupation of the Balkans in their hit-and-run tactics against their conquerors of a foreign faith. For five centuries, they were 'the highest form of primitive banditry, the one which comes closest to being a permanent and conscious focus of peasant insurrection'.

Led by elected *voivodes* or dukes, the *Haiduks* were male military communities, who recruited young men in trouble with the state. They were free and rootless outlaws, whose rare allegiance was to their group. 'The *Haiduk* ballads sing of the men whose swords were their only sisters, whose rifles their wives.' When the comrades broke up, they had to disperse 'as lost individuals to the four corners of the earth. Death was their equivalent of marriage', although some *Haiduk* young women dressed as men and picked up a rifle, partisans before their due time. And yet, as the ballad sang of them:

> We have made many mothers weep,
> We have widowed many wives,
> Many more have we made orphans,
> For we are childless men ourselves.

As the robber 'moss troopers' were recruited as light cavalry by contrary sides during the English Civil War, so the *Haiduks* and the neighbouring Cossacks might serve the state or in major revolutions against it, before the rebels became the new administration. That would be the case for Pancho Villa, who served as a general in the Mexican Revolution and was rewarded with a *hacienda*, so joining the landowners, whom he execrated. In the early stages of the Russian Revolution, Trotsky would use Cossacks and brigands in the fight against the White armies, while Mao in the formative years of the Chinese Revolution would recruit 'declassed elements' of deserters and robbers, beggars and Manchurian 'Red Beards' or horse-thieves, sworn to attack all government officials. As pollen attracts bees, so rebellion attracts outcasts, until they are cast out. For no high command can long put up with such unreliable courage.

To the oppressed, the raider and avenger became a symbol of the struggle for justice. From medieval *troubadour* to Border balladeer, from Chaucer to Schiller to Victorian novelists, the appeal of the free man of the woods and plains has been broadcast through songs and plays and romances. Robin Hood was, indeed, commemorated in 1420 by Andrew de Wyntoun, who celebrated him as active in the 13th century:

> Then Little John and Robin Hood
> As forest outlaws were commended good.

Their tactics were praised by Langland in *Piers Plowman*:

> And some to ride and recover what was wrongfully taken
> He showed them how to regain it through hands of might
> And wrest it from false men . . .

And in the *Prologue to the Canterbury Tales*, Chaucer gave a description of the freeholder and yeoman, which would have suited any mounted Borderer, armed with quiver and bow, shield and sword and dagger:

> And he was clad in coat and hood of green
> A sheaf of peacock arrows right and keen
> Under his belt he bore full carefully.
> Well could he dress his tackle yeomanly:
> His arrows drooped not with feathers low,
> And in his hand he bore a mighty bow.
> A cropped head had he with a brown face.
> Of woodcraft well knew he all the usage.
> Upon his arm he bore a gay bracer,
> And by his side a sword and buckler,
> And on the other side a gay dagger.
> Harnessed well, and sharp as point of spear;
> A Christopher on his breast of silver sheen.
> A horn he bore, the baldric was of green;
> A forester was he, truly, as I guess.*

The Border ballads never lost their sense of mystery and fate, the love and loss of marginal folk on the frontier of existence. The 'halfpenny literature' of the English streets, however, was hardly more than doggerel, though Shakespeare might ironically proclaim: What hast here, ballads? I love a ballad in print; for then we are sure they are true.' To Henry Mayhew in his *London Labour and the London Poor*, they were 'certainly the rude uncultivated verse in which the popular tale of the times is recorded'. And these tales were mostly of calamities and scandals and rapes, of robbers and celebrities, of executions and supposed last confessions in front of the noose. The broadsheet of the street ballad of William Nevison, the great Robber of the North, showed the level of the descent into bathos. According to his street biographer in 1685, Nevison, and not the later Dick Turpin, rode his mare from London to York between sunrise and sunset:

> In all his exploits, Nevison was tender to the fair sex, and bountiful to the poor. He was also a true loyalist, and never levied any contributions upon the Royalists. His life was once spared by the royal clemency . . . His name became the terror of every traveller on the road. He levied a quarterly tribute on all the northern drovers, and in return not only spared them himself, but protected them against all other thieves, and the carriers who frequented the road willingly agreed to leave certain sums at such places as he appointed, to prevent their being stripped of them all.

In the popular mind, Nevison was the supreme outlaw, who respected God and the King, while extending for a fee to cattle drovers his protection from more unscrupulous highwaymen. The ballad of his last words hymned his virtues:

> He maintained himself like a gentleman,
>   Besides he was good to the poor;
> He rode about like a bold hero,
>   And he gain'd himself favour therefore . . .

> 'Tis now before my lord judge,
>   'Oh! Guilty or not do you plead';
> He smiled unto the judge and jury,
>   And these were the words that he said.

'I never robbed a gentleman of twopence,
But what I give half to be blest,
But guilty I've been all my life time,
So gentleman do as you list.

'It's when I rode on the highway,
I've always had money in great store,
And whatever I took from the rich,
I freely gave to the poor.

'But my peace I have made with my Maker,
And to be with Him I'ready to draw;
So here's adieu! To this world and its vanities,
For I'm ready to suffer the law.'

The theatrical success of the 18th-century *The Beggar's Opera*, satirised British justice as much as the criminal hero. As the Duke of Queensberry told its author, 'This is a very odd thing, Gay. I am satisfied that it is either a very good thing or a very bad thing.' Certainly, the highwayman Captain Macheath exposed the corruption of the government of Sir Robert Walpole as much as the happy depravity of the London underworld. Even Dr Johnson had to admit that the play might have 'some influence by making the character of a rogue familiar, and in some degree pleasing'. Two centuries later, Bertolt Brecht, in his *Threepenny Novel* and *Opera*, would convert Gay's work into a savage indictment of the oppressive exploitation, wrought by capitalism. The bitterness of the worker was never better expressed than in the revolutionary song of the kitchen-maid Jenny, when she is asked who has to die by pirates firing from a black ship with fifty big cannon. She replies, 'All of them!' And as their heads fall, she cries: 'Hoopla!' And who can answer Macheath's question, 'What is robbing a bank compared to owning a bank?'

Two highwaymen of Georgian times, Dick Turpin and Jack Sheppard, would be elevated to their roles in popular nostalgia by the dandy Harrison Ainsworth, a Victorian writer, under the influence of the Gothic romances and Sir Walter Scott's historical novels.* In his serial drama, often set in the family vaults of *Rookwood*, the title of the epic, Dick Turpin was the hero of the peripheral plot. 'Rash doing was the main feature of Turpin's character,' Ainsworth wrote. 'Like our great Nelson, he knew fear only by name . . . With him expired the chivalrous spirit which animated so many knights of the road.' Although no sentences could be further from the truth, Ainsworth made Turpin state: 'It is as necessary for a man to be a gentleman before he can turn highwayman, as it is for a doctor to have his diploma, or an attorney his certificate.'

As for the ride from London to York on the faithful Black Bess, who died at the knell of the tolling bells of the Minster, Turpin never did it, except in the imagination of the novelist of *Rookwood*, who recorded the gallop in one sitting himself: 'So thoroughly did I identify with the highwayman, that, once I started, I found it impossible to halt.' Indeed, imagination was the whip of fact. And the crime novel sequel of 1839, entitled *Jack Sheppard*, outsold *Oliver Twist* by Charles Dickens; dramatised in eight versions that same year, it proved the appeal of the condemned villain to the people. Thackeray might thunder in *The Times* that 'Ainsworth dared not paint his hero as the scoundrel he knew him to be. He must keep his brutalities in the background.' But a contemporary lampoon, *Flowers of Hemp: or the Newgate Garland*, better caught the public mood in a parody of Wordsworth's ode to Milton:

> 'Turpin, thou should'st be living at this hour:
> England hath need of thee . . .
>
> Great men have been among us – names that lend
> A lustre to our calling – better none:
> Maclaine, Duval, Dick Turpin, Barrington,
> Blueskin and others, who called Sheppard friend.'

Perhaps the outsider and opium addict and supreme essayist, Thomas de Quincey, would best describe the hold, which the bandit and the highwayman retained over the populace of every country, where the poor were oppressed by the rich, and where central urban control pressed upon the traditional values and liberties of the country. To de Quincey, the Gentleman of the Road –

> Followed a liberal profession, one which required more accomplishments than either the bar or the pulpit, since it presumed a bountiful endowment of qualifications – strength, health, agility, and excellent horsemanship, intrepidity of the first order, presence of mind, courtesy, and a general ambidexterity of powers for facing all accidents and for turning to good account all unlooked-for contingencies.

The finest men in England, physically speaking, throughout the last century, the very noblest specimens of man, considered as an animal, were the mounted robbers who cultivated their profession on the great roads. When every traveller carried firearms the mounted robber lived in an element of danger and adventurous gallantry.

CHAPTER ELEVEN

The American Horse

Before they set sail for the New World, the explorers and the Conquistadors were already thinking of native Americans as naked, well-made, propertyless, and as free of age and disease as Adam and Eve – yet as red, barbaric, anarchic, immoral, aggressive and cannibalistic as a Lucifer or Beelzebub. Policy or fantasy often made invisible the western 'Indians', so miscalled because Columbus believed he had reached Asia. The greatest river in South America is still named the Amazon because its discoverer thought that he had seen the one-breasted race of warrior women.

Yet the classical and biblical myths, which the Spanish and the Portuguese imported in their minds into the New World, harmed the native peoples less than the past experience of the Iberian empires. As the shock troops of the Pope against the Arabs, the Spanish and Portuguese were used to conversion by the sword. The Moors had both civilised the petty warlords of Spain and had taught them to accept slaves taken in war as natural. The Conquistadors brought with them a tradition of slavery – and baptism – for the defeated. The famous Bulls of Pope Alexander VI, which split the unknown world between Spain and Portugal in 1493, charged the two empires with making the heathen world Christian.

Justification follows the act. Those original Americans, who were not exterminated by the sword or disease, were turned into serfs on a Spanish *hacienda* under the followers of Cortes or Pizarro. The champion of the *colons*, Sepúlveda, knew nothing of the American tribes, but he did know that a crusade justified all. The destruction of half the native population was merely the necessary stage before the salvation of the other half. They were *homunculi* or little men, inferior to the Spaniards 'as children are to adults, as women are to men', and only by obedience could they be saved. Their defender Las Casas, who had spent twenty years preaching among them, argued the opposite – that they compared well with the Greeks and the Romans, were rational and religious by nature, were more virtuous than the Europeans, and were highly urban and organised as was seen in the great cities of Mexico and Peru. And what about the benefit to Europe from the imported maize, potato, tobacco and cocoa of the Americas?

The Spanish Crown backed Las Casas and wrote laws to protect the native peoples, but the *colons* ignored Madrid and bounced the head of the first Viceroy to Peru on the end of a string for trying to protect the Inca and other tribes. Whatever Europe thought, the men on the spot did what they liked. If the Europeans could believe two opposite versions of the local Americans, what could the victims believe but one version of the early white invaders? The first Spaniards were taken to be gods, which helped to explain the feebleness of the resistance to Cortes. In 1508, the inhabitants of Puerto Rico decided to test the immortality of some Spaniards by holding them under water; the Spaniards proved mortal.

Never has a god fallen so fast in the mind of his believers into mere man, if not a beast. The ferocity and rapacity of the Conquistadors was such that Benzoni reported from Peru that the Incas 'not only would never believe us to be Christians and children of God, as boasted, but not even that we were born on this earth or generated by a man and born of a woman; so fierce an animal, they concluded, must be the offspring of the sea'.

As with the early Mongols, the advent of iron and cattle and the horse, and now the dog, changed life for the native peoples of the Americas. The only metals worked in the Americas before the coming of Columbus were gold and silver and a little copper, and these were used mainly for ornament. Being soft metals, they were often beaten rather than fired. After the Indians first met the exploring Spaniards, they would trade any quantity of gold for what they called white metal, iron and tin. The initial effect of the Spaniards' cannon and armour and crossbows and swords was decisive against semi-naked tribes armed only with stone-tipped spears and wooden clubs and bows and arrows.

In Alvarado's massacre of the sacred dancers in Tenochtitlan, the Aztec chroniclers recorded the terrible slashing of the iron. The Spaniards 'attacked the man who was drumming and cut off his arms. They then cut off his head, and it rolled across the floor.' They attacked all the dancers, 'stabbing them, spearing them, striking them with their swords. They attacked some of them behind and these fell instantly to the ground with their entrails hanging out.' Others were beheaded or had their skulls split into pieces. The Spaniards 'struck others in the shoulders, and their arms were torn from their bodies. They wounded some in the thigh and some in the calf.' Others had their stomachs cut open. 'Some attempted to run away, but their intestines dragged as they ran; they seemed to tangle their feet in their own entrails. No matter how they tried to save themselves, they could find no escape.'

The Spaniards in their turn had to watch the sacrifice of their fellows by the obsidian knives of the Aztecs. Once fifty-three Spanish prisoners and four of their horses were cut open by the Aztec priests, who removed their smoking hearts and set up their heads on pikes facing the sun, the heads of the horses below those of the men. But in the pitched battles, obsidian was no match for iron, while the quilted armour of the mounted Spaniards could absorb arrows better than naked flesh. At first, indeed, the Aztecs had thought horse and rider were one like a Centaur. Later, they thought the horse was a giant stag, which snorted and bellowed and sweated and foamed with its iron bells ringing at its neck. The shock of the horses was like the force of a storm or an earthquake. 'They make a loud noise when they run; they make a great din, as if stones were raining on the earth. Then the ground is pitted and scarred where they set down their hooves. It opens wherever their hooves touch it.'

Although iron vanquished the stone empires of Mexico and Peru, the use of the animals of Europe, the trained horse and the dog, caused the most terror in the Mayan tribes. When Ponce de Leon was putting down a revolt in Puerto Rico, he had a fierce hound called Bezerrillo, which tore open the inhabitants and knew 'which of them were in War, and which in Peace, like a Man'. The Puerto Ricans were more afraid of 10 Spaniards with Bezerrillo than of 100 without him, and he received his share of the spoils with the rest of the soldiers. Cieza de Leon once met a Portuguese 'who had the quarters of Indians hanging on a porch to feed his dogs with, as if they were wild beasts'.

When the Aztec emperor Motecuhzoma's messengers first reported to him the armaments of the Spaniards under Cortes, they described the cannon, the iron weapons, the horses, the blond hair of the white men, their sweet bread, and finally their dogs, which were said to be enormous with burning yellow eyes, tireless and powerful and swift and fierce and spotted like an ocelot. This last description terrified Motecuhzoma and helped to make him the indecisive puppet, resigned to his fate, whom Cortes manipulated so successfully on his first advance on the Aztec capital. Then the dogs were sent running ahead of the Spanish column: 'They lifted their muzzles to the wind. They raced on before with saliva dripping from their jaws.' And who will ever forget the sight, in Werner Herzog's film *Aguirre: The Wrath of God*, of the armoured Conquistador with his single horse and cannon floating on a raft down the Amazon, to search out another mine of jungle gold?

Ironically, the savagery of the trained beasts of Europe broke the Aztecs as much as the technology of iron. The hooves of the cavalry and the teeth of the wolfhounds were as destructive and more terrible than the long-range death flying from cannon mouth and musket and crossbow. The monsters of war were imported into the Americas, where the great city of Tenochtitlan was larger than any in Spain and boasted at least a quarter of a million inhabitants. As Bernal Diaz de Castillo reported, when Motecuhzoma first showed the Spaniards the sights of the white-stuccoed city from the top of the sacrificial pyramid in its centre, 'some of the soldiers among us who had been in many parts of the world, in Constantinople, and all over Italy, and in Rome said that so large a market place and so full of people, and so well regulated and arranged, they had never beheld before'. In Herrera's opinion, Tenochtitlan surpassed Venice as a city built on water and was twice the size of Milan.

Yet the sacrificial pyramid itself was enough to confirm the righteousness of Christian conquest. Gómara, who was later the secretary of Cortes and his biographer, claimed that the skulls of 136,000 sacrificial victims were exposed near the great pyramid of Tenochtitlan, and that the entrance to the temple dedicated to Quetzalcoatl – the white bird-god whom Motecuhzoma confused with the Spaniards – was like the muzzle of hell. The door of the temple was carved 'in the form of a serpent's mouth, diabolically painted, with fangs and teeth exposed, which frightened those who entered, especially the Christians'. Every chapel inside the temple was crusted with blood and stank with human sacrifice. The worship of snake and jaguar gods seemed to be the worst of idolatry and a confusion of bestial with human nature. The main duty of the Aztec warriors was to capture victims for the knives of the priests. They believed that the source of life, the sun, needed regular infusions of human blood to renew itself.

So the clash of European and American confirmed the worst fears of either culture. The ruthless slaughter by Alvarado of the sacred dancers seemed as shocking to the Aztecs as the human sacrifices to the war-god Huitzilopochtli seemed to the Spaniards. Both peoples were treacherous and deceitful in war, both tortured prisoners by flaying or the rack if they needed information, both used massacre and terror as instruments of policy and strategy. Both cultures were urbanised and organised and cruel, but the collapse of the Aztec Empire, soon followed by the collapse of the Incas before a few hundred Spaniards, can only be explained in terms of the sense of Christian mission of the more moderate Conquistadors, such as Columbus and Cortes, and the ultimate ferocity and avarice of such mass-killers and plunderers as Alvarado and Pizarro.

The Aztec chroniclers, indeed, mocked the greed of the Europeans, which they found inhuman. When Motecuhzoma first sent gold in quantity to the Spaniards, they were seen to be transported with joy, fingering the gold like monkeys. 'Their bodies swelled with greed, and their hunger was ravenous; they hungered like pigs for that gold.' When the Spaniards searched Motecuhzoma's personal treasure-house, the Aztecs saw that the Spaniards 'grinned like little beasts and patted each other with delight'. Later, when Pizarro seized the Inca Atahualpu and made him fill a large room with gold and silver to the height of his reach, the Inca did not gain his liberty with his ransom, but his death.

The great object of the Spanish expeditions to the New World was bullion, and their success almost matched their avarice. Their transport by sea of this loot transformed the European economy and led to future global domination by means of maritime trade. And by land, their introduction of Spanish longhorn cattle and the hardy North African pony changed the ecology of the Great Plains above the Rio Grande river. Cortes had landed in 1519 with ten stallions and five mares and a foal. Within fifty years, mustangs were spreading from the Panhandle of Texas to the further prairies, followed by breakaway cattle, looking for the liberty of the wild grasses. Within 200 years, the indigenous prairie tribes had mastered the horse and acquired the musket and powder and ball.

The Great Plains were now dominated by some nine tribes of buffalo killers or cattle rustlers. They had long lived as the Mongols; their tipis, made from twenty dressed hides, created a family room, some fifteen feet wide. The lodge poles were sledge runners to drag the moveable camps behind the horses in the necessary pursuit of game. The Sioux and the Crow and the Blackfeet in Montana and Wyoming, the Cheyenne and the Arapo and the Pawnees in mid-prairie, the Kiowa and the Comanches and the Apaches to the south, these tribes of some 20,000 people roamed between the Rockies and the Mississippi river, warring more fiercely on each other than ever the Reivers in their interminable feuds.[*]

Outside California, such aggressive peoples defeated the Spanish probes to the northlands. First, Cabeza de Vaca wandered into New Mexico and returned with tales of the seven gold Cities of Cibola. Then in 1540, Coronado led a large force of more than 200 cavalry, 1,500 horses and 500 cattle in search of chimeras and glory. Except for the sack of many *pueblos*, Coronado achieved little in his two years' expedition as far as Kansas, except replenishing the wildstock. As his chronicler Pedro Castañeda wrote of the landscape: 'This country is like a bowl, so that when a man sits down, the horizon surrounds him all around at the distance of a musket shot.'

Later in 1598, the explorer Juan de Oñate took formal possession of New Mexico in the name of the Spanish king. Settlements were set up at a capital at Santa Fe, while a trail led to El Paso in the south; also Albuquerque and Santa Cruz would be established on the upper Rio Grande. The ranchers or *ecomenderos* set up plantations and ranges for producing wheat and maize, beans and squash, as well as grazing for cattle. After limited rebellions, the local *pueblo* peoples were turned into devout labourers, as subservient to their priest as to their landlord. Although the Spanish failed to exploit the Great Plains, they did establish most of the trading trails across the South-West. Only in California did they set up remarkable ranching communities of long endurance.

To the first European colonists landing on the Atlantic Coast, the threat of an intrusive barbarian horse culture was cut off by mountain and forest. Indeed, the trees were the opportunity of the Pilgrim Fathers and their successors. Available timber was the material of houses and stockades and ships. The barrier of the backwoods created the means of progress. Once the descendants of the Puritans had broken through the fir mountains on to the Great Plains – making the trees their familiar in the process and displacing the forest tribes in their advance – then they lost all direction, faced with a new hostile environment which terrified them. The gigantic oval of the dry grasslands between the forests of the eastern seaboard and the Rocky Mountains was already the home of a great beast. There lived one animal 'that came nearer to dominating the life and shaping the institutions of a human race than any other in all the land, if not in the world – the buffalo'.

As the new American colonists displaced the timber tribes and drove them on to the prairies, some of these adapted and some were decimated by the mounted plainsmen. The Saukees of the high forest were warned of their future fate. 'When hunger drives you from those woods, your bodies will be exposed to balls, to arrows, and to spears. You will only have time to discharge your guns, before, on horseback, their spears will spill your blood . . . As you have seen the whirlwind break and scatter the trees of your woods, so will your warriors bend before them on horseback.' These tribal tactics were so similar to clan fighting along the Scottish Borders. Following the Saukees came the European culture of the white pioneers, moving west, so helpless on the grasslands outside the wheeled wooden waggons, which served as defence and shelter and transport for tools and goods.

Industrial civilisation in America began with the building of log cabins, but faltered on the edge of the prairie in the sod hut. There was little wood or water in this new hostile country, which the early Americans thought uninhabitable and called the 'Great American Desert'. Two thousand miles of space had to be passed through, not occupied. There was no place for the settler, only for the vagrant. An army captain was to observe in 1852 that the last strip of forest before the Great Plains, named the Cross-Timbers, seemed 'to have been designed as a natural barrier between civilised man and the savage'.

The Plains were not to be the final barrier. The Rocky Mountains and their foothills lay between the prairies and the Pacific coast. And these peaks, thickly wooded up to the height of the timberline, above which the cold and the wind ensured that no tree grew, turned the pioneer American trappers into a bestial form of humanity. The 'Mountain Men' were the walking fears of the pioneers – anarchic savages dressed in skins and living on raw meat, without law or conscience, almost as fierce as the grizzly bears that disputed their hunting rights.

To exist in that environment, the Mountain Men slipped backward in the scale of civilisation until their wilderness skills equalled those of the peoples already there. Moreover, hunting alone rather than in tribes, their reversion to the primitive could be at a lower level of savagery than the red men. One was called 'Cannibal Phil' because he survived the winter by eating his squaw. All of them ate 'anything that walked, swam, wriggled or crawled'. Like beasts, they lived between famine and feast, drinking the blood of the buffalo and eating its liver raw, spiced with the gall from its bladder. The time of the annual sale of their beaver pelts was a time of drunkenness and orgy and killing and waste. The rest of the year was an animal life on the mountains that made a man forget that living might be more than survival.

The beaver were overtrapped and the Mountain Men passed away, to be followed by the waggons of the overland pioneers, making to the sunset. The Rockies were to stop the Mormons, seeking Zion and religious freedom, and they in their turn were to help and prey on the later caravans, lumbering through the passes on the Oregon and California Trails. When Cheyenne attack or internal quarrels or lack of supplies did not cause the wheeled villages of the pioneers to break up into quarrelling groups which forgot the conventions of social life, a winter besieged by snow and want in the mountains could lead even Victorian women into a recognition of the ferocity within their niceties. The notorious Donner party lasted through the winter on the high sierras by consuming one another dead and alive. Its only concession to civilisation was to label the remains so that a man or a woman might not consume their own kin.

Each new barrier that confronted the immigrant became the receptacle of his fears. To the first European settlers, the ocean was the prime wilderness to be survived, and the fierceness of storms seemed to be reflected in the rapacity of the pirates who preyed upon sea traffic. Then to the settlers on the coastline, the forest with its beasts and its red men was the frontier of terror. Once the woods had been cut and used and controlled, then the prairies became the new horror and their horsed tribes the most implacable and cruel of all. And finally, there was the obstacle course of the western mountains, which could turn Europeans themselves into cannibals before they might reach the west coast with its opportunity for a life of some ease.

Where Spanish culture had penetrated the southern Great Plains, a Mexican cattle country lay below San Antonio in a diamond, cut between Laredo and Brownsville and Indiana on the Gulf Coast. Between the Nueces river and the Rio Grande, the *ecomenderos* and mixed cowboys had corralled the wild longhorns on the open range. As J. Frank Dobie described them, these cattle were mightily antlered and wild-eyed:

> This herd of full-grown Texas steers might appear to a stranger seeing them for the first time as a parody of their kind. But however they appeared, with their steel hoofs, their long legs, their staglike muscles, their thick skins, their powerful horns, they could walk the roughest ground, cross the widest deserts, climb the highest mountains, swim the widest rivers, fight off the fiercest bands of wolves, endure hunger, cold, thirst, and punishment as few beasts of the earth have ever shown themselves capable of enduring.

The invaders of this cattle paradise would be Yankees. Before the white Americans arrived in Texas, some 4,000 ranchers and Mexican cowboys with the Comanches had occupied this empty wilderness. The Spanish governors knew that the intruders would come; just so, the barbarians had attacked the Roman Empire. As the wise historian of *Pioneer America* wrote, the rulers decided to 'tame the Goths':

> That is, to invite some Americans to come to Texas to domesticate them, and to convert them into defenders of Texas against their brethren. That policy saved neither Rome nor Texas from the barbarians. When Moses Austin, a Connecticut Yankee who had settled in Missouri when it was Spanish, asked permission, in 1820, to found a colony of three hundred 'Goths' in Texas, its governing council quickly consented. Moses Austin died soon afterward, but his son Stephen pursued his scheme. He won the respect and affection of both Latins and rough American frontiersmen, and he was almost astonishingly successful.

As with Hengist and Horsa and the Danes, who expanded their first agreed landing space into a county, so Stephen Austin – his name would become a city – encouraged American settlers to flood into the dry cattle land. Within twenty years, there were 30,000 immigrants in villages and on farms and ranches above the Rio Grande. As with the ancient Danes flooding over the North Sea, their presence only encouraged more invaders to arrive across the Mississippi river. Skirmishes began between the new Texans and the Mexican authorities, culminating at San Antonio in the deaths of two fabled frontiersmen, David Crockett and Jim Bowie of the long hunting knife. Later, Sam Houston defeated the Mexican army, while it was having a siesta. A cavalry charge overwhelmed dismounted men. And the brief independence of Texas developed into an American war against Mexico, which ended in the acquisition of the whole of the South-West of the United States for a mere $15,000,000, almost a better deal than President Jefferson's previous purchase of Louisiana from Napoleon.

Only in Oregon did the British Empire thwart American expansionism. The failure to take Canada after the American Revolution and the War of 1812 was galling, but this final compromise was something of a humiliation. A pretty straight geographical survey was drawn as a frontier from the Great Lakes to below Vancouver, an invisible barrier which both nations had to respect. Indeed, the harried Plains tribes south of that dotted border called it the 'Medicine Line'. If they reached it ahead of the US Cavalry, they were merely at the distant mercy of the Mounties and British justice.

The Spaniards had set the example. More than cattle and horses, precious metal remained the chief attraction for the new vagrants across the Great Plains. As in Peru, the discovery of gold and silver in the sierras of the Rocky Mountains seduced prospectors in swarms across the Great American Desert. With horse or pack mule, they followed the older ways, such as the Oregon Trail along the Platte river or the Santa Fe Trail along the Arkansas river to Colorado Springs. New trails were blazed, the Smoky Hill beside the Kansas river to eastern Colorado, and a Mormon route by Salt Lake City to Montana. The rush of miners to California swamped the old Spanish laws and administration. Even so, another code of the West developed in the mining camps of the ravaged gulches.

The tens of thousands of prospectors, named the Forty-niners, were a wild bunch, trying to hack and dredge an individual fortune out of a wilderness. Their poet Fitz James O'Brien, sct in a lyric the mood of the times:

> Up in a wild Californian hill,
> Where the torrents swept with a mighty will,
> And the grandeur of Nature filled the air,
> And the cliffs were lofty, rugged, and bare,
> Some thousands of lusty fellows she saw
> Obeying the first great natural law.
> From the mountain's side they had scooped the earth,
> Down to the veins where the gold had birth . . .
> They rocked huge cradles the livelong day,
> And shovelled the heavy, tenacious clay,
> And grasped the nugget of gleaming ore,
> The sinews of commerce on every shore.

Such naked greed was greeted with mockery in the naming of some of the mining camps:– Mad Mule Gulch and Loafer Hill, Slapjack Bar and Chicken-thief Flat, Git-up-and-Git and Rat-trap Slide, Sweet Revenge and Shirt-tail Canyon, You Bet and Gouge Eye. Faced with bandits and outlaws, the miners developed a vigilante society, where rough justice could develop into mob rule and lynch law. In the absence of any authority from central or state government, for it hardly exited in pioneer days, the miners executed those who were thought fit to kill. Their first historian celebrated, in the language of the time, 'the rude mountain courts, truth reached by shortcuts, a rough-hewn sturdy system':

We are irresistibly compelled to think of the whole race of American pioneers, from the days of Boone and Harrod to the days of Carson and Bridger; heroic forest chivalry, heroic conquerors of the prairies, heroic rulers of the mountain wilderness, ever forcing back the domains of savage and wild beast. Well did one of the most eloquent of American lecturers once exclaim:

'Woe to the felon upon whose track is the American Borderer! Woe to the assassin before a self-empanneled jury of American foresters! No lie will help him, no eloquence prevail; no false plea can confuse the clear conceptions or arrest the just judgment of a frontier court.'

To the indigenous peoples of North and South America, such a method of debased European justice was as alien as the avarice, which brought the intruders into the Great Plains. They had initially met the fur trappers and traders, who were outnumbered and had to depend on the compliance of the wilderness tribes. Early Jesuit missionaries, such as Father Nicolas Point, made distinctions between the virtuous Flatheads, the vicious Coeur d'Alenes, and the Blackfeet, 'notorious for being bloodthirsty and well-known for their pillaging'. In common, all these tribes had 'an unrelenting spirit of independence, cruelty to the vanquished, forgetfulness of the past and improvidence for the future'. And the fur trader Henry Boller could paint two pictures:

The One would represent the bright side of Indian Life, with its feathers, lances, gayly dressed & mounted 'banneries', fights, buffalo hunting &c.

The Other, the dark side, showing the filth, vermin, poverty, nakedness, suffering, starvation, superstition, &c. Both would be equally true – neither exaggerated, or distorted; both totally dissimilar!

The clash between European and primitive perception led to the revival of a historical tradition, which saw societies, chiefly as the products of their environment. The spread of a horse culture from Asia and the ocean voyages of the rigged ship had led to the global expansion of a Great Frontier. By saddle and sail, the civilisations around the Mediterranean Sea had permeated Europe, which was stretching its boundaries to the Americas and South Africa and Australasia. The Atlantic Ocean was more significant a shifting border than the Great Plains, for Europeans in body and spirit brought their settled traditions to the wilderness.

As Walter Prescott Webb wrote: 'Man stood naked in the presence of nature, (which) gives no orders, issues no proclamations, has no prisons, no privileges; it knows nothing of vengeance or mercy. Before nature all men are free and equal.' The pioneer was caught in the trap of liberty. He did not have to win his freedom, which was imposed upon him. Independently, he had to create a small society, given the conditions and the natural wealth of these vast marginal spaces. The poet Robert Frost would comment: 'The land was ours before we were the land's.'

'The Significance of the Frontier in American History', a paper of 1893 by Frederick Jackson Turner, was the most influential thesis for a generation. As Ibn Khaldun, he emphasised geography and movement as the determining factors in his nation's growth. The first frontier was the Atlantic shoreline, which gave opportunities to fur-trader and miners, to herders of cattle and farmers.

> Each type of industry was on the march towards the West, impelled by an irresistible attraction. Each passed in successive waves across the continent . . . The Indian trade pioneered the way for civilisation. The buffalo trail became the Indian trail, and this became the trader's 'trace'; the trails widened into roads, and the roads into turnpikes, and these in turn were transformed into railroads . . . Thus civilisation in America has followed the arteries made by geology, pouring an ever richer tide through them .. The exploitation of the beasts took hunter and trader to the west, the exploitation of the grasses took the rancher west, and the exploitation of the river valleys and prairies attracted the former.

For Turner, his frontier heroes derived from families, who had fled the troubles in Ireland and Scotland, and now they burst from the mountains of Kentucky and Tennessee into the opportunities of the plains and politics. David Boone, the great backwoodsman, varied his roles as hunter, trader, cattle-herder, farmer and surveyor, ending in Missouri as a pioneer of new trails across the Mississippi river. His son was a trapper in the Rocky Mountains, his grandson an Indian agent, while a kinswoman married the frontier leader, Kit Carson. In three generations, one family had crossed the continent.

Another of Turner's heroes was the President Andrew Jackson from the mountain state of Tennessee. The historian linked Jackson to the Reivers' Trail. 'This six-foot backwoodsman, with blue eyes that could blaze on occasion, this choleric, impetuous, self-willed Scotch-Irish leader of men, this expert duelist, this ready fighter, this embodiment of the tenacious, vehement, personal West, was in politics to stay. The frontier democracy of that time had the instincts of the clansman in the days of Scotch Border warfare . . . Each man contended with his neighbour for the spoils of the new country that opened before them.' In Kentucky and Tennessee, the raid and the blood-feud continued. The Westerner defended himself and had little time for central government or the law. Andrew Jackson personified the unchecked development of the individual.

The concept of nature changing character and politics has persisted in American history. While the primitive horse culture of the Mongols and the Huns to the Blackfeet and the Apaches made them more obviously the creatures of their environment, a case would be made for those pioneers from Europe, who had crossed the Atlantic Ocean, and now burst over the Appalachians and were ferried across the Mississippi river. 'Spiritually, as well as geographically, they had come further from Europe. They had a stronger belief in political democracy and in equality of opportunity. They were also more individualistic and more self-assertive.' They did not respect tradition, but rather invented their own codes of conduct. They were engaged on one of the larger enterprises in human history. The transformation, within two generations, of tens of millions of acres into ranches and farms, towns and even cities, was 'so unprecedented that it produced a kind of permanent spiritual intoxication'. From this ferment, the facts and the legends of the Wild West were brewed.

CHAPTER TWELVE

The Scotch-Irish

The Norman invasion of Leinster and Meath in the 12th century had been recorded by Gerald of Wales, and he stressed the importance of horsed archers in combat with hostile foot soldiers. 'In any fighting in Ireland,' he wrote, 'we must be particularly careful to ensure that archers are always incorporated in the mounted formations.' The enemy could cause great damage by hurling stones at close range, 'alternately rushing forward and retreating without loss to themselves because they are so mobile'. The only counter-measures were volleys of arrows, aimed at the lightly-armed Irishmen. Although these invading *arcarii equestres* originally came from Gwent, as did the majority of the longbowmen in the campaigns of other early Anglo-Norman kings, by the time of King Richard the Second, such early Reivers were recruited from Cheshire near the Borders. They used a special barbed birch arrow, an ell in length, and flighted with red peacock feathers. Overseas, they earned a dubious reputation for extreme thuggery.

In 1315, after the victory of Bannockburn, Edward the Bruce had landed in Ulster with 6,000 veteran soldiers to harass the English across the Irish Sea in their area of influence, the Pale around Dublin. A dashing and ruthless cavalry leader, Edward defeated the Anglo-Norman barons and had himself crowned as High King of all Ireland. Yet three years later, a reckless charge into a superior enemy force saw his body hanged and drawn and quartered, as that of William Wallace had been. Although some of his scattered army remained in Ulster, no real effort was made to establish a Scots colony there until the end of the reign of Queen Elizabeth the First of England. Using the old raiding tactics of the Borders, Lord Mountjoy laid waste to Ulster, killing off the cattle and the people. When James the Sixth of Scotland and First of England succeeded to the two thrones, a brilliant strategy solved both the problems of the anarchic Borders and of rebel Northern

Ireland. The worst of the Reivers, led by the Grahams, were shipped with their families to form a Plantation in Antrim and Down counties on fertile ground, seized from the Irish warleaders. The new landlords were called 'undertakers', as if their expertise in killing matched their skills in farming and herding cattle.*

Trade with the Lowlands of Scotland was encouraged by King James, because their ports 'lye so neir to that coiste of Ulster' for the transport of 'men and bestiall'. Horses, stolen in the Borders, were shipped to Carrickfergus for a safe sale. And, indeed, the Reiver culture was transported to Northern Ireland, as though a moveable theft. The Irish were driven off their lands and the produce stolen. Taking advantage of the English Civil War, a revolt in 1641 against the Presbyterian Scots incomers by the militant Catholic downtrodden led to a guerrilla war that lasted eleven years, in which one in seven of the colonials went to the grave. After crushing the Scots Covenanters in their homeland, Cromwell and his army crossed the sea to pacify Ireland. Over half a million people died of the sword or famine or plague, while 50,000 fled or were deported. The tribal organisation of the island was destroyed, and two-thirds of the land passed into Protestant hands.

The Presbyterian immigration to Ulster increased in the reign of King Charles the Second, who began a campaign to drive from their pulpits all ministers who would not accept an Episcopal Church, subject to royal authority. Seventeen years of 'killing times' began, when the Covenanters of the Western Lowlands reverted to guerrilla tactics against the King's soldiers. Some were killed or tortured or hanged, while hundreds were sent to gaol. Finally, the Covenanters stopped behaving as believing Reivers, stealthily defending their faith, and they stood in 1679 in a pitched battle at Bothwell Bridge, where they were easily defeated. Most of the survivors sped, as King Charles had once done, in a bonny boat like a bird on the wing, over the sea to Ulster, where they might elect their pastors in peace.

Even so, they still had to suffer for their belief. When King James the Second ascended the British throne, he loosed upon Ireland the dreaded slash-and-burn James Graham of Claverhouse, whom the historian Macaulay called 'rapacious and profane, of violent temper, and of obdurate heat, who has left a name which, wherever the Scottish race is settled on the face of the earth, is mentioned with a peculiar energy of hatred'. But after the Battle of the Boyne in 1689 and the defeat of the Catholic marauding royal army by the Prince of Orange, the immigrant Lowland Borderers dominated Ulster and began that inevitable process of all conquering peoples, intermarriage with the women of the place. The struggle between the Catholic and the Protestant Masonic lodges in open and clandestine wars would persist for more than 300 years. In one decade before 1700, however, 50,000 Scotsmen would take up the lands and trade of Ulster, bringing with them their considerable skills. And so the Plantation prospered with the wool and linen trade, until it began to threaten the industry of the mother country. As with the later unfortunate tax on tea in the American colonies, restrictions were passed on the export of Irish cloth, while rack-renting landlords rendered smallholdings untenable. As Archbishop William King observed of those now leaving for North America, 'it is impossible for people to live or subsist on their farms'.

These ills were followed by a biblical long drought and the Test Act of 1703, which required all office-holders to take the Anglican church sacrament. This discriminated against Catholic and Presbyterian alike. In the first sixty years of the 18th century, some 200,000 people from Ulster took passage across the Atlantic Ocean. And as the historian Froude wrote, this Great Migration 'robbed Ireland of the bravest defenders of the English interests, and peopled the American seaboard with fresh flights of Puritans'.

Still in search of good land, these Scotch-Irish incomers pushed up from the settled tidewater into the Appalachian Mountains through the Susquehanna and Cumberland Valleys, or down the Great Valley into Virginia and the Carolinas. They brought their hymns and their Border ballads with them. As a verse of one of them was to be sung:

> Daniel Boone on Pinnacle Rock,
> He killed Injuns with his old flintlock.
> Cumberland Gap, Cumberland Gap,
> Hmmm . . . way down yonder in Cumberland Gap.

Although beyond the law, these frontier settlers set up their own community rules, based on several 'rights'. A 'corn' right gave the sower a hundred acres of virgin soil for each acre he planted. The 'tomahawk right' established a claim by blazing the bark on a circle of trees, rather as Hengist and Horsa had delineated their landing place in England with a perimeter of strips of cowhide. A 'cabin right' asserted as property the tract around a log shack, and if the home-owner upped sticks in the restless fashion of the time, he could sell his 'rights' to the next taker.

As for the old reiving tactics of Border skirmishes, the immigrants applied them in the 'French and Indian' War, which began in 1755 and lasted with Pontiac's War for nine cruel years. The burning and scalping and torture used by the Ottawas and the Shawnees was reciprocated. The worst incident occurred when the Scotch-Irish rangers, named the 'Paxton Boys', wiped out a peaceful village in the Congesta Massacre. Afterwards, 500 armed mountaineers delivered a Remonstrance, demanding more self-rule, to the Philadelphia authorities. There was to be little peace on the turbulent frontier.

Even in the hills and forests, these colonials lived, rather as the Reivers had, in huts of poles and bark; they were wrapped in a blanket for the night beside a dying fire. Their food was mainly salted beef or pork and maize bread, instead of oatmeal. Their transport was still the horse and the ox; their guardian the watchdog. Their defences were the rifle and the powderhorn and the knife, the axe and the spade and the hoe. As in former times, these were the necessities of survival and made the pioneers into the right stuff for the winning of the West.

Before the American Revolution, these backwoodsmen were already rebelling against taxation in a movement; their title was not Covenanters, but Regulators. Their violent protests led to the 'battle' of Alamance in 1771 in North Carolina, after which five of the leaders were hanged and hundreds fled to Tennessee. And so with the beginning of the War of Independence, the mountain Scotch-Irish already found themselves at odds with the Tory plantation owners of the tidewater. A succession of observers attributed the outbreak of hostilities to a sequel of the English Civil War. 'There is no use crying about it,' Horace Walpole declared at Westminster. 'Cousin America has run off with a Presbyterian parson.' And a Hessian captain refused to name the conflict 'an American rebellion; it is nothing more or less than a Scotch Irish Presbyterian rebellion'.

Other Scots immigrants had crossed the Atlantic, many of them Catholic Highlanders, fleeing from the scorched-earth policies of the 'Butcher' Duke of Cumberland, who had ordered, after his victory at Culloden in 1745, that the cavalry 'drive the Cattle, turn the Plough and destroy what you can belonging to all such as are or have been in the Rebellion by burning the Houses of the Chiefs' all the way across the Grampians to Fort Augustus. This rough policy was still worrying to Cumberland, for later he wrote back to the Duke of Newcastle: 'All the good we have done is a little blood-letting, which has only weakened the madness, not cured it.' He trembled for fear 'that this vile spot may still be the ruin of this island and our family'. But the old clan system was destroyed by forts and rocks and sheep, its chieftains bought by the chance to turn common land into personal property. Yet the American Revolution would change ancient wrongs and grudges into another battle, this time for the liberty of a continent.

In the Highlands of Scotland and in Ireland, there was much support for the Declaration of American Independence. 'Here are none but rebels,' a clergyman of the Church of Ireland wrote back in 1775 to the Under-Secretary for the Colonies in London. 'All our newspapers abound with intelligence favourable to the rebels. The King is reviled, the ministry cursed, religion trampled under foot.' Early in the struggle, the young Lieutenant Ridsdale informed the *Hibernian Magazine* that the troops which 'kept up the spirit and life of the rebellion were totally Scotch and Irish'. And, as Ebenezer Wild noticed in Valley Forge, St Patrick's Day produced a noticeable change in camp, a celebration by the Irishmen born in America or settlers there, reinforced by deserters from the British lines.

Although Scottish regiments under British officers fought their fellow-countrymen in the colonial war, as did some of the Loyalist Volunteers of Ireland, there were six mutinies among Scottish troops raised for America, which resulted in the discharge of the levies. Without doubt, the Declaration of American Independence provoked strong support from the Gaelic nations. 'Here we sympathise more or less with the Americans,' an Irish Member of Parliament wrote from Dublin. 'We are in water colour what they are in fresco.'

Tactically, neither the American nor the British generals appeared to appreciate the lessons of the previous 'French and Indian' War. The Massachusetts militias did inflict the first defeat on the Redcoats of the regular army by using concealed tactics on the enemy march to Concord and the retreat to Boston. 'The country was an amazing strong one,' Lieutenant Barker of the King's Own regiment recorded, 'full of hills, woods, stone walls, etcetera, which the rebels did not fail to take advantage of, for they were all lined with people who kept an incessant fire upon us, as we did so upon them, but not with the same advantage, for they were so concealed there was hardly any seeing them'. The Americans suffered a hundred casualties, the British three times that number before reaching the safety of Bunker Hill. There, the rebels later entrenched themselves in their folly, but a third red wave of frontal attacks by the Redcoats led to their flight. 'One cluster', a Connecticut Captain wrote of his militiamen, 'would be sneaking down on their bellies behind a rock, and others behind hay-cocks and apple trees.'

Yet the British losses had been heavy, and neither side had learned to avoid a pitched battle at all costs. The mistaken rebel expedition through the wilderness under Benedict Arnold to assault Quebec ended in the disaster of street-fighting, with the British sharpshooters hidden behind doors and windows, and grapeshot ruling the roads. On the route home, smallpox and malaria and dysentery thinned the rebel ranks, until there were less than 3,000 survivors. Yet even with this example, the worldly General John Burgoyne, once a Light Horse commander of the 16th Dragoons, allowed himself to be trapped in a counterattack in 1777 from Canada; he was surrounded in the forests and forced at Saratoga into a humiliating surrender. Even with artillery, columns of marching men with horse-drawn supply trains were extremely vulnerable to those bred in the backwoods.

For the Westerners among the rebels, there was a revival of previous frontier wars with the local tribes, recruited by both the combatants. The charismatic George Rogers Clark struck with unexpected raids into Kentucky and probed at Illinois, with the aim of attaching both future states to Virginia. To the pioneers, warfare was another means of expansion. Clark killed and scalped any tribesman, who aided the English: no prisoners were taken. The formidable Senecas and the other Five Nations ravaged the Wyoming Valley in Pennsylvania with an allied Royalist force, but General Washington's orders to a larger American expedition were those of 'Butcher' Duke of Cumberland after Culloden. The lands of the Six Nations were not to be 'merely over-run but destroyed'. And so it was harshly done, although the sluggish American columns still carted along their cannon and their baggage waggons and their pack horses. Fire and sword and lead ball and famine destroyed the Six Nations for ever, and the way to the West lay open.

The most effective cavalry Commander was Lieutenant Colonel Banastre Tarleton, whose speed and strike became the terror of the Continental armies in the Southern States. His small squadron of dragoons had lost its chargers to fever, and were mounted on mere 'swamp tackies', when he charged at dawn into an American camp of 500 troopers at Biggin's Bridge in South Carolina, seizing all their horses and fifty waggons of ammunition and supplies. A few weeks later, Tarleton covered over 100 miles in two nights and a day, and he massacred a rearguard of some 300 men, killing all the survivors by sabre and bayonet. And then at the Battle of Camden against an American army, led by General

Horatio Gates, the victor at Saratoga, the British General Cornwallis found the right position for regular troops to break the southern militiamen – an open pine forest flanked by two swamps. The bayonet charge of the Redcoats on the narrow ground led to panic, with Gates observing that his men 'ran like a Torrent and bore all before them'. Tarleton was now unleashed with his dragoons to ravage the rout, while Gates fled on a racehorse, hardly stopping for three nights at a canter of 60 miles a day. 'Was there ever such an instance of a general running away,' Colonel Alexander Hamilton asked, 'from his whole army?'

In 1781, however, the Americans inflicted a reverse on Tarleton's 'Legion' at Cowpens, and for the first time, he was defeated by Washington's cavalry. In spite of a drawn battle at Guildford Court House, the commanding General Cornwallis made the cardinal mistake of retiring on Yorktown in Virginia, harried by the mobile Nathanael Greene and 'Light-Horse Harry' Lee. He allowed himself to be surrounded by 6,000 regular French troops with experience of siege warfare, as well as the more seasoned brigades of George Washington. He depended for supplies on the British navy with its usual supremacy over the French fleet and relief by General Clinton's army; but this time, the Count de Grasse blockaded the port with thirty-two ships of the line. Invested by land and sea, the cornered Cornwallis had to follow the example of Burgoyne and surrender. Had he kept to the field, he might have fought on. But the American colonies were now forever lost. And to the tune of 'Killiecrankie', Robert Burns wrote a 'Ballad on the American War' which hardly seemed to regret the outcome too much:

> Burgoyne gaed up, like spur an' whip,
>   Till Fraser brave did fa', man;
> Then lost his way, ae misty day,
>   In Saratoga shaw, man.
> Cornwallis fought as lang's he dought,
>   An' did the Buckskins claw, man;
> But Clinton's glaive frae rust to save,
>   He hung it to the wa', man.*

Although the Scotch-Irish were the sinews of George Washington's army, and also strong democrats, they were not important in the later Constitutional Convention or in the ordering of the infant United States of America. Even during the Revolution, gangs in South Pennsylvania did good business by stealing horses. The backwoodsmen remained lawless and led the Whisky Rebellion against the new national government. When they crossed the Alleghenics into Ohio and the Great Plains, they reverted to lynch law, meting out summary justice in the absence of a sheriff or a court. 'Self-discipline seems to have been the hardest lesson the Scotch-Irish had to learn,' their historian Leyburn noted 'from the time of their barbaric ancestors in Scotland to the end of their frontier days in America'.

In the future, eleven American Presidents were to claim Scotch-Irish ancestry, from Andrew Jackson to Richard Nixon, although their Border genes would hardly explain or excuse their behaviour in office. Another American President of Dutch-American descent, Theodore Roosevelt, would be their apologist in his defence of Manifest Destiny, *The Winning of the West*:

> That these Irish Presbyterians were a bold and hardy race is proved by their at once pushing past the settled regions, and plunging into the wilderness as the leaders of the white advance. They were the first and last set of immigrants to do this; all others have merely followed in the wake of their predecessors. But, indeed, they were fitted to be Americans from the very start; they were kinsfolk of the Covenanters; they deemed it a religious duty to interpret their own Bible, and held for a divine right the election of their own clergy. For generations their whole ecclesiastic and scholastic systems had been fundamentally democratic. In the hard life of the frontier they had lost much of their religion, and they had but scant opportunity to give their children the schooling in which they believed; but what few meeting-houses and school-houses there were on the border were theirs.

Yet perhaps in his haunting *Cities of the Plain* in his Border Trilogy, the novelist Cormac McCarthy best summed the predilection to violence of the Scotch-Irish, as they migrated from the hill country to the prairies and the sunset. An old ranch hand, Mr Johnson, is being asked about the old days.

> . . .Tales of the old west, he said.

> Yessir.

> Lot of people shot and killed.

> Why were they?

Mr Johnson passed the tips of his fingers across his jaw. Well, he said, I think these people mostly come from Tennessee and Kentucky. Edgefield district in South Carolina. Southern Missouri. They were mountain people. They come from mountain people in the old country. They always would shoot you. It wasn't just here. They kept comin west and about the time they got here was about the time Sam Colt invented the sixshooter and it was the first time these people could afford a gun you could carry around in your belt. That's all there ever was to it. It had nothing to do with the country at all. The West.

CHAPTER THIRTEEN

Warriors into Outlaws

The American Civil War saw the beginning of the end of an effective cavalry. Artillery and trench warfare largely took over from the charge of the horsemen, who were often dismounted to bolster the infantry. The dragoons and the light horse were used mainly in reconnaissance and protecting communications, although a series of devastating long-distance raids, laying waste enemy railroads and supplies, proved that Reiver tactics were still useful in this dogged war of attrition. Occasionally, the massed riders of Jeb Stuart would still prove crucial in battle, but even they fell to the Union cavalry, once it was supplied with the Spencer carbine, which could loose off its seven bullets in a minute, as fast as a Mongol had shot his arrows from his saddle.

In the Chattanooga campaign, the Union advance with 150,000 men was halted by the hit-and-run tactics of Southern partisans and the Confederate horse under the command of Nathan B. Forrest and John H. Morgan. As armies now depended for transport on steam engines rather than pack mules, the destruction of the vital supply depot at Murfreesboro by a night attack stopped the Union forces in their destroyed iron tracks. The invading troops were forced to split in order to guard their supply lines, and soon they had to rely on swift riders to deliver messages, rather as the future Pony Express of the West. When General Bragg took over the Army of the Mississippi, he insisted that each corps should organise 'a company of cavalry of not less than fifty effective men assigned to their headquarters to act as escort and couriers'.

Before the crucial battle of Gettysburg, Jeb Stuart with three brigades of troopers went on a circling movement round the Union army, crossing the Potomac and reaching Rockville, only 13 miles from Washington. He fell in with a huge supply train and took over, in his words, 'more than one hundred and twenty-five best United States model wagons'. Encumbered by his loot, Stuart ignored the gathering battle, in order to destroy rail tracks and telegraph wires. Units of Union cavalry rallied and counter-attacked and held the town of Hanover, blocking Stuart's short route to Gettysburg. And now, after thirty-six hours in the saddle, Stuart's riders could hardly continue. As he reported: 'It is impossible for me to give you a correct idea of the fatigue and exhaustion of our men and beasts at this time. From our great exertion and constant mental excitement, want of sleep and food, the men were overcome and so tired and stupid as almost to be ignorant of what was taking place around them.'

After another cavalry encounter on a thirty-mile march, Stuart and his troopers did reach Gettysburg, before the battle was lost. Positioned on the left flank of the Confederate forces by General Robert E. Lee, he awaited his opportunity to defend or attack. While the march of Pickett's Virginians moved uphill to their doom, Stuart tried to roll up the enemy's right flank. At first, he succeeded with his tired horsemen, observing that 'the impetuosity of those gallant fellows after two weeks of hard marching and hard fighting, was not only extraordinary, but irresistible. The enemy's masses vanished before them like grain before the scythe.' Unfortunately, a counter-charge by the 1st Michigans, led by a later Western hero, Brigadier-General George A. Custer, decided this classic cavalry encounter. As a Federal Captain Miller declared of the two opposing columns galloping into each other, 'so sudden and violent was the collision that many of the horses were turned end over end and crushed their riders beneath them. The clashing of sabres, the firing of pistols, the demands for surrender, and cries of the combatants, filled the air.' But Custer's shout of 'Come on, you Wolverines!' and a final thrust broke the Confederates, who turned back to their former posts.*

In fact, the Southerners were also beaten by dismounted cavalrymen, firing the Spencer repeating rifle, which Stuart thought, 'in the hands of brave, determined men . . . the most effective firearm our cavalry can adopt'.' In another encounter, one of his officers, Colonel Harry Gilmore, also praised the Spencer carbine and noted the coming finale of the charge on horseback against riflemen ranged behind a stone wall:

The gallant 3rd dashed on in splendid style, with their long bright sabres raised in *tierce point*, and with a wild ringing yell, to rouse the horses and carry dismay to the hearts of their foes. But when within a hundred and fifty yards of the barricade, a deadly fire poured into their ranks, which emptied many a saddle, and threw the column into some confusion. They pushed on, however, *right up to the fence*, killing men behind it with the

pistol, and tried to make a gap; but that it was impossible for mounted
men to do, and the poor fellows were forced to fall back out of range and
re-form the regiment, now looking no larger than a good squadron.[*]

On one of the greater and celebrated search-and-destroy missions, the
'March through Georgia' in 1864 towards the end of the war, General
Sherman detached his best cavalry to raid down into the Deep South,
because his army had to live off the devastated land and could not find
enough forage for its 35,000 animals, which were pulling some 2,700
supply waggons. General James H. Wilson, however, on his raid down
to Selma, proved the effectiveness of massed riders in destroying the
Confederate industrial base behind the lines. With 12,500 mounted
men, Wilson and his Federal forces covered 20 or more miles a day.
Meeting only scattered resistance, the Union general destroyed the
Selma Arsenal in what was called the most successful cavalry operation in American history. They captured or paroled 65,000 prisoners,
destroyed numerous iron works and foundries and steamboats and
locomotives, and seized nearly 300 pieces of artillery and 100,000
stands of small arms. Their losses were only 100 dead and 600
wounded. This was the Great Raid of the American horse.

The chief problem of wars is what to do with the troops, once
the war is over. Inevitably, as at the close of the Hundred Years War
between Britain and France, so it was when General Robert E. Lee
laid down his arms. Trained brigands and freebooters continued to
plunder the land. To commandeer in combat may be necessary, but to
plunder in peacetime is a capital offence. While the defeated South had
to suffer the looting of the northern carpet-baggers, the West became
the riding ground of some of the more notorious bandits of all time.
During the fighting they had operated as guerrillas along the Missouri
and Kansas Border, where the land was disputed between the pro-slav-
ery Confederates and the 'free soil' Jayhawkers. More murderous than
even the Reivers, these mounted terrorists totted up a crimson calendar
of crime.

Most rebel movements work with extremist elements, which they
later disclaim as beyond control. The most important of the Southern
guerrilla leaders was William Clarke Quantrill, who was a horse thief
and cattle rustler before the Civil War. Claiming to have the sanc-
tion of the Confederate President Jefferson Davis himself, 'Captain'
Quantrill enlisted some fifty raiders. His most notorious exploit was
the sacking of Lawrence in Kansas in the summer of 1863, burning and

looting 190 buildings and killing 140 men and women and children. He claimed that this was in revenge for the Jayhawkers driving off herds of cattle and horses and reducing Harrisonville to ashes. Tit-for-tat as in all frontier wars, both sides sought to excuse their barbarity under the name of retaliation.

'Bloody Bill' Anderson had learned his trade in fighting the Plains tribes, and he used to scalp and cut off the ears of his victims; these trophies were hung on his horse's bridle, as the Celtic warriors had done in their wars against the Roman invaders. Riding with him was a future generation of bank and train robbers, who included the James and Younger brothers. On one occasion, Coleman Younger lined up fifteen Jayhawker prisoners and used their bodies to test the penetrating power of an Enfield rifle. In another experiment, the boyish Jesse James wore a calico dress to tempt a dozen Federal soldiers into a whorehouse, where they had their throats cut.

Ambush and dispersal remained the preferred tactics of the partisan commanders. After the Lawrence raid, Quantrill disbanded his riders with the statement: 'More men; more trails for the bluebellies to follow.' A future rendezvous was agreed, but until that place and day, the bandit fighters had to hide and ride in small units. After three raids into Kansas on pickets and troop-transporting locomotives, Jesse James was credited with seventeen kills or executions, when a Federal leave train was overwhelmed at the Centralia depot, and its seventy-five soldiers forced to kneel by the tracks before being dispatched by a Colt bullet in the skull. According to a US Military Telegrapher, 'a full head of steam was turned on and the engine sent flying tenantless away to the north'. In a following cavalry action against the local militia, the Jayhawkers were lured forward, until they had to dismount to resist a counter-charge. They broke under the attack and were massacred with James notching up another nine dead men.

After further bloody skirmishes, the guerrilla bands heard of the peace, and most of them rode towards a surrender. On his way, James met a US cavalry detachment and was shot through his right lung. Given no hope of living, he was sheltered and cured in a cousin's house. He survived the blood-feuds of the Kansas 'free soil' men against the Missouri rebels, which reduced the Southern State to a fearful wasteland. Still fighting in what they saw as a defence of their homeland, some of Quantrill's band shot up towns and created a little night's havoc to prove their presence, now that they had lost their dominance.

With his brother Frank James, the recovered Jesse set about forming a new gang. Although some of them were put on trial, the verdict of the jury was 'there wasn't any charge against them, for what killing and robbing they had done had been committed in the war and as an act of reprisal on the enemy'. The James brothers, however, were to invent a fundamental American western myth – bank robbery, a manner of stealing from the rich to give to the poor, if the proceeds ever reached that far. At Liberty and Lexington, Missouri, the James gang, mounted on fine Kentucky horses, robbed the banks and killed a schoolboy. Their fourth bandit raid on Richmond resulted in three more murders; pursuing *posses* lynched three of the gang, but the James brothers were not named and disappeared in their usual fashion.

Joined by the four Younger brothers and other former combatants, the James bandits continued their career of crime for sixteen years. They also pioneered the robbery of trains, carrying gold from California, and of their passengers, as the old English highwaymen had plundered the stagecoaches. They also followed the example of the Royalist brigands returning valuables to any other Stuart supporter, in that they often gave back their plunder to fellow Southerners, claiming that they were still fighting in the Confederate cause. Followed by detectives from the Pinkerton Agency, who killed one of the Youngers and blew up innocent people in a 'safe' farm, which had sheltered him, Jesse James became the victim as well as the outlaw. An Amnesty Bill was even passed by the Missouri State Legislature, but it was quashed on a technicality. And so the James legend grew as he added to his catalogue of violence.

After many more robberies, the citizens of Northfield, Minnesota, finally struck back in 1876 against the James-Younger gang. An unsuccessful hold-up of the bank was followed by a battery of rifles and shotguns pointed at the escape of the robbers. Two of them were killed, but the James brothers evaded the following *posses*, who did seize in a blaze of Colt revolvers the much-wounded three surviving Youngers. Coleman kept on insisting that he and his siblings were driven to banditry and were the victims of circumstances. Sentenced to life imprisonment, he declared: 'If it had not been for the war, I might have been something, but as it is I am what I am.'

With new members of their marauding band, Frank and Jesse James resumed their train and even stagecoach raids. But once a reward of $10,000 was offered for their capture, dead or alive, betrayal was a swarm of wasps over their scalps. A distant relative, Robert Ford, shot

Jesse (alias Mister Howard) in the back, as he was straightening a picture hanging on the wall. Frank James surrendered himself, asking for a fair trial, tired of being hunted and living in the saddle for twenty-one years. 'There is not a drop of blood on my hands,' he protested, 'except that shed in open and honourable war. I was a guerrilla. I fought the best I knew how with Quantrill, Anderson . . . but I never in all my life slew an unarmed man or a prisoner.' After an extraordinary trial, a Southern jury acquitted the former Confederate officer. Trials for war crimes were not yet legitimate.

The next troop of Western brigands were modern 'moss troopers', as much committed to reiving or rustling herds as to raiding western communities from their lairs. The Wild Bunch were all working cowboys or *vaqueros*, preying on the cattle of the open range or those being driven to the railheads at Abilene or Dodge City along the Chisholm and Panhandle and Peqos Trails. After the droughts and agricultural Depressions of the 1880s, the unemployed cowpunchers drifted towards the Hole-in-the-Wall Valley of northern Wyoming, near the excellent grazing land of the Powder river country. Crevices and canyons ate into the red sandstone walls surrounding this dry place. A group of raiders formed there, while an outlaw trail to Brown's Hole by the Colorado and Utah borders led on to the almost inaccessible Robbers' Roost in Wayne County. Such hiding-places attracted hundreds of thieves on horseback, including Nathan Champion, 'the King of the Rustlers' with his Red Sash gang, and Butch Cassidy and Harry Longbaugh, known as the Sundance Kid. The reiving of cattle and horses was on such an immense scale that the state militia and hired gunfighters were called out against the Wild Bunch by the Wyoming Stockgrowers Association. The deaths of Champion and his partner summoned a ragtail army of outlaws and homesteaders to fight off the big cattle ranchers, but the confrontation was stopped by the intervention of the US Cavalry, trying to enforce a truce.

Quitting the cattle wars, Butch Cassidy and the Sundance Kid turned back to assaulting banks and locomotives in the style of the James brothers. A Train Robbers' Syndicate plundered the Union Pacific Railroad, but the Wild Bunch was penetrated and scattered by Pinkerton detectives. In a celebrated crossing of the final frontiers, Cassidy and the Sundance Kid, with the hard-riding and shooting Etta Place, sailed for Buenos Aires and bought an *estancia*, later sold to a beef syndicate. The trio resumed their career of robbing banks and trains and now mining operations in Argentina and Chile and Bolivia, riding the high trails over the Andes, until the two men were surrounded in 1911 by a company of cavalry; they killed themselves along with many of the enemy. And so, the eve of the Great War saw the grand finale of the last of the American legendary outlaws.

More illustrative of the Border wars in Scotland and Ireland than the actions of the Wild Bunch was the career of William H. Bonney, or Billy the Kid. Born of a devout Irish Catholic mother, Bonney drifted from Silver City in New Mexico into stealing horses and rustling steers on a small scale. He killed three of the Chirocahua Apaches for twelve ponies and five saddles and loads of pelts. 'Here were three blood-thirsty savages, revelling in all this luxury,' Bonney was said to declare. 'The plunder had to change hands.' After murdering a few more tribesmen and gamblers, and so earning a reputation as a gunman, Bonney returned to work as a cowboy in the 'Lincoln County War'. The large rancher John S. Chisum was opposed by Murphy & Dolan, Irish-American Catholic merchants, who represented the small stockbreeders. The Protestant Chisum accused the lesser cattle owners and homesteaders of rustling and rebranding his steers for sale, while his huge 'round-ups' were said to sweep up thousands of the beasts of the scattered herders. Bonney found himself in another Border conflict of raids and reprisals on the side of the poor people and his blood line, and he was credited with eight more kills. As so many of the Reivers, he switched sides after three years on the range, revenging himself for the murder of one of his new employers, and he began to rustle Chisum's cattle. In these frontier circumstances, unconditional loyalty was no priority.

In many ways, one commentator observed, 'William H. Bonney symbolised the whole pastoral epoch doomed by the railroad, tractor, and homesteader.' Forged by the open range, and a product of its wars, he was pursued by Pat Garrett, who was hired by the Panhandle Livestock Association to lead a *posse* of gunslingers called the Home Rangers, in order to terrify the nester ranchers and small-time rustlers, such as Billy the Kid, whose popular reputation was based on his fearlessness in taking on the firepower of the cattle barons. Under the guise of a Sheriff's authority, Garrett stalked Bonney and killed him at Fort Sumner, a belated victory for property law.[*]

Another Reiver survival in the Far West was the blood feud. The Graham family of Arizona had been immigrants a long while back, but they had brought to the Tonto basin their Scots habits. After working for a cattle baron in 1885, they began to steal his stock, rebranding the steers in the name of a company, which they shared with the Tewksburys. The thieves fell out, as thieves do. The Tewksburys drove a herd of sheep into the open range, and a seven years' war of murder ensued. The Tewksburys had the better of the feud, killing twenty-two Grahams for the loss of four dead. In truth, the manner of the Far West was not far from that of the divided Borders of the British Isles.

Of course, in that masterpiece *Huckleberry Finn*, Mark Twain almost seemed to go along with the blood feuds and honour system of the Southerners. The killings between the Grangerfords and the Shepherdsons were memorably explained by Buck, who said: 'Well, a feud is this way – A man has a quarrel with another man, and kills him; then that other man's brother kills *him*; then the other brothers, on both sides, goes for one another; then the *cousins* chip in – and by-and-by everybody's killed off, and there ain't no more feud. But it's kind of slow, and takes a long time.'

The American author positively fawned on Colonel Sherburn, who had shot a villain called Boggs with his pistol in the main street, and then faced down a whole lynch mob. He was carrying a double-barrelled gun in his hand, and he shouted at the unruly crowd: 'The idea of *you* lynching anybody'! It's amusing.' Yet such summary justice before a trial was not amusing to those who were murdered in the South and the West, where the cowboys often felt they had the right to execute malefactors with an occasional noose or a frequent gun.

The leading 'civilisers' were made by the Four Horsemen of the Automatic Apocalypse – Messrs Colt and Winchester, Remington and Maxim. Their predecessor was Eli Whitney, who turned his attention from processing cotton in gins to making standard parts for all carbines in moulds and jigs. Samuel Colt adapted the methods of the production line to a revolver with six barrels, which could be fired quickly from the saddle, faster than the arrows from the Apache bows. The Texas Rangers had the answer to tribal archery and the muskets of the Mexicans. So the South-West of the United States was won, while Samuel Colt concentrated on making machinery to cast accurate and replaceable spare parts for his weapons. When he set up a factory in London, he was asked whether his pistols were better processed rather than hand-made. 'Most certainly,' he said. 'And much cheaper.'

The Winchester repeating rifle was the Second Horseman of the Automatic Apocalypse. The United States cavalry used it against the Plains tribesmen, and they used it against the buffalo. The President of Mexico bought it to defeat the invading Emperor Maximilian, and

the Riffs to resist the intrusive French again in North Africa.* The
Third Horseman Eliphalet Remington had a rifle just as good, and
he sold it in tens of thousands to Madrid and Stockholm as well as
to Washington, to Cairo and Havana and also to Peking. Although
his company spread into the tools of peace, typewriters and sewing
machines and reapers and binders, it diversified by producing cartridges and percussion caps. In the Russian War against the Turks of
1879, the Remington factory at Bridgeport in Connecticut produced
the bullets for both sides, more than 200 million rounds for Istanbul,
slightly less for St Petersburg. Both nations kept their quality control-
lers at the works in New England, but these did not come to blows.
They exchanged greetings of good will.

Yet the Fourth Horseman, Hiram Maxim, was the true creator of
the age of empires and the apostle of death. Who were Clive of India
and Rhodes of Africa compared to the inventor of the machine gun? As
a country boy in Maine, Hiram had begun by inventing a mousetrap.
When he tried to perfect a medical inhaler, he was told he should not
waste his time on such quackery. He knew the answer. 'It will be seen',
he said, 'that it is a very creditable thing to invent a killing machine,
and nothing less than a disgrace to invent an apparatus to prevent
human suffering.'

Actually, there was a trinity of Maxims in the family. While Hiram
invented the machine gun, his brother Hudson thought up smoke-
less cannon powder, and his son Hiram Percy discovered the Maxim
Silencer. They exported their intelligence and weapons to most sides in
most wars. The British would massacre the Zulus with the circling and
spitting chambers of Hiram's creation, while the Boers would pepper
the British with the American Pom-poms. The Russians would kill half
their Japanese victims with tiny missiles of murder, while a reporter
noticed that 'a visible wave of death swept over the advancing host' of
Sudanese on camels, charging the machine guns at Omdurman. Tens of
millions would die from the Maxims' fortunate inspirations in the First
World War, and thousands of millions were made: the first number was
men, the second was bank notes.

Such possibilities of massacre nullified the Second Amendment to
the American Constitution, the right of the citizen militia to bear arms
in an age of muskets and hunting knives. But at least the weapons in
the hands of the Western outlaws and frontiersmen and ranchers were
only repeating rifles and revolvers. The machine-gun was merely used
to wipe out the last late Sioux Ghost Dancers. Although the new killing

and transport technology won the West, it was not sufficient to obliterate the tribesmen of the Plains, only the hordes of the buffalos and the clouds of the pigeons. Yet within the first two decades of the 20th century, the Automatic Revolution would put an end to the warrior on horseback, who had charged past the millennia to glory or death.

CHAPTER FOURTEEN

Print the Legend

The cattle kingdoms of the West evolved from destruction and creation. The Plains tribes had to be defeated and coralled in Reservations along with the slaughter of their main source of food, the buffalo. The railroads had to be built from the Atlantic to the Pacific Coast to supply a world market with beef and hides. In the driving of great herds on long trails, the unique culture of the cowboy emerged. In the words of Walter Prescott Webb:

> In this evolution the Plains worked their will, and man conformed. The Plains put men on horseback and taught them to work in that way. The southern Plains offered the natural conditions in which cattle could breed and multiply without care . . . carrying with them ranchman and cowboy with lariat, six-shooter, and horse. In the end the cattle kingdom occupied practically the whole Great Plains environment; it was the most natural economic and social order that the white man had yet developed in his experiment.

In the middle of the 19th century, American forces had been dispatched to the West to keep the warring tribes under some sort of control. These peoples not only threatened the white settlers breaking free from the eastern mountains, but also they fought among each other, the Cheyenne against the Crow and the Comanche and the Kiowa, while the Apache cut down all they could find. With lawlessness spreading behind the frontier in the Civil War, most of the Plains tribes took the opportunity to attack the oncoming pioneers and settlers.* Within thirty years, the US Army and the state militia had a thousand encounters with the Plains warriors. Kit Carson, with a few homespun volunteers from New Mexico, managed to win against some 10,000 Navajo men and to force a lasting peace upon them.* Yet decades of ferocious combat were necessary to ensure the removal to Reservations of the Apache and the

Cheyenneand the other Plains warriors.. Although the best light cavalry of the time, the various tribes were too few in numbers to do much more than harass the millions of pioneers, heading towards the sunset.

One victory was won by the Sioux in 1874 at the Little Big Horn against General George Custer and his 7th Cavalry, who had already subdued the Cheyenne at the Washita battleground. Surrounded by the warriors of Sitting Bull and Crazy Horse, the dismounted cavalrymen were reduced to an open defence against mounted foes, who pierced and hacked them to pieces in a few minutes. Subsequently, the might of the US Army and the need to protect the gold-miners, plundering the Black Hills, put an end to most Sioux resistance; the tribe was penned in or fled over the Canadian border. A final massacre of Sioux Ghost Dancers at Wounded Knee in 1890 by the Hotchkiss machine-gun riddled all protest. Three centuries of horse and man and culture were gone, as tumbleweed in the wind.

The onrush of the railroads had already eliminated the Great Southern herd of more than five million buffalo. Their meat was needed to feed the navvies laying the iron tracks; their hides were valued at a dollar and their tongues at a quarter. In testimony to the Smithsonian Institution in Washington a report declared: 'The man who desired buffalo meat for food almost invariably killed five times as many animals as he could utilise, and after cutting from each victim its very choicest parts – the *tongue alone*, possibly, or perhaps the hump and hind quarters, one or the other, or both – fully four-fifths of the really edible portion of the carcass would be left to the wolves.'

Until the locomotive reached the Plains, the two trails from Texas, through to California and to the violent Missouri and Kansas area around Baxter Springs, were bristling with danger. The western route had long stretches of hot dust, where the cattle died of thirst; shale and cacti cut up the hooves of horses; and the Apache and outlaws took a running toll of man and beast. A drive to the east met swarms of the Civil War freebooters, who demanded passage money to round up herds, which they had deliberately stampeded. As the founder of the rail stocktown of Abilene wrote, if the prairies could talk, 'they could tell many a thrilling, blood-curdling story of carnage, wrong, outrage, robbery and revenge not excelled in the history of any *banditti* or the annuals of the most bloody savages'.'

Joseph G. McCoy with his two brothers selected Abilene as the site of the meeting of cattle trail and railtrack, because it was unsettled with excellent Kansas grass and good water. Within two months, he had built stockyards and pens and loading chutes that could deal with 3,000 head of cattle. His purpose was 'to establish a market whereat the Southern drover and the Northern buyer would meet upon an equal footing, and both be undisturbed by mobs or swindling thieves'. A scout was sent into Indian Territory to explore a new trail and induce the owners of the moving herds to deviate to this safe place towards the north. 'This was joyous news to the drover, for the fear of trouble hung like an incubus over his waking thoughts alike with his sleeping moments.' In the refrain of a cowboy ballad:

> Drive up your steers from the long chaparral
> For we're far on the road to the railway corral.

Although Abilene was as corrupt and lurid as Brecht's imaginary western city of *Mahogonny*, it stood, in the opinion of the historian of the Great Plains, 'for all that happened when two great civilisations met for conflict, for disorder, for the clashing of great currents which carry on their crest the turbulent elements of both civilisations – in this case the rough characters of the plain and the forest'. In his superb study of how the environment outweighed human endeavour, Walter Prescott Webb put geography above economics, and he stressed the reasons for the spread of the cattle kingdom from Texas over what had been called the Great American Desert.

Abilene offered the market; the market offered inducement to Northern money; Texas furnished the base stock, the original supply, and a method of handling cattle on horseback; the Plains offered free grass. From these conditions and from these elements emerged the range and ranch cattle industry, perhaps the most unique and distinctive institution that America has produced.

There would be a change of name. While the railroad owners would rake in wealth and the ranchers would be ruined by blizzards and drought and low stock prices, the term 'robber barons' would now be applied to the East Coast financiers rather than the rustlers. Populist revolts would incite the Western farmers and herders into near rebellion, just as their ancestors in the Appalachian mountains had turned against tidewater exploitation. Discontented cowboys even joined sections of the early union, the Knights of Labor. And from the realities of life on the open range would grow an enduring myth and legend of the most celebrated nomadic horse and cattle culture in all the world.

Although some of the cowboys were Mexican or even Yankee, the majority were Southerners; they made the best hands, in the testimony of one of them:

> Now our cowboys had to be bred and raised with wild cattle and when the cattle business came into Texas and Colorado and the cows got into the brush or out on the plains with the buffalos, then it was that the real cowboy work commenced . . . The real cowboy was first made in the New Country. The way of rounding up and roping calves and branding cattle out in the open, was done there. There were no corrals and the Indians were so bad that people just got their cattle branded up and left them to increase until next branding time.

The cowboys had a code, which was to inspire the later myths of them. To the remarkable Charles Siringo, who was both a cowpuncher and a Pinkerton detective, those rules consisted of pride in skill and daring, endurance and loyalty to an outfit and the job, not to an employer. There were no given orders, for each man knew the role assigned to him by the trail boss. So individualistic were the cowboys that they preferred guarding the steers on the open range to the loose command of ranch life. Although they stuck together on a cattle drive, they practised a collective anarchy, each man for himself under the wide protection of his comrades.

The distance of the trails and their appearance were hardly better described than in one of Webb's favourite works on the American cowboy:

> Ninety days it took to get from San Antonio to Abilene – five weeks from the Red River to the Kansas border – six months from Texas to the High Plains. Days and weeks and months of snailing along a trail whose sides ravelled out like the strands of a torn rope or a piece of unhemmed burlap, a trail anywhere from fifty yards to two miles wide, a chocolate band threaded across a green prairie, a trail without soil, pushed lower than the surrounding country by the seemingly ceaseless pounding of thousands of sharp hoofs, . . . a dilapidated wagon frame beyond going on, or the barren circle of a bending ground telling that a herd had stopped here a night before. Here along these trails passed the wealth of an empire.

Some of the cowboys could equal the Mongols in their dexterity on a horse. One *vaquero*, John Young, told of the 'brush popper', who ran wild cattle through the thorn scrub of the Nueces Valley:

> In running in the brush a man rides not so much on the back of his horse as under and alongside. He just hangs on, dodging limbs as if he were dodging bullets, back, forward, over, under, half of the time trusting his horse to course right on this or that side of a brush or a tree. If he shuts his eyes, he is lost. Whether he shuts them or no, he will, if he runs true to form, get his head rammed or raked . . . Man and horse hit the brush as one. They understand each other. They may get snagged, knocked by limbs that will not break, cut, speared, pierced, with black thorns . . . No matter. The horse and rider go like a pair of mated dogs charging a boar. The brush hand is in his element.

This was the ultimate symbiosis of horse and man. If there was any rest in camp on the trail, the cowboys would behave as if they were back in the Appalachians or on the small farms of the South. They would have wrestling matches or listen and sing to music from the fiddle or the mouth organ. Their own chants derived from the British Border ballads, which had crossed the Atlantic with the migrants from Ireland and Scotland. One of these even celebrated the concocted ride of the highwayman Dick Turpin, who was said to say in 'Bonnie Black Bess':

> No poor man I plundered
> Nor e'er did oppress
> The widows or orphans,
> My Bonnie Black Bess.

Many others told of the hard existence of the steer herder:

> The cowboy's life is a dreary, dreary life,
> He's driven through the heat and cold;
> While the rich man's a-sleepin' on his velvet couch,
> Dreamin' of his silver and gold.

In his extraordinary encyclopaedic work, *The Folksongs of North America*, Alan Lomax showed the permeations of the horse and cattle culture across boundaries and oceans. As assiduous as Sir Walter Scott, his collection showed more Border ballads extant in the mountain chains and the prairies than were still sung in the British Isles. In the winning of the West by pony and steer, waggon and railtrack, 'rough campfire balladry is the best account of the feelings of the men who tamed the continent, and its quietly factual, humorous, or sentimental tone indicates that they found plenty of aggressive outlets in everyday life . . . If they seem pre-occupied with death, perhaps it is because death stared them in the face every day.'

Some of the songs referred directly to the Irish migration to fight for the French King and later for the American rebels against King George the Third, in particular the popular 'Johnny Has Gone for a Soldier':

> Oh, Johnny dear has gone away,
> He has gone afar across the bay,
> Oh, my heart is sad and weary today,
> Johnny has gone for a soldier.

> Shoole, shoole, shoole agro,
> Time can only heal my woe.
> Since the lad of my heart from me did go,
> Oh, Johnny has gone for a soldier . . .

As Lomax pointed out, the old Border ballad tradition, which linked love and death, fitted the code of the backwoods and the cowboy, where justice so often lay in the hands of the kinfolk or the outfit. He quoted a Carolina man: 'The best way is to trust in God an' your gun.' As in 'The Dying Cowboy' and 'Charlie Quantrill' and 'Jesse James', the outlaw became the hero, who robbed the rich to befriend the poor, and paid for his charity with his life:

> Now Jesse goes to rest with his hands upon his breast
> And the devil will be upon his knees.
> He was born one day in the county of Clay
> And he came from a solitary race.

> O Jesse leaves a wife, she's a mourner all her life,
> And the children, they were brave,
> But the dirty little coward, he shot Mister Howard,
> And he laid poor Jesse in his grave . . .

One of the most redolent of the cattle drivers' chants was 'The Old Chisholm Trail', because it adapted the Confederate rebel cavalry battle-cry into the cowpuncher's yell at his breaking steers:

> I never hankered for to plough or hoe
> And punchin' steers is all I know
> With my knees in the saddle and a-hangin' in the sky
> Herdin' dogies up in Heaven in the sweet by-and-by
> Come-a ki-yi-yippee, a ki-yi-yippee, a ki-yi-yippee, yippie-yay . . .

Equally powerful was the chorus of 'Go On, You Little Dogies' with its lament for the poorer cowboys.

> O hoop-an-li-ay, go on, you little dogies
> O hoop-an-li-o, Wyomin's your home
> It's whoopin' an' yellin' an' drivin' the dogies
> Ever makin' sad fortunes where its none of our own.

One piece of the wandering gypsy music survived in the Ozarks in America, fit to match the gypsy Border 'Ballad of Johnny Faa'. Yet 'The Horse Trader's Song' had far more to do with methods of dealing than the love of a lady.

> It's do you know those horse traders
> It's do you know their plan?
> It's do you know those horse traders
> It's do you know their plan?
> Their plan is for to snide you
> And git whatever they can
> Lord, Lord, I been all around this world . . .

Another world-wide wanderer, William F. Cody, turned the cowboy into a Wild West Show in his re-invention as Buffalo Bill. Earning his nickname as the slaughterer of thousands of the big beasts in order to feed the transcontinental railroad builders, he had actually been through most of the frontier rites of passage. He had served against the Plains tribes and had scouted for the US Cavalry, he had freighted goods and ridden on cattle drives. He was to become the greatest

Western celebrity of the dime novel, which also hailed the exploits of such English criminals as Jack Shephard.* After 1869, he was serialised in the New York Weekly under the title: *BUFFALO BILL, THE KING OF THE BORDER MEN: The greatest Romance of the Age.** Although his original appearances were in comic books, the image of Cody was changed by Prentiss Ingraham, his chief ghost-writer, into 'one of America's strange heroes who has loved its trackless wilds, rolling plains and mountain solitudes of our land, far more than the bustle and turmoil, the busy life and joys of our cities, and who has stood as a barrier between civilisation and savagery, risking his own life to save the lives of others'.

As early as 1887, a British visitor to the actual West was already aware that the cowboy was rapidly becoming mythical. 'Distance is doing to him what lapse of time did for the heroes of antiquity.' He was being invested with every romantic quality, in tales of impossible daring and endurance and skill at riding. He was being pictured as an alternative Buffalo Bill, 'a long-haired ruffian who, decked out in gaudy colours, and tawdry ornaments, booted like a cavalier, chivalrous as a Paladin, his belt stuck full of knives and pistols, makes the world to resound with bluster and braggadocio'.

The cowboy hero would progress from pulp fiction into the Western novel. In his Leatherstocking tales, J. Fenimore Cooper had already followed *The Last of the Mohicans* with *The Prairie*. He had resolved, as early as 1827, 'to cross the Mississippi and wander over the desolate wastes'. His wife said that 'he could see the Apollo in the young Mohawk'. Certainly, in the climactic struggle between the honest Pawnee chief Hard-heart and his crafty Sioux rival, the two men on horseback fought with the tactics and weapons of the early Reivers. 'Each had his spear, his bow, his quiver, his little battle-axe, and his knife; and each had, also, a shield of hides.' Unhorsed, the Pawnee flung his knife into the naked breast of his enemy. On his fall, a *mélée* ensued between the mounted warriors. Falling back, the Pawnees were saved 'by a volley from the fatal western rifles' of the white pioneers, shooting from outside their tents. Now the Pawnees massacred the routed Sioux, and 'the knife and the lance cut short their retreat'.

This early and classic tale of Western conflict was made more sophisticated by Owen Wister, who had a *summa cum laude* from Harvard, and turned his leading men into brooding creatures, dominated by the wilderness. For him, cow-punchers were not a race. 'They gallop over the face of the empty earth for a little while, and those whom rheumatism or gunpowder does not overtake, are blotted out by the course of empire, leaving no trace behind.' Later, in *The Virginian*, Wister created a graceful and virile and shrewd and uncultivated hero, who won a Southern schoolmistress in the style of Walter Scott's Young Lochinvar. This novel was only to be outclassed in appeal and reality by Andy Adams' *The Log of a Cowboy*, the meticulous record of a trail drive of longhorn cattle from the Rio Grande to the Blackfoot Agency in Montana State.

The twenty-five novels of Zane Grey, such as *The Lone Star Ranger*, illustrated a fictitious West for the rest of the world. His characters defined themselves by deeds rather than thought. They were primitive archetypes, who might have come from a Norse saga. And with their lack of speech and their fierce action, they were the darlings of the new silent cinema, which invented a *genre*, which has persisted to this day. When the word became the moving picture, the West was changed into a country of the imagination. As the early screen cowboy Tom Mix was to declare: 'The Old West is not a certain place in a certain time, it's a state of mind. It's whatever you want it to be.'

The first American story film was a Western, made by Edwin S. Porter in 1903, *The Great Train Robbery*. Although it had actually been shot for the Edison Company near the Lackawanna tracks in New Jersey, it was a visual dime novel about bandits like the James Brothers plundering the railroad that linked the continent. But as trade follows the flag, so movies follow the finance and the location. The cowboy and bandit film would travel to Hollywood in California, and the studios there would make the product look more authentic. As the creator of the horse culture of the Western movie, John Ford was to say: 'In the East, they think what I show is false, but I want to show them what happened. That's the way it was. I'm interested by the folklore of the West . . . showing what really happened, almost a documentary.'

As a young director in Hollywood, Ford stitched an Irish realism and ritual into the embroidery of the past. However sentimental he may have been, he became a popular artist because of his earthy and comic love of naturalism. The cowboy may have already become in the mass mind the romantic hero described by Walter Prescott Webb:

> He lives on horseback as do the Bedouins; he fights on horseback, as did the knights of chivalry; he goes armed with a strange new weapon which he uses ambidextrously and precisely; he swears like a trooper, drinks like a fish, wears clothes like an actor, and fights like a devil. He

is gracious to ladies, reserved towards strangers, generous to his friends, and brutal to his enemies. He is a cowboy, a typical Westerner.

Yet Ford's genius lay in making his stereotype into an archetype and a legend. His first epic picture of 1924, *The Iron Horse*, followed James Cruze's *The Covered Wagon*, and both derived from D.W. Griffith's *The Birth of a Nation*. In that melodrama, which created the grammar of the American cinema, the cavalry charge was unfortunately the ride of the hooded Ku Klux Klan, desperate to save the purity of Southern maidenhood. In Ford's case, he presented the building of the transcontinental railroad as American history. In the opening sequence, Abraham Lincoln was shown, taking time off from directing the Civil War to talk to the rail engineers about a great nation pushing through the Great Plains on an 'inevitable path to the West'. With the father of the nation supporting Manifest Destiny, the building of the track to link the United States could be presented as a mission of strong men and metal machines against the resistance of the wilderness and the mounted tribes standing in their way.

The dialectic of John Ford was already apparent in *The Iron Horse*. He praised the progress of the pioneers, yet he understood their inevitable conflict with the threatened Sioux and Cheyenne braves, led by the Chiefs Big Tree and White Spear. Although Ford had not yet adopted his later subtle approach to the conflict between primitive horse culture and forged transport, he did make his villain a white man, masquerading in the costume of what was then called a 'Red Indian'. In the attack of the mounted warriors on the first train to cross the prairies, the monster was the iron steam engine, halted in its tracks, although not by an attempt to lassoo its high funnel.

Fifteen years later, Ford defined the Western film in *Stagecoach*, also creating its ultimate hero, John Wayne in the role of the Ringo Kid. Based on Maupassant's *Boule de Suif*, a savage attack on hypocrisy in which a prostitute gave herself to an enemy officer in return for a safe conduct for a coachload of bourgeois passengers, the script of *Stagecoach* had more to do with cowboy ritual and the myth of the outlaw than with European class divisions. As the drunken Doc Boone declared: 'We have been struck down by a foul disease called social prejudice. Come, be a proud, glorified dreg like me.' Those words suggested that true esteem and glory came from individual defiance of the conventions of the misguided town, which judged the outcasts, and was called Tonto, meaning 'stupid'. The journey of the mixed bunch of passengers away from prejudice on their Stagecoach of Fools lay through the purgatory of Monument Valley and Apache attack towards a heavenly goal with the name of Lordsburg.

On the way there, the travellers would meet their fate or redemption. The three outcasts were saved by love or generosity after helping at the birth of a baby. The false clergyman and the gambler fell to the Apaches, the banker was arrested, the Ringo Kid was avenged on his accusers for his brother's death. He and the prostitute were allowed their liberty by the sheriff, in order to spare them the dubious 'blessings of civilization', as Mark Twain had allowed his hero in *Huckleberry Finn*.

Ford loved the scenario of *Stagecoach*. Before shooting began, he announced with glee that there was not a single respectable character in the cast. His admiration for the outcast and for the victim of society had also become respectable during the Great Depression, when tens of millions were jobless and put outside the pale through no fault of their own. Poverty was no shame then, bankers were considered crooks with vaults, and human decency was the best hope of group survival. So *Stagecoach* also somehow represented within its small wooden walls on wheels the whole bandwagon of the Roosevelt years, rolling towards some resolution in the future Lordsburg of prosperity and social justice.

The Apaches were the wild forces of nature and nemesis – yet they were less terrifying than the verdict of society. They stood in the landscape as if they were mere bleak bluffs of sandstone in Monument Valley, then whirling clouds of dust on their pursuing horses. They were as quick and beautiful as the attack of the elements, and even their savagery in the killing of a family of settlers was shown in a posed martyrdom, with their woman victim kneeling like a penitent at the altar of misunderstanding.

Ford specifically used his mounted Apaches as natural avengers. The opening titles set them in history without any judgement of their struggle for independence. Ford's statement about them informed his audience of their hopeless war against the new vehicles, which allowed the white immigrants to dispossess them:

Until the Iron Horse came, the Stagecoach was the only means of travel on the untamed American frontier. Braving all dangers, these Concord coaches – the 'streamliners' of their day – spanned on schedule wild, desolate stretches of desert and mountainland in the Southwest, where in 1885 the savage struggle of the Indians to oust the white invader was drawing to a close. At the time no name struck more terror into the hearts of travellers than that of GERONIMO – leader of those Apaches who preferred death rather than submit to the white man's will.

In this declaration, Ford praised the remorseless wheels of change that had brought him and previous pioneers across the wilderness, yet he admitted that the white people were the invaders and the mounted tribesmen were brave and terrible in their struggle for independence. Himself an Irish rebel at heart, he could only admire Geronimo's long guerrilla war. Played by Chief White Horse, Geronimo himself appeared briefly in *Stagecoach*, dominant on a sandstone cliff. Ford was criticised for the last-minute charge of the 7th Cavalry to save the stagecoach by a slaughter of the attacking Apaches. To some modern critics, it smacked of racism as much as the gallop of the Ku Klux Klan in *The Birth of a Nation*. Yet this was a false interpretation. Historically, the US cavalrymen did defeat the Plains tribes, and mythologically, their intervention was as classical gods from a machine, arriving in the nick of time to save the stagecoach from the Furies.

They were a dramatic device, put by Ford in a historical context and made human. Their massacre of the Apaches was glorified by no words at all, only by the sound of the bugler blowing the charge and the images of troopers at the gallop with sabres drawn and their flag held high. They were no nobler than Geronimo and his braves, high on their monumental sandstone bluff. In fact, they seemed alien to the very landscape, from which the Apaches seemed to grow. By setting the artificial transport and the uniforms of a regular army against eroded crimson and scarlet buttes and bluffs, the gigantic sculptures of time and weather, Ford reduced the image of human progress to a few insects crawling beneath the indifferent stone faces of the ages.

The Apaches, however, were never presented as intruders upon the majesty of the landscape, but as its true inhabitants, painted like the rocks and the desert and the eagles and the wildcats, a part of the scale and ferocity and liberty of the place. They were as large as their own land or they vanished within it. When once their scouts were seen on the rim of the crevasse through which the stagecoach passed as into the entrance to hell, they appeared a distant warning to the eye of the intruder upon their horsed space, as the danger signal a ship might fly in the vast expanse of the ocean.

So John Ford defined the code of the West and its rituals, for *Stagecoach* was truly *The Pilgrim's Progress* of its genre. Thousands of derivatives reached the flicker of celluloid films, and John Ford himself – a US Navy Admiral in the Second World War – glorified the procedures and honour system of the American Cavalry beyond the call of patriotism. Yet in his last and minimal Western film, *The Man Who Shot Liberty Valance*, he boiled down the cowboy myth of his creation to its bare Shinbone, the name of his archetypal town. This was the whole skeleton of the settling of the legendary West, as fundamental and cursory as the writing on a pioneer grave. The film opened with a mocking credit sequence – the names of John Wayne and James Stewart and John Ford and the film title set on broken wooden crosses, as if they had been abandoned in some forgotten desert cemetery. The first shot was, indeed, another Fordian epigram and epitaph – an old train puffing through cacti and sand in the dreck of the wasteland.

The film dealt with the killers, hired by the ranchers, to break up the sheepherders and farmers, and so maintain the open range. There were lessons in schoolrooms on frontier history, calling for statehood, so that dams and fences and towns and churches might be built for the new immigrants. Liberty Valance and his gang tried to terrorise the citizens' meeting, with Valance shouting: 'You sodbusters are brave in a bunch, but alone –' Yet the sodbusters elected the local lawyer and newspaper editor to represent them and end the reign of terror of the cattle barons.

In the necessary shoot-out between the enforcer Lee Marvin and the lawyer James Stewart, the rancher John Wayne killed Marvin, although Stewart appeared to do so. 'Cold-blooded murder,' Wayne was made to say, 'but I can live with it.' Stewart became a distinguished Senator and attended Wayne's funeral. He confessed that Wayne, and not he, had killed Liberty Valance. The press was not interested, and Ford's last judgement was spoken. 'This is the West, sir. When the legend becomes fact, print the legend.'

The final shot of the film explained Ford's ultimate message. As the train rounded a curve in the line, going away, it was surrounded by wheatfields. Grain grew where the desert was. The film needed no analysis, because it had expressed all of the statements that Ford had spent forty-five years in making, the themes of the law against the outlaw, the town against the wilderness, the civilized man against the savage, the farmer against the rancher, the family against the loner, the church against wicked liberty. Everything was pared down to the bone, only the necessary was shown. 'He shot them bare,' Lee Marvin said. 'If it ain't out there, you ain't going to have it at all . . . He really knew the binoculars he was looking through – in specifics.'

In the 1950s, a New Western was emerging in *High Noon* and *Johnny Guitar*. The leading man did not fight for the community, but for his own beliefs or purposes. More and more, the hero was a Billy the Kid, a professional gunfighter, killing for wages as had the *condottieri* of the Renaissance. They had few social values, if any, and no commitment to the law or the family. In the Italian westerns of Sergio Leone, from *A Fistful of Dollars* to *My Name is Nobody*, Clint Eastwood played the supreme and amoral bounty hunter, unscrupulous and deadly in revenge. And yet, he succeeded later in becoming the worthy heir of John Ford, as a director. For he recreated in *Pale Rider* the cowboy as a Horseman of the Apocalypse, come again to cleanse the earth of evil, with no hope of redemption. And so the romantic myth of the American cowhand passed through pulp fiction into ritualised exorcism, as if the ghost were being laid of the memories of all those deaths and endurances on the long trail nowhere. And all the remembrances would be gathered by e.e. Cummings in an affectionate and ironic elegy:

> Buffalo Bill's
> defunct
>> who used to
>> ride a watersmooth-silver
>>> stallion
> and break onetwothreefourfive pigeons justlikethat
>>>>>> Jesus
> he was a handsome man
>>>> and what i want to know is
> how do you like your blueeyed boy
> Mister Death

CHAPTER FIFTEEN

Horse Culture

In symbol and art and literature, the horse was shown as almost a god and far more than a mere beast, chomping on the grass. In India and in the Greek and Roman Empires, seven horses pulled the chariot of the Sun, the divine light. Their names had to do with Thunder and Lightning, Blaze and Fire, Red and Daybreak and Earthlove. In Norse mythology, only two shielded horses drew the incandescent solar chariot, the Early Waker and Speedy Goer, while Dag, the god of the Day, rode behind a single milkwhite stallion, which scattered sparkling rays from its golden mane down to earth. As Matthew Arnold wrote his *Balder Dead*:

> Forth from the east, up the ascent of heaven,
> Day drove his courser with the shining mane.

In Egyptian and classical reliefs and sculptures, the horse was celebrated in war. In the funeral passages of kings to the afterworld among the Persians and the Armenians, there were many equine sacrifices, to carry the royal bodies to the life-giving Sun. The Roman emperor Caligula was said to have raised his wise charger Incitatus to the rank of consul. Yet no greater remembrance of the mystical horse was ever created than the chalk White Horse of Uffington Hill, supposedly to commemorate the mounted King Alfred's victory at Ashdown against the armoured Danes on foot. And in terms of terror and prophecy, the Four Horsemen of the Apocalypse and the Pale Rider of Death were fearsome revelations and the inspiration of medieval artists and sculptors from the Low Countries to High Germany.

While the great equestrian statues of the heroes of Greece and Rome had hardly survived except for the Charioteer at Delphi and the Roman mounted bronzes of Marcus Aurelius and the Regisole, the four bronze horses, stolen by Venice from Byzantium after the Fourth

Crusade took that fabled city, now grace the façade of the basilica of San Marco. These proved to be an inspiration for the Renaissance and the age of the *condottieri*, the great cavaliers of the wars between the Italian cities and with the Papal States. Verocchio's statue of the mounted Bartolommeo Colleoni was the crux of harsh magnificence, the overpowering sternness of the face of the armoured conqueror staring down at the wrinkled mane and head of his dominant charger. For brute force, none of the myriad equestrian statues of princes and generals in the following centuries has ever equalled this display of raw power. In his Florentine fresco of 1436 of the greatest of the *condottieri*, Sir John Hawkwood of the White Company, Paolo Uccello showed a different aspect of a warrior, almost melancholy after his many cautious victories. Holding his marshal's baton above his scarlet saddle, the stately British captain rides a greenish pale charger in front of a dark red penumbra. Yet he was the warleader, said to have inspired the Italian proverb, which was to be applied to Lord Byron:

> Inglese italianato
> È un diavolo incarnato.

Such incarnate devils are frozen in Uccello's later triptych of *The Battle of San Romano*, when another *condottieri*, Niccolò da Tolentino, routed the battalions from Siena. On the left panel, Tolentino rides with his charging knights on a rearing horse. The foreground is a directed mess of pieces of armour and shattered lances, a helmet and the corpse of the back of a mailed attacker. In the centre, an unhorsed knight is in a mass of infantry and cavalry, their lances and spears and crossbows projecting towards the viewer. On the right flank, reinforcements arrive from Florence, their commander on a black horse among fluttering banners. The three panels with their lines of direction converge on the curve of a human eyeball.

This design of battle invented the perspective of war. The still thrust of the spearshafts, the raised or broken lances, pierced the stuck attack of the knights in the middle distance against the small far cypresses beyond. The sight was that of the blink of a mercenary pikeman, frozen in an attitude of horror, before the charge of the enemy struck him down. Uccello was the genius of the centrifugal force. He aligned all the pointers taking the eyes to the centre, whether these were dead or dying cavaliers or broken lances or furrows in the fields. His clarity of vision was as a strategy or a battle map, as direct as the advance at

Trafalgar of Nelson's two columns on the vitals of the spread French and Spanish battlefleet.

The great equine statues and paintings of Leonardo da Vinci were never to be realised. From drawings now at Windsor Castle, we can see that his genius would have captured the mettlesome beast and man in the glory of their ferocity. Leonardo had studied at Verocchio's workshop, and in the sketches for *The Battle of Anghiari* and the bronze Francesco Sforza and Trivulzio Monuments, he exceeded the example of his master. If Ernest Hemingway was correct, and genius is grace in motion, then Leonardo made the paper move with his careering studies of horse and rider.

Except for one flamboyant stallion from Rubens, paintings and sculptures of equestrian subjects generally became tamed and rigid for more than two centuries, as if they had congealed. Then another amateur butcher, as skilled as Leonardo in his dissection of the human body, applied his studies to the stallion. The drawings of George Stubbs in *The Anatomy of the Horse* of 1765 were the result of his flaying of dead horses and stripping off the flesh to analyse their muscles and bones. As he wrote to his subscribers: 'All Gentlemen who keep Horses, will by it, be enabled not only to judge of the Structure of the Horse more scientifically, but also to point out the Seat of Diseases or Blemishes, in that noble Animal, so as frequently to facilitate their Removal.'

In his paintings, George Stubbs set out the two sides of horse culture. His classic racing pictures, such as *Gimcrack with John Pratt Up* and *Whistlejacket*, showed a civilisation turning the stallion from the battle charger into the groomed mount, bred for gambling and speed, the epitome of wealth and sophistication. Yet in his canvases of *Horse Frightened* and *Devoured by a Lion*, also of the lion rending a white courser, the fear and turbulence and ferocity of the two beasts were shocking and exaggerated and 'sublime', a prelude to the Romantic age to come, which linked such visual cruelty to the nightmares of Henry Fuseli and the popular Gothic novels of that era.

After the French Revolution, Jacques-Louis David would achieve the same transition, particularly in his celebrated painting, *Napoleon Crossing the Alps*. In his previous neo-classical works, such as the *Oath of the Horatii*, David had produced a static dignity for his heroes, as if they were caught in freeze frame. Yet his portrait of *Count Potocki* showed an aristocrat, who had just broken a wild horse, its mane tossing and forelegs pawing the ground. Napoleon, however, was depicted in a swirling cloak on a rearing charger, driving his artillery forward up the mountains into Italy, almost a force of nature, an imperial will dominating the elements and his army.

The French commander failed in 1812 in his attempt to overwhelm Russia, but its superb Romantic poet Pushkin found his inspiration both in his five years of exile among the Cossacks near the Crimea, also in the statue of another harsh Tsar, who had created St Petersburg on the River Neva, set towards the Baltic and Europe. This Falconet monument inspired a poem from the Polish patriot Mickiewicz and later Pushkin. Both wrote of the effigy of Peter the Great, riding a courser, loosed on a bridle towards a revolutionary future:

> His charger's reins Tsar Peter has released;
> He has been flying down the road, perchance,
> And here the precipice checks his advance.

Pushkin's gloss was as accurate a prophecy, in *The Bronze Horseman:*

> Proud charger, where are you ridden,
> Where do you leap? And where, on whom
> Will your hoof strike? You lord of doom
> And potentate, when appearing
> Above the void, you had in hold
> A curb of iron and sat in old
> On Russia, her haunches rearing.

In two other rebellious poems *Ode to Liberty* and *On The Dagger* of 1821, Pushkin offended the authorities. He seemed to praise the sudden assassin, who was 'the secret punisher of freedom's rape'. Exiled to the Caucasus, he was seduced by the Romantic poetry and attitudes of Lord Byron. A verse epic, *The Prisoner in the Caucasus*, reflected the current fashion and passion. An egoistic Russian lieutenant has a Circassian girl fall in love with him, when he is captured. He swims to safety, abandoning her to suicide. Another poem on *The Gypsies* repeats the theme of civilised *ennui*, revived by mountain wanderers. The hero Aleko declares of the stuffy cities:

> What have I left? Bitter treachery
> And prejudice and calumny,
> The persecuting mob and blame,
> Or else the gilt-edged sword of shame.

Lord Byron was the touchstone of the Romantic Revolution, that denial of the Industrial Revolution which would transform the western world. He inspired Mary Shelley to write *Frankenstein*, the epic modern struggle of good against evil in mankind, wishing to play god and create its own destructive monsters. By his person and pen, Byron made the outlaw respectable and notorious. Nothing more strangely represented his admiration for the primitive man, whom he could never be, than his curious eulogy of Daniel Boone in a world-weary and final poem, *Don Juan*. There the cult of nature reached its apogee through the aristocrat, whose lordly way contradicted his values, and whose wasted death made him the symbol of a freedom that he never lived nor possessed. Byron was always a peer in life, if a bandit in spirit. His Daniel Boone was conceived in an Italian villa at an extreme remove from the American forest and the author's style. Personal luxury dreamed of a thicket Utopia.

> Of the great names which in our faces stare,
>> The General Boone, back-woodsman of Kentucky,
> Was happiest amongst mortals anywhere;
>> For killing nothing but a bear or buck, he
> Enjoy'd the lonely, vigorous, harmless days
>> Of his old age in wilds of deepest maze . . .
> 'Tis true he shrank from men even of his nation
>> When they built up unto his darling trees,
> He moved some hundred miles off, for a station
>> Where there were fewer houses and more ease . . .

Yet Byron's Boone was not all alone, but the progenitor of a new race. This 'sylvan tribe of children of the chase' lived in a young unawakened world, where there was no sorrow.

> The free-born forest found and kept them free
> As fresh as is a torrent or a tree . . .
> Simple they were, not savage; and their rifles,
> Though very true, were not yet used for trifles . . .
> Serene, not sullen, were the solitudes
> Of this unsighing people of the woods.

Byron continued to state, however – so much for Nature. Civilisation had both its variety and its joys, such as 'the sweet consequence of large society, war, pestilence, the despot's desolation'. The best answer to the Malthusian and mechanical tragedy to come was his own Romantic revolt against the age of overpopulation, even if it meant an exaggeration of the threatened pleasures of a free and roving life. Hardly able to ride with his crippled foot, he became the bard of the horse culture in his surge of a poem to the Cossacks, *Mazeppa*. His hero is a seventy-year-old Hetman, who is defeated at Poltava, while fighting for a Swedish king against the Russians in the Ukraine. 'Shaggy and swift, and strong of limb, All Tartar – like he carried him.' Byron took his inspiration from a *History of Charles XII* by Voltaire, who described Mazeppa's splendour and courage. And so Byron praised the Cossack chieftain in words, put in Charles's royal mouth:

> In skirmish, march or forage, none
> Can less have said or more have done
> Than thee, Mazeppa! On the earth
> So fit a pair had never birth,
> Since Alexander's days till now,
> As thy Bucephalus and thou:
> All Scythia's fame to thine should yield
> For pricking on o'er flood and field.

As a penalty, the captive Mazeppa is lashed under the belly of an untamed horse, which gallops across the steppes to the forests and the mountains. Mazeppa manages to struggle onto the back of his tiring steed, which joins

> A thousand horse, and none to ride!
> With flowing tail, and flying mane,
> Wide nostrils never stretch'd by pain,
> Mouths bloodless to the bit or rein,
> And feet that iron never shod,
> And flanks unscarr'd by spur or rod,
> A thousand horse, the wild, the free,
> Like waves that follow o'er the sea.

The herd swerves off to the forest, and Mazeppa's stallion dies of a broken heart and wind. Chained to his mount, Mazeppa is rescued by a Cossack maid, 'a slender girl, long-hair'd, and tall'. And so he lives to become the prince of his people in this romantic paean to horse culture.

With Byron as his model and Pushkin as his spur, Mikhael Lermentov also found relief from gentlemanly *angst* among the Cossacks. A cavalryman, he wrote passionate verses about Pushkin's death in a duel, and so he also incurred the Tsar's anger, and was sent to the Caucasus rather than Siberia. One year before he himself died in 1841 in a duel at the age of twenty-six, his masterpiece was published, *A Hero of Our Own Times*. His death paralleled that of his despairing *alter ego* Pechorin. If hit by a bullet in the *pas-de-deux* of trial by pistol, he had to fall from the rocky platform of the encounter into an abyss.

Among beautiful descriptions of the border mountains, 'inaccessible reddish cliffs, hung with green ivy and crowned with clumps of oriental plane; yellow slopes streaked with ravines; and there, at a great height, the golden fringe of the snows', Lermentov described the alternative means of local transport – cart-oxen and camels and horses, which were valued more than women. The Chechens and the Cossacks ruled the ranges outside the occasional Russian forts. Horse rustling was even more important than cattle and sheep raiding. The Byronic and bored Pechorin epitomised the vices of his age, and he only escaped them by hunting or galloping across 'the wide, free, and open steppes'. He could not commit in love for a Circassian beauty or a princess from St Petersburg. As a conversation made clear:

'I suppose the French made boredom fashionable.'

'No, it was the English.'

'Ah, that explains things, for the English have always been heavy drinkers.'

This reminded me of a man I had known in Moscow, who assured me that Byron was nothing more than a drunkard.

This was not true for Lermentov or his creation, Pechorin. In memory of the British aristocrat, they took disdain and detachment to the limit. Living was worthless, only the wild horsemen gave an example to existence:

I mounted, and cantered off into the steppe. I love riding a spirited beast through long grass against the wind that whistles across the wild. In all that concerns my military attire I am most fastidious – expensive weapons in a plain setting; the fur on my cap of exactly the right length; boots and gaiters must fit perfectly; inner white tunic, outer tunic dark brown. I have carefully studied the riding of these mountaineers, and nothing can tickle my vanity more than to be told that my seat resembles that of a native of the Caucasus.

Pechorin dies for the honour of a woman he does not love, while refusing the love of a former mistress, because she understands him – 'weakness, evil, passions, and all. Is evil really so attractive?' He has an insatiable eagerness to grasp every sensation in life, and then to discard it. His role is always that of executioner or traitor to the passions of other people. Pushkin had written in *Eugene Onegin* of Pechorin's part – 'the mind's cold observations, and the sorrowful teachings of the heart'.

For Pechorin as for the Cossacks, his craving for freedom was inborn, a sort of inexplicable prejudice. And if he died, he died. This was not the philosophy of Tolstoy in *The Cossacks*, the longest work he wrote before starting *War and Peace*. This inept novel again pits an urban young man Olenin against the natural Cossacks, whose free virtues are opposed by the savage Chechens, ferocious Tartar tribesmen. Olenin falls for a Cossack maiden Maryanka, who spurns him for a Cossack lover, saying, 'Do gentlemen marry Cossack girls? Go away.' The contrast between the constrained city dweller and the wild liberty of the Caucasus is unconvincing, as is another extraordinary Tolstoyian exercise, *Strider: The Story of a Horse*. Tolstoy's natural altruism could not cope with raw Darwinism. Even he had to recognise that foals would grow up to be cruel to their mother mares, who would turn towards other stallions.

The fourth supreme Russian writer, who dealt with the Cossacks, was Isaac Babel, who rode with the Red Cavalry and Budyonny's Invincible Brigades against the Poles after the Russian Revolution. His collection of dispatches and short stories, taken from his diaries in the front line, were see-saws of contradiction, published under the original title of *Horse Army*. A young revolutionary Jew from Odessa, whose father had knelt before and kissed the *knout* of one of the Tsar's storm-troopers during a *pogrom*, Babel was now riding with newly-indoctrinated Cossacks, invading the heartland of the old Hasidic communities of Galicia and the Ukraine. For him, these towns reeked of dung and frontier misfortunes. His own ambiguity was expressed in a reproach from an old Rabbi: 'You shoot because you are the Revolution. But surely the Revolution means joy. And joy does not like orphans in the house. The Revolution is the good deed of good men. But good men do not kill.' To which, Babel had himself reply: 'The International is eaten with gunpowder and spiced with best-quality blood.'

As for his comrade Cossacks, Babel noted in them 'layers of worthlessness, reckless daring, professionalism, revolutionary spirit, bestial cruelty'. One of them nearly shot Babel for riding into battle with no rounds in his revolver, and the Jewish intellectual lamented that he did not have 'the simplest of proficiencies – the ability to kill my fellowmen'. Unlike Byron and Tolstoy, Babel could not hymn the Cossacks as noble savages of nature. He had suffered from their brutality in peace and had joined them half-heartedly in war. As the critic Lionel Trilling noted of Babel's mixed feelings about both his own people and those of the Caucasus, the violence of the Americas was nothing to that of the East of Europe, and the Cossacks were not exceptional in their ferocity. Babel was drawn by what went with the brutality, the boldness, the passions, the simplicity and directness – and the grace. In two phrases, Babel wrote of 'ambushes about his heart' and of night flying towards him 'on mettlesome horses'; in another sentence, he looked on the world with his comrades, as 'a meadow in May, a meadow traversed by women and horses'. And yet he could never master the hereditary skills of his curious chosen companions with their 'Cossack trot, the peculiar Cossack gallop – dry, furious, abrupt . . . I would wobble like a sack on the stallion's long lean spine'.

Even stranger was the modern preoccupation with the *gaucho* myth of the myopic national librarian, Jorge Luis Borges. His own disability made him far-sighted in his views on family and Argentinian history. On his pages, we read of ancestors, who founded Buenos Aires or fought and died in civil wars and rebellions. In one symbolic story, *Pedro Salvadores*, the outriders of the dictator Rosas come to seize the rancher, who hides in a dark cellar for nine years in order to avoid his fate, while his wife earns their keep by sewing uniforms for the army. Speaking for his subject, Borges questioned his own blindness about the troubled politics and coups in his country. 'Who was he? Was it his fear, his love, the unseen presence of Buenos Aires, or – in the long run – habit that held him prisoner? . . . His dreams, at the outset, were probably of that sudden night when the blade sought his throat, of the streets he knew so well, of the open plains. As the years went on, he would have been unable to escape, even in his sleep.'

Even more than Byron or Babel, Borges might escape from the stifling city to the open plains through his imagination. He was fascinated by the code of the *gaucho* and the gangster in the duel by dagger. Seeing himself as another librarian with military ancestors, a certain Juan Dahlmann, Borges sent his fictional self on a progress to *The South* from a debilitating sanatorium on a quest to find the shell of an inherited ranch. The train grinds to a halt in the middle of the *pampas*. In the general store, the civilised Dahlmann is challenged to a knife fight by a drunken *peon*; he is thrown a naked dagger by an ancient *gaucho*, seeming 'outside time, situated in eternity':

> If Dahlmann was without hope, he was also without fear. As he crossed the threshold, he felt that to die in a knife fight, under the open sky and going forward to the attack, would have been a liberation, a joy, and a festive occasion . . . he felt that if he had been able to choose, then, or to dream his death, this would have been the death he would have chosen or dreamt.
>
> Firmly clutching his knife, which he perhaps would not know how to wield, Dahlmann went out into the plain.

In his cerebral blindness, Borges was particularly fixated by an elemental *gaucho*, Martín Fierro, celebrated in the folk poem by José Hernandez. To meet his death in *The End*, Fierro rides towards his doom across a shimmering plain beneath the final sun of the day. Fierro greets the black avenger waiting for him with the words, 'Destiny has made me kill, and now, once more, it has put a knife in my hand.' The two men go to fight under the moon, their ponchos wound round their forearms as shields against slashes. This time, Fierro falls, yet Borges has already imagined him dreaming of a knife fight in the eighteen-sixties, when he did in his killer's brother:

> A *gaucho* lifts a black man off the ground with the thrust of his knife, drops him like a bag of bones, watches him writhe in pain and die, squats down to wipe off his knife, unties his horse's bridle and swings up into the saddle slowly, so no one will think he's running away from what he's done. This thing that was once, returns again, infinitely; the visible armies have gone and what is left is a common sort of knife fight; one man's dream is part of all men's memory.

CHAPTER SIXTEEN
Outback and Backlands

The Australians have always seen their colonisation of a continent, only populated by 300,000 Aborigines, as the terminus of the Last Frontier. The first settlers were mainly British convicts and their keepers: the conflict between the law and the lawless and the primitive was initially worked out in Van Diemen's Land, later Tasmania. The prison at Hobart was brutally operated with chain gangs for the worst offenders; when they broke out, they became bushrangers; they were faced by vengeful police behind and ravenous beasts and aboriginals in the wilderness. A series of early place names was a list of events – Murderer's Plains, Killman Point, Hell Corner, Four Square Gallows. Convicts on a Ticket-of-Leave, such as the notorious Michael Howe, plundered and looted the bush farmers and later the mail coaches and miners on the mainland, in the way that their mounted models, the English highwaymen, had done.

As two Victorian ethnographers noted, 'the advance of settlement has, upon the frontier at least, been marked by a line of blood'. Another Tasmanian historian wrote of the island colonists 'suffering from a guerrilla war'. The Aborigines fought back against the invaders. They had no villages or fields. They lived off the land with their superior bushcraft. 'Their movements were unpredictable, adopting the classical stratagems of the weak when pitted against the strong – stealth, surprise, secrecy.' They attacked, when at an advantage, and they retired, when they were overmatched. There was no front line or imaginary dotted frontier between the opposing forces, only the contours of a common landscape, in which the settlers had the advantage of guns and horses. 'Now every man travels well-armed,' the *Cooktown Courier* noted, 'and a carriers' camp at eventide is a regular school of musketry'.

Some thousand miners and farmers and stockmen, some of them Aborigines, were killed in these frontier wars, while at least 20,000 of the tribesmen were exterminated in various campaigns of terror, beginning with the infamous Black Line or Tasmanian Drive, which sent nearly all of the native population to prison in the stockade or the grave. As the Governor of the colony wrote, 'Terror may have the effect which no proffered measures of conciliation have been capable of inducing.' As in the American South and West, there was a pricking excitement in tracking and murdering a fellow man, because he was black. The Aborigines appeared to be doomed, anyway, for in the words of the *Sydney Herald*, 'they will and must become extinct'.

Across the Great Plains of the United States, the advance of the frontier was inexorable behind the armed horse and cattle culture, which was followed, where the land allowed, by sheep herders and wheat farmers. Such also was the advance of civilisation in Central Australia. However much the environment shaped the characters of the pioneers, significant patterns of behaviour split the experiences of the two continents. In the United States, the open ranges were invaded by barbed wire and fenced crops and grazing land for sheep. These led to the wars of the cattlemen against the intruders in the 1890s, shown as a petty *Iliad* in a multitude of Western films. The cowboys won, and most of the flocks retreated to Wyoming under the care of immigrant Basque proprietors. In Australia, only the Aborigines killed the stockmen in open warfare. The distribution of sheep and cattle depended upon rainfall, and in those even wider open spaces, there was room enough for all herders. Any rancher could find the land, which he could use, if not always the needful water in this wilderness of many a drought. Even though the 'Father of His Country for the Sheepmen', John Macarthur, shot and killed his superior officer, he was pardoned in London, because he introduced the Merino breed to Australia, and so reduced the dependence of the English textile mills on Spanish wool.

A further difference between the prairie and the outback lay in a radical revision of Turner's frontier thesis, that the conditions created a person hell-bent on making something of himself. In *The Australian Legend*, Russell Ward presented an opposite theory, that the typical Australian frontiersman was a wage-worker, who did not usually expect to become anything else. The loneliness and hardships of range life taught him to value his mates, but his economic interests told him to stick with them collectively, not to strike out on his own. 'By loyal combination with his fellows he might win better conditions from his employer, but the possibility of becoming his own master by individual enterprise was usually a remote dream.' At the ranch he joined a 'primitive organisation of nomad tribesmen, if one can conceive of a tribe without women and children'. The divergent frontiers in America and Australia produced differing breeds of cowboys and pioneers, so similar in presence, yet sometimes so far apart.

This was proven in the Eureka Rebellion of 1854, when the Australian miners, who had shipped to California during its Gold Rush, returned to dig for their home nuggets in Victoria. Directed by a brother of the Irish Potato Martyrs of 1848, 1,000 miners were involved in Ballarat at the battle of the Eureka Stockade. Assaulted by government troops, the pistol-packing diggers fought for a few minutes and were overwhelmed and their leaders captured. Hardly a 'trap' or gold field policeman was injured, but many ballads from Ballarat turned the losing miners into victors. The legend was printed and sung:

> Oh, the traps, the dirty traps!
> Kick the traps whene'er you're able
> At the traps, the nasty traps,
> Kick the traps right under the table.

In the Great Riot of Kalgoorie in 1894, the loss to the police, after 'carefully checking the lists of the slain', was five brass buttons. Such outbreaks could not compare with the dozens of dead in the coal-and-iron mining wars of the past two centuries in the Appalachian mountains, where the Molly Maguires and their successors fought the company police in a series of bloody private wars.

What the outback and the prairie frontiers had in common was the sad song and the myth of the bandit hero. The Border ballads of the Reivers were translated into the country-and-western music of the hill-billies, and then they were passed on to the cowboy refrains of the prairies and the lyrics of the cattle drovers and the oxcart drivers of Central Australia, who were still cattle nomads, bound to their bul-locks and horses on a rotten diet. As one chronicler wrote:

One of the more widespread hobo songs in the United States is 'The Great American Bum', found in Australia as 'Hang the Man Who Works'. The bushman complains about his monotonous diet of 'Tea, Damper, and Mutton', while the American outbacker complains about 'Beans, Bacon, and Gravy' . . . Where the whole country is poor, songs like 'The Arkansas Traveller' or 'Charlie Brannan' are typical responses in America; comparable areas in Australia produce songs like 'The Cockies of Bungaree':

Well, when I'd done my first week's work
    I reckoned I had enough.
I went up to that cocky and I asked him for my stuff.
I came down in Ballarat and it didn't take me long –
I went straight into Sayers Hotel and blued my one pound one.

The cultural flow has been steady in one direction – from America to Australia, though Americans have versions of 'The Wild Colonial Boy', 'Bold Jack Donohue', 'Bound for South Australia', 'Botany Bay' and two or three other Australian compositions. 'Click Go the Shears' is sung in Australia to the tune of a song written by Henry Clay Work, the popular post-Civil War American composer, [who also wrote] the recent Australian plaint 'Pub with No Beer', a sozzled 'Beautiful Dreamer' . . . The Australian 'Wild Rover No More' is the American 'Strawberry Roan'; that delightful bush character Sam Holt has his ribald adventures sung to the American tune 'Sweet Alice, Ben Bolt'; and 'The Old Bullock Dray' is the American fiddle tune, 'Turkey in the Straw'.

Lawless, the Border Reivers had always celebrated in their ballads and folk memory, those who were without the law. Was not wee Jock Elliott a riposte to King Edward the First of England, the Hammer of the Scots? And so the legend of the bandit as hero sprung from the freewheeling conditions of the Australian frontier. The bushrangers of folklore, Ben Hall and Daniel Morgan and Ned Kelly behaved and lived as if they were translated 'moss' bandits from the Scots Borders. In the Harley and Fish river districts, full of wild cattle, one of their hideouts was a limestone cavern, named the Devil's Coach House. Ravines and forests hid the Davis Gang from pursuit in the Brisbane Water and Hunter river districts, while its seven members rode out 'well-mounted and well-armed with double-barrelled guns and pistols, and supplied with packhorses to carry swag'. They were eventually hunted down by the local Marchers, the Mounted Police, established in Sydney in 1825; this force could call upon some 150 troopers to man important posts in the interior. They were armed with a sabre and a carbine and horse pistols, and they wore a light dragoon uniform. As with the red-coated Mounties in Canada, the Australian Police had to kill or capture the bushrangers and take them back to formal justice and execution on the gallows. There was no mining-camp or mob or lynch law, as in the American South and Western Lands.

The adventurous Ben Hall and his gang were hailed as latter-day Robin Hoods, in spite of an occasional atrocity. As their biographer noted:

One prided himself on courteous behaviour to women; another boasted of his kind-heartedness, declaring that he had never 'pulled trigger on any unarmed cover'; a third claimed credit for robbing only those who could afford to part with that which he took from them; and a fourth avowed that he had 'never shot anyone, not even a "bobby"'.

Such excuses contributed to the legends of the bushrangers, although these pleas were hardly accepted at their trials.

Daniel Morgan, however, was considered a gangster and a monster rather than a man – 'who tortured his victims because the sight of their writhings gave him pleasure –who committed murder from sheer wantonness, and a tigerish lust for blood'. He and his men attacked wool stations at shearing time, burning down the sheds, as well as mail-coaches.* He even claimed to raid the whole state of Victoria. When finally he was cornered, he was tricked into an ambush and shot in the back, as Jesse James had been by Bob Ford, the dirty little coward. And the last words of Morgan, too, were in the traditional mode: 'Why didn't you challenge me fair, and give me a chance?'

Of the last and most notorious of the bushranging gangs, that of the Kelly brothers, it was said that they were working out 'the old leaven of convictism' – also, of the centuries of the Irish Troubles, set against the invasive English Law. They had been condemned to become bandits. The father of the family, 'Red' Kelly, had been transported to Tasmania in 1841 for trying to shoot his landlord. Released into Victoria State, he settled at Wallan, an out-station, which was 30 miles from Melbourne. He married into the Quinn family, and the bonded Irish clan moved to Glenmore and Greta in the north. Their income came from 'duffing' or reiving cattle and horses. One of Red's sons, Ned Kelly, admitted to stealing some 300 horses when he was a bushranger; he had helped to steal many more as a lad.

When Ned was only sixteen, he was taken as a mate by an experienced bushranger, Harry Power, who taught him the techniques of highway robbery and the whereabouts of mountain safe caves. His younger brother Dan was already an experienced cattle 'lifter' in 'Kelly Country', where so many of the drovers' herds lost their stock. Another cattle-thief and an educated conman, Joe Byrne, made up the gang. After a Constable Fitzpatrick tried to arrest the Kelly brothers on charges of horse-theft, he was shot in the wrist. The two youths escaped, but three of their relatives were put in gaol for aiding and abetting an attempted murder. Swearing revenge, Ned and Dan took to the bush. Acting on information that the Kelly Gang was in the Wombat Ranges, two *posses* were sent after the bushrangers. One was led by a Sergeant Kennedy along with three constables. They were surprised and shot with only a single survivor.

There could be no mercy now for the Kelly Gang, which turned from rustling to sophisticated robberies. They took prisoners and set up bases and cut telegraph lines, before they cleaned out the bank at Euroa. Another raid on Jerilderie began with the occupation of the local watch house, where the two constables and their families were locked up in the cells. Putting on police uniforms, the outlaws surveyed the town on the following Sunday and took over the Royal Hotel, which became a second lock-up for its guests. On the Monday, the Kellys stuck up the bank and looted it and seized the telegraph operators. Ned Kelly then spoke to a crowd of the citizens, declaring himself and his family to be the victims of injustice. He even handed to the editor of the local newspaper a short autobiography, probably written by Joe Byrne as an exoneration. He claimed to be a martyr to police interference and persecution. At the age of fourteen, he had been imprisoned for three months for 'using a neighbour's horse without his consent'. The police had pinned many other misdeeds on the Kellys, and 'became a nuisance to the family'. Even the killings on the Wombat Ranges were unintended. The gang shot the constables because they believe the constables had come out to shoot them.

After murdering an informer, the Kellys wanted revenge on their worst enemies, the aboriginal black-trackers, whose uncanny skills had led to the capture and death of most of the earlier bushrangers. Among their harbourers and supporters near Greta, the gang had spent an extraordinary season, turning plough-shares into plate armour. As mailed and helmeted as any Arthurian knight, they would defy a shoot-out in Glenrowan, the town chosen for their ultimate defiance of the law. They seized some line-repairers to help them wreck the railtrack to Benalla, from which a special train of police and black-trackers must arrive, once the presence of the Kellys was known. Putting on their armour, the outlaws waited for the relief train to turn over before assaulting the waggons.

For once, the surveillance over the citizens of Glenrowan went awry. A local schoolmaster warned the oncomers of the destroyed railtrack, and the expedition steamed safely to the dark station. Surprised and surrounded at Jones' Hotel, Joe Byrne was shot in the groin by a police volley. Ned Kelly broke out, wounded a superintendent, was clipped in the arm, and galloped away to Morgan's Lookout; but in the morning, he returned in his armour for the final confrontation.* As the *Melbourne Age* stated of Ned Kelly:

> It was nearly eight o'clock when his tall figure was seen close behind the line of police. At first it was thought he was a black fellow. He carried a grey coat over his arm, and walked coolly and slowly among the police. His head, chest, back and sides were all protected with heavy plates of quarter-inch iron . . . The contest became one which, from its remarkable nature, almost baffles description. Nine police joined in the conflict and fired point-blank at Kelly; but although, in consequence of the way in which he staggered, it was apparent that many of the shots hit him, yet he always recovered himself, and, tapping his breast, laughed derisively at his opponents, as he coolly returned the fire, fighting only with his revolver. It appeared as if he was a fiend with a charmed life.

Now Constable James Arthur took up the story of the encounter at Glenrowan, as he gazed at:

> A madman who had conceived the idea of storming the hotel with a nail-can on his head. I then said to him, 'Go back, you d--- fool, you will get shot.' The figure replied, 'I could shoot you, sonny' and at that moment fired his revolver at me, but missed. He evidently was crippled, and did not take proper aim. We were then only between twenty and thirty yards apart. I levelled my Martini rifle, and fired at his helmet, thinking I would knock it off. It only staggered him slightly. An opening in the helmet looked like a huge mouth, I fired at that and hit him again. He still came on. I fired a third shot at his body, and heard it hum off him. I was completely astonished, and could not understand what the object I was firing at was. The men around me appeared astonished too. Someone said, 'He is a madman!' Dowsett, the railway guard, said, 'He is the devil!' Sergeant Kelly exclaimed, 'Look out, boys, he is the bunyip!'

For half an hour, the firing went on until another police Sergeant closed on the armoured man and fired two shots into Ned Kelly's legs, which brought him down. Yelling and cursing, his revolver wrenched from him, the outlaw was captured. Jones' Hotel was fired, and the charred skeletons of Dan Kelly and his associate were raked from the ashes. The wounded Ned was taken away for trial and execution in a quiet and almost philosophical mood. When asked what had brought him to

Glenrowan, he replied that it did not matter much. 'I do not know, or I do not say. It does not seem much any way.' Such imperturbability and refusal to apologise made Ned Kelly even more of a hero before his conviction, when he interrupted the Judge who was delivering the verdict. He declared that there was no flashness or bravado about him.

> THE PRISONER: My mind is as easy as the mind of any man in this world, as I am prepared to show before God and man.

> HIS HONOUR: It is blasphemous for you to say that. You appear to revel in the idea of having put men to death.

> THE PRISONER: More men than I have put men to death, but I am the last man in the world that would take a man's life.

There were even efforts for a reprieve of Ned Kelly, but he was duly hanged. The last exhortation of his mother, who was also put in gaol with him, were the words: 'Mind you die like a Kelly, Ned!' And so he did, the noose about his neck. His legend persisted into the iconic paintings by Sidney Nolan, two films and one fictitious diary by Peter Carey. With him ended the era of the bushrangers in Australia, who had contributed so little outside the myths of the outback. The real creators were the overlanders and the drovers and the 'bullockies', who had been plundered while they made the continental trails, which later developed into settlements and townships and roads. The cattle rustler Harry Redford had actually established the Strzelecki Track by stealing 1,000 head from a station in Central Queensland and driving them 1,500 miles along four river-beds: at his trial, the jury acquitted him for his daring. Other herd trails were the Murranji Track from the Victoria river in Northern Territory to Newcastle Waters in Queensland; the Birdsville Track, still the only road from the Simpson to the east coast; and the Canning Stock Route, in its way as renowned as the Chisholm Trail from Texas up to the stockyards.

For outlaws, the trails led to the borders, over which they were safe from justice, although not always from pursuit, as with the *hot trod* of the Reivers. Many a bandit crossed the Rio Grande down Mexico way with a *posse* on his heels. The horse culture extended both sides of this porous frontier. The *ranchero* was something of a Border warlord in his cattle kingdom, and his support with hundreds of light cavalry was important to many insurgents, such as Pancho Villa or Emiliano

Zapata, who might bring down governments, but who proved unable to run them. As with the Moss Troopers, there was a fine line, drawn between banditry and serving as mercenaries in a rebel cause; there was no loyalty given to any authority except the local boss. In only one case did the outlaws back a millennial movement in Canudos in the Brazilian heartlands. There they died to the last man, woman and child.

'We are condemned to civilization,' Euclides da Cunha wrote of his masterpiece of 1902, *Os Sertões*, translated as *Rebellion in the Backlands*. This poetic description of a peasant millennial revolt in a labyrinth of clay huts at Canudos is the supreme statement of nature and the nature of the northern Brazilian *vaqueiro* or cowboy. The destruction caused by the clash of two cultures, the Europeanised sea-board and the retrograde interior, is made into a deterministic drama, which has been compared to Tolstoy's *War and Peace*. A military engineer, who covered the turmoil, da Cunha was both a geographer and a sociologist. For him, the rugged land forged the intractable people. His style suited the terrain, the 'barbaric yawp' of another Walt Whitman. As he wrote, his hues were taken from the earth, from the black mud of the pits, with vermilion from the coagulated blood of the wilderness ruffians, and the sepia of bandit affrays in the hinterland.

Despite his profession, da Cunha thought that war was monstrous and illogical, 'with the stigmata of original banditry behind it'. Whether soldiers or *vaqueiros*, they were all Reivers. In a harsh scrubland riven by ravines, a cattle-herding economy had superseded another deluded Gold Rush near the São Francisco river. The whelp of the backlands, the *vaqueiro*, was the product of an unforgiving landscape, prone to famine and drought; he was harder than the swaggering *gaucho* of the grassy *pampas* to the south. Clad in cowhide armour against cacti and thorn bushes, as was his loping mount, man and beast appeared inseparable to da Cunha, a crude sort of Centaur. His weapons were as the Borderers and the North American pioneers; the long-barrelled rifle or the antiquated musket; the sticking sword or 'alligator knife'; the prong or *guiada*, a lance three yards long; and even a crossbow. His temporary cottage was a clay tent, daubed on wooden stakes and covered with thatch. Often he was indolent, but in the cowhunt of the branded steers, the *vaqueiros* of the wilds had 'all the fierce and terrifying movement that one associates with a band of Tartar horsemen'. Yet when the herds were separated and being driven home, a melancholy lullaby soothed the dry scrub:

E cou mansão
E cou . . . cão

Just as in the Texan refrain.

Get along, little dogie,
Get along.

A wandering prophet, Antonio Conselheiro, cast a religious spell over some 20,000 of these desperate and rootless people of the wasteland. They built a clay-and-wattle labyrinth of 5,200 dwellings around a central church, dedicated to Jesus and the Resurrection. The fissured outlands were honeycombed with pits and trenches, while a belt of scorched earth, seven miles in width, surround Canudos. All property was held in common, as in the Anabaptist communities of Luther's Germany, while fasting and suffering were exalted as bridleways to heaven. 'Canudos was the refuge of renowned criminals,' da Cunha observed. 'These heroes of the knife and gun came there to mingle with the credulous back woodsmen and the deluded *vaqueiros*, for this weird sect . . . found its natural representatives in these truculent John the Baptists, capable of loading their homicidal blunderbusses with the beads of their rosaries.'

Four military expeditions were sent against these fierce and dismounted bandits and cowboys and their women. The harsh land, which had produced a 'wandering and dissolute, restless and combative, society' provided free ammunition, saltpetre and charcoal, brimstone and lead for bullets. The first sortie against Canudos consisted of little more than a battalion of regular troops, equipped with two Krupp cannon and two machine guns, which dismayed the rebels with their noise and summary execution. The artillery, however, slowed the advance of the column and was useless against the pits and trenches and ambuscades of these supreme guerrilla fighters, whose strength lay 'in their very weakness, in systematic flight, in a baffling strike-and-run attack, with the enemy making his escape by scattering out over a friendly terrain which serves as his protector'. On the outskirts of the rebel shanty city, the troops ran out of supplies and were forced to retreat with heavy losses.

The next expedition was an infantry brigade with fifteen million cartridges and four Krupp field guns and a squadron of cavalry to protect the supply train of ox-drawn waggons. After a march through ambushes from scrubland and mountain pass, the soldiers reached the clay walls of Canudos with its labyrinthine ways. In this maze of tortuous alleys, they were shattered and scattered, bewildered and butchered. As the knights of St Louis had charged from open desert victory into the killing-ground of the narrow streets of Mansourah on the Seventh Crusade, now the Brazilian regulars were ripped apart, piecemeal and higgledy-piggledy. With their commander dead, they fled in a panic-stricken mob back over the wasteland, discarding their weapons as they ran. Only the Krupps cannon defended the rout, until the artillery men were overwhelmed. The rebels were now fully equipped with modern guns and munitions, and they lined the trails to Canudos with the decapitated heads of their victims, whose slashed uniforms were left to flutter on the spines of the thorn bushes.

Da Cunha compared these lost battalions to the Roman legions of Varus, and the tactics of the rebels to those of the Parthians. Such one-time cattle-herders still fought on the move, if not on the hoof, because of the terrain: yet 'these dismounted Centaurs attack the enemy in the same manner in which they would ride down the wild horses of the *pampas*'. The next larger expedition of 5,000 men against Canudos set out in columns of three brigades without scouts, and so fell into the dozens of traps, sprung against them. The soldiers in their cloth uniform were torn apart by cacti and jags of rock, while the leather armour of their foe was never penetrated. The supply train was too heavy and slow, and the troops marched without water in an arid land. As for the heavy guns, da Cunha referred to them as 'Pyrrhic elephants in the form of an artillery which, however imposing it might be, was useless under such conditions as these'. One squadron of lancers, however, was recruited from southern *gauchos*, who could ride the pits and gullies of the northern backlands, and their reconnaissance and sallies were the salvation of the strike force, particularly in rounding up wild cattle for the spit or the pot.

After a series of inconclusive combats, with the rebel snipers flushed out by bayonet charges, two of the columns reached the out-reaches of Canudos and became paralysed in a siege of the twisting city.

This was the struggle of the sinuous boa with the mighty bull. Coiled and captured, the former had but to uncoil its links . . . after which it would seize its prey in those contractile coils, constrict him, then relax its hold and let him once more exhaust himself by pawing up the earth with his horns; and this process of attracting, retracting, leading on, would be continued until the victim had been completely drained of his strength.

The third column came to the rescue and opened a supply route for the relieving waggons. Until their arrival, foraging for the starving troops proved discouraging and murderous. 'The lancers' squadron alone proved effective to a degree. It would daily gallop far and wide over the neighbouring trails. Astride crippled mounts that broke into a limping canter when the spur was applied, the *gauchos* performed true cowboy exploits. Without thought of distance or the changes to be met with, they roamed a region which was wholly unknown to them.' In one action, the lancers came on the rear of a rebel entrenchment and rode down the enemy across the tableland. Yet usually in this war of attrition, all was brutal close encounter, in which the soldiers found the ferocity of the foe offset 'by the savage cruelty of the earth'.

After months of siege, only a thousand of the clay shanties had been taken, and a large force of Brazilian army reinforcements had to be mustered. Even the death of the Prophet Antonio Conselheiro did not quench the fanaticism of his followers: he was believed to have gone as an ambassador to heaven, where God would guarantee him a victory down below. Hovel to hovel, the clay shacks were reduced in what da Cunha saw as a huddled and 'enormous bandits' den'. There an atavistic, obscure and bloody drama of the Stone Age was taking place with the sword and the rifle taking the place of the stone hatchet and the harpoon made of bone, 'but the knife was still there to recall the cutting edge of the ancient flint'. As the Jewish Zealots at Masada, the rebels fought to the last living being. Their tangled skein of a city was reduced to dust and ashes. And the general might report as the Roman did, when salt was sown over the ruins of Carthage: *Delenda est Canudos*.

In his illuminating book on *Primitive Rebels*, Eric Hobsbawm pointed out that the outlaws of Canudos were the only millennial sectarians who were not disappointed. They all died in their Zion, expecting a resurrection, unlike other chiliastic groups, who were given a series of dates for a Second Coming, which never quite came. There were also two extreme types of outlaws. One was as Ned Kelly, who fought for and with his kin, and who worked on blood-feud and revenge as much as on robbery. The other was the 'social' brigand, 'the classical Robin Hood who was and is essentially a peasant rebelling against landlords, usurers, and other representatives of what Thomas More called the "conspiracy of the rich".' Both the bandit and the peasant rebel could become brilliant guerrilla fighters against oppression and poverty. Yet their outbreaks were short-lived. For they could not organise in a sustained political movement.

And so they were butchered along with the cattle, which they tended with more care than the state tended to their welfare.

Two later inspiring bandits of the backlands were celebrated in song and ballad. The first of these was Captain Limpião, whose ferocity against the ranchers instilled some courage in the poor labourers:

> Where Limpião lives
> Worms become brave,
> The monkey fights the jaguar,
> The sheep stands his ground . . .
>
> He killed for play
> Out of pure perversity
> And gave food to the hungry
> With love and charity.

As for his contemporary, Antonio Silvino, his marauding with his gang was worthy of an Armstrong or a Scott with a band of Reivers on the Borders:

> He spared the skin
> Neither of soldier nor civilian,
> His darling was the dagger
> His gift was the gun . . .
> He left the rich as beggars,
> The brave fell at his feet,
> While others fled the country.

CHAPTER SEVENTEEN

Commandos and Camels

The belligerent horse and cattle culture, which had begun in Mongolia some 4,000 years ago, came to a lingering end in Asia and Africa. As on the Great Plains of America, the rifle and the machine-gun and field artillery would vanquish the outriders with their bows and spears and sabres.* On the North-west Frontier of India, the Great Game was being played in the 19th century between imperial Britain and Russia through the mountain passes and among the tribes of Afghanistan. There, Alexander the Great had fought his most difficult battles with the Scythian horsemen. There, the Bengal Lancers and other cavalry regiments would encounter their most intractable foe.

The main Afghan tribes, the Pashtuns and the Baluchis, were still nomads, living beside their flocks in black goat-hair tents, while the northern herders lived in their felt yurts. The two million tribesmen depended on caravans of camels and horses, ponies and donkeys, for trade and warfare. They had antiquated *jezail* muskets and a few rifles and cannon to add to their daggers and swords and spears. Russian meddling in Afghan affairs resulted in an unwise military expedition in 1838 by the Army of the Indus to capture Kabul, a force of 60,000 men with 30,000 camels to carry the provisions.

The occupation of the Hindu Kush, however, proved impossible, as it would prove for other future invaders. The British garrison of 16,500 soldiers and collaborators was penned in an indefensible cantonment near the Royal Gardens on a marsh beneath two mountain ridges. Faced with a widespread rebellion, a withdrawal to the east was negotiated for the January of 1842, a Death March through the snows of the rugged winter passes. Harassed all the way, as Napoleon's army had been on the retreat from Moscow, the British and their followers were finally wiped out in a last stand at Gandamak, near friendly Jalalabad, where the sole survivor escaped to bear news of the disaster.

Colonel Lewis Robert Stacy was the chronicler of the counter-attack on Kabul in 1842, followed by a more organised retreat. After years of wily diplomacy and broken treaties with the frontier tribesmen in an endeavour to secure their support for the British cause, Stacy became a brigade commander in another advance into Central Asia. Usually surrounded by horsemen on the high hills above the passes, the British used shrapnel and grapeshot from their field-pieces to disperse the enemy, who occasionally charged their attackers and were met by machine-gun and rifle fire from the infantry and dismounted cavalry. When the Indian army horsemen attacked, they had the wrong equipment. For in Stacy's opinion, the sword was 'not the weapon for a trooper in Asia; had our men been armed with lances, they would have killed many more and suffered less'.

The expedition to Kabul consisted of two troops of horse artillery, three detachments of light horse, a brigade of infantry and two regiments of grenadiers, and the Madras sappers and miners. Camels and cattle were part of the supply train, which needed constant protection against the many raids in that desolate terrain. Christie's irregular cavalry proved brilliant in their sorties, particularly in an Afghan retreat. So the harriers might be harried. In one encounter, the light horse met a massed force of 5,000 of the enemy mounted men and were put to flight. However valuable were the tactics of the skirmishers, the heavy gun now ruled the field and the mountain. As Colonel Stacy recounted of a final battle, before Kabul fell and had then to be evacuated:

The cavalry this day were of the greatest service. The main body of the force, led by the Major-general, was never less than three miles ahead of the rear-guard, and generally five miles. If the enemy had cut in between the General and the baggage, they would have had comparatively no force to oppose them, and might have caused us considerable loss. In consequence of this distance between the two bodies, our cavalry could not be permitted to charge when Turner's shrapnels made havoc and scattered confusion amongst the enemy; it was as much as the cavalry could do to keep the flanks clear . . . The enemy's cavalry were distinctly seen drawn up with as much regularity as Afghan manoeuvres admit, their right resting upon a very high and precipitous hill, and their left upon a deep *nullah*, with a shallow running stream, the banks in most places perpendicular . . . Leslie's troop of horse artillery was the first to open, and every shot told admirably. The enemy were immediately in confusion; the horse went about, taking a direction between the two ranges of hills, and never pulled bridle until they were well out of shot.

Although there were occasional cavalry charges, mobile field artillery was the beginning of the end of the effective light horseman and raider. This proved to be the shell-case in the second Anglo-Afghan War, which began in 1878 after more Russian intrusion into affairs across the Caucasus. After the murder of the British resident and his entourage, Major-general Roberts marched again on Kabul and put a collaborating Khan in power. Again, Roberts and his force were surrounded by rebels in their cantonment, while a relieving force lost a thousand men to a superior army with thirty field guns at the battle of Maiwand, near to Kandahar, which would be besieged in its turn. The Afghan cavalry enveloped the static British lines, and even the rapid fire of the Martini-Henry breech-loading rifles could not contain their assault, while the big guns were running out of ammunition. In spite of a cavalry charge against the onrush, the British were overwhelmed by a mass assault and forced into a headlong retreat to Kandahar with small rearguard actions holding back the pursuit and another massacre.

Advised of the defeat, Major-general Roberts began a forced march from Kabul with his Bengal Division, for he did not trust the allied Pashtuns to fight against their own countrymen. The British military column covered the route to Kandahar in a mere twenty-two days at a rate of thirteen miles each twenty-four hours without much opposition. The steady Indian army with its artillery reduced the enemy ranks until they fled, pursued by the Bombay cavalry brigade for fifteen miles back into the mountains. This last major action ended the Afghan wars, in which five British and twenty-five native cavalry regiments were involved.* The lessons of these encounters were not learned in time for the next major colonial conflict.

The Boer War began with a botched Border raid. In the Victorian era, the discovery of precious metals and diamonds in the Orange Free State had led to a mining stampede, as had taken place in the Gold Rush to California. Yet the incoming prospectors, now called Outlanders, were not exploiting a wilderness. They were invading a federated state of expert cattlemen, somewhat after the breed of Austin's early ranchers in Texas. On the Great Trek, the original Dutch colonists in South Africa had struck out from British control. Across desert and plain and mountain, they had been seeking their liberty on a long passage in their covered waggons, and as the American pioneers had to fight their way past the Sioux and the Comanches, so the Boers had gunned down the Hottentots and then the Zulus in the battle of Blood River. They had set up a puritanical South African Republic above Cape Colony and

Natal on the sea, and they strove to control and tax the flood of free-booters in pursuit of personal riches and imperial greed.

Following his dream of a railroad, bisecting all Africa and stretching from Cape Town to Cairo, Cecil Rhodes had already outflanked the Boer Republic by sending his outriders through Bechuanaland and north of the Limpopo river to a country, which would be named after him – Rhodesia. One of his colonels in the defeat by machine-guns of the Matabele chief Lobengula was a Dr Jameson, whose easy triumph flattered his vanity, while his grasp of reality was as substantial as a mirage in the Kalahari Desert. In the fresh mining city of Johannesburg, the Outlanders promised to rise against the Boers on New Year's Day, 1896, if Jameson led a raid of the Bechuanaland and Mashona Border Police to the rescue. A clever and cynical petition for help was concocted for this pre-emptive attack:

> The position of matters in this State has become so critical that we are assured that, at no distant period, there will be a conflict between the Government and the Outlander population . . . Thousands of unarmed men, women and children of our race will be at the mercy of well-armed Boers; while property of enormous value will be in the greatest peril. We feel that we are justified in taking any steps to prevent the shedding of blood, and to ensure the protection of our rights.

The Jameson Raid was a fiasco, and the Johannesburg rising fizzled out. Across the frontier, Jameson could only muster 500 mounted men. His advance was met by gathering Boer forces. Surrounded on a farm at Vlakfontein, the British Maxim machine-guns proved ineffective against accurate rifle-fire from weathered ranchers, used to killing quick wild game for the pot. With seventy casualties against eight Boers, Jameson surrendered and soon started a war, which would develop the best horse guerrilla tactics yet seen in the *commandos*, and the notorious means of their whittling down, the concentration camp.

The British generals had little idea of how to cope with the mobile and largely self-sufficient Boer trooper, used to living off the land. Generally equipped with a superior Mauser rifle instead of the lances and sabres and revolvers of the outdated and imported cavalry from the Indian Army, the free-wheeling member of the *commando* lived on ground meal and fresh or dried meat, *biltong*. As the Border Reivers, he attacked in ambushes and slipped away from the charges of his pursuers. Those best equipped to counter this wily strategy were the Australian and Canadian volunteer cattlemen. As one wrote in *Digger*:

> Ex-frontier cavalryman myself, with further experience as cowboy in both the United States and the north-west Canada, and also as stockrider in Australia, I have never for a moment doubted that in the raising of an irregular force lay the solution of England's problem . . . With inherent horsemanship, inherent wild-land craft, mounted on his own pony-bronco of Canada or brumbie of Australia – the Canadian ranch-hand, the Australian stockrider, shearer, station rouseabout might easily become the quintessence of a useful and operative force against a semi-guerrilla enemy.
>
> A pair of cord breeches, a couple of shirts, his big hat, and a cartridge-filled belt, Winchester carbine, a pony of the sort that can be run into a white sweat, and staggering, tremble, and then be kicked out to nuzzle for grass or die – that's what your man wants. . . Why, each is of the other, horse and man, each apart, a thing inept.
>
> Orthodoxy against the Boers in military operations doesn't wash. Aldershot-cum-Sandhurst-cum-Sudan-cum-India and War Office tactics fall flat. The Boer is here, there, and everywhere, not to be followed by 'crushing forces' – only to be checked and turned and tracked and harried and hustled by a brother Boer. There is scarce a Canadian ranch-hand but owns a pony of bronco breed, scarce an Australian station-hand of any decent calibre but owns or can procure a tough and serviceable semi-'brumbie' mount.
>
> And will these men volunteer? Yes, plenty of them, and those that won't, can't . . . Arm them and saddle them, men of the wild-lands and prairies, Work them van, flank, and rear . . . Even where the war is over, and our regulars and reserves must return, make these men into protective police for a while, officered not by orthodoxy but by knowledge and experience. They will 'learn the country'. They will evolve scouts from among them who shall make no mistakes. They will give to England what she needs in times like these – to come again or not.

The author of *Digger: The Story of the Australian Soldier* offset two actions in the Boer War, the defeat at Stormberg and the victory at Sunnyside. In the first action, a large British force, on duty for thirty hours, was marched on a seven-hour trek without scouts into a Boer ambush. Ordered into a frontal attack, the English soldiers were massacred by rebel rifles and pom-poms and machine-guns. As long-range weapons had been invented, no modern light horseman could understand why the British generals acted 'as if they were storming a citadel defended by men with clubs'. Even the retreat was organised in columns on the road. The troops did not scatter, making themselves difficult targets and sniping back from safe places. Their close formation was still their murder.

At Sunnyside a year later in 1900, the Queensland Mounted Infantry attacked the Boer position on three sides under cover, 'cautious as tigers and nimble as cats'. Given this persistent and deadly advance, the Boers retired from their *laager* – wagons drawn in an armoured circle as on the pioneer prairies – and then they retreated, as those fighting a guerrilla war should. The official Report declared: 'The dexterity of the Queenslanders was remarkable; they stalked the enemy as a sportsman would stalk a deer, criticizing their own fire and the fire of the foe with coolness and interest.' They lost only three dead.

When the aged General Cronje was trapped at Paardeberg by Lord Roberts, the veteran of the Afghan campaigns, he had to surrender with 4,000 men, only to be told: 'You have made a gallant defence, sir.' Yet Cronje should have trusted to the Boer genius for light cavalry tactics. A pitched battle had to be avoided at all costs, as the British army had most of the big guns. One war ballad praised the artillery:

> We three! We three!
> Grim Trinity!
> The Common and Shrapnel and Lyddite Shell
> Shriek over the blue,
> Terrible, true,
> With our summons to heaven or hell.

With the inexorable British advance to the heart of the Transvaal, what the young war correspondent Winston Churchill most feared came to pass. 'We desire a speedy peace,' he wrote in the *Morning Post*, 'and the last thing we want is that this war should enter on a guerrilla phase.' Under four brilliant commanders, Christian de Wet and Louis Botha and J.C. Smuts and de la Rey, the *commandos* ranged the length and breadth of South Africa for the first three years of the twentieth century. Forty thousand troopers ran rings round the heavier British cavalry and marching columns. Botha's mounted infantry charged at Bakenlaagte in a sweep a mile long, destroying the British guns and a company of the Buffs. At Groenkop, de Wet's *commando* overwhelmed a whole camp of Yeomanry in a night attack. And at Tweebosch, de la

Rey and his mounted horse surprised Lord Methuen's column of local outriders and Northumbrian infantry, taking 600 prisoners and waggonloads of necessary munitions.

Yet these were some of the few major actions. Every week, there were dozens of skirmishes between the marauding and scattered *commandos* and the less mobile imperial forces. The new commander-in-chief, Lord Kitchener, had to find a policy, which cut off supplies from the scavenging Boers, who were living as the Reivers had, raiding horses and cattle, but welcome in most of the friendly farmhouses of the *veldt*. Kitchener applied what had been done by the Romans and suggested by Elizabethan commanders for the northern Marches. He gave orders to ravage the homesteads and destroy the crops and drive off the stock from the Boer ranches. He had the wives and children rounded up, as herds of sheep and cattle, and then penned into large *laagers*, now called concentration camps. And he had constructed a modern Hadrian's Wall, blockhouses of corrugated iron filled with shingle and connected by telephone and barbed wire in a barrier that stretched from Portuguese East Africa to the western Bushman Territories of the Atlantic coast.

The concentration camps led to international infamy, and would inspire the modern strategies of mass murder and regroupment. By October, 1901, there were 118,000 white and 43,000 black people herded into disease-ridden encampments. The Boer children were dying faster than flies of chicken-pox and enteric, malaria and pneumonia, fever and measles. At one time, one-third of the occupants of some camps were not surviving, while by the close of the war, at least 20,000 prisoners were dead. Although this policy of containment and scorched earth was quite effective, its brutality fired the resistance of the *commandos*, determined to continue their raids to the bitter end, and some of them, beyond that.

The most remarkable account of the life of a guerrilla in the saddle was written by Deneys Reitz, a member of the Africander Cavalry Corps, formed after Cronje's defeat and the assault on the Boer homeland. In Reitz's first two actions, the British field-guns swept away the skirmishers, and they were pursued by enemy dragoons, their sabres in their hands. The following day, Reitz managed to help bring down a couple of troopers by rifle fire. 'They were both Canadians, badly wounded, one of whom told me that many thousands of their people, as well as Australians and other Colonial forces, had volunteered for the war, as if the odds against us were not heavy enough already.'

The retreat into the Transvaal went on, with the Africander Cavalry Corps losing a third of its strength within a week of fighting. Stocking up his saddle-bags with meal and *biltong*, Reitz and a comrade ran into an English patrol and brought down another two troopers with Mauser-fire, before managing to escape. They galloped away across the sodden *veldt*, outpacing 'five hundred English horsemen, for in spite of our long night's journey, their heavy troop horses were no match for our hardier and lighter mounts'. Having had his commander captured, Reitz did not fret, for 'with the Boers each man is practically his own commander, so the loss did not weigh heavily upon us, and having shaken off our pursuers, we rode along westward at our leisure'.

The reformed *commando* now saw pillars of smoke rising behind the advancing English columns. The farmhouses were burning in the rear of the enemy. 'Towards noon word spread that, not only were they destroying all before them, but were actually capturing and sending away the women and children.' A more terrible chapter of the war was opening. If the intention was to undermine the morale of the *commandos*, it had the opposite effect. 'Instead of weakening, they became only the more resolved to hold out, and this policy, instead of shortening the war, prolonged it by a year or more.'

The English could only crawl in the wake of the Boer horsemen, but when the news spread that the English were clearing the country, the plain became 'alive with wagons, carts, and vehicles of all descriptions, laden with women and children, while great numbers of horses, cattle, and sheep were being hurried onward by native herdboys, homes and ricks going up in flames behind them'. General Botha directed the refugees to make for Swaziland, while his forces scattered and retired before the slow and leaden progress of the enemy, expending 'their blow in thin air'. This strategy made the drive go to pieces during the next few days with the foe groping after the elusive Boers, who 'easily evaded the lumbering columns plodding through the mud far in the rear'.

The large *commando* was now split up into smaller groups, which had to live by foraging for sheep roaming about the *veldt*, and by gathering the maize from uncropped fields. Reitz and his comrades decided to free-lance in a raid south into the imperial centre of Cape Colony. They protected another escaping waggon train from the English cavalry, and they broke in remounts from the wild horses, common on the mountainsides by the Elandsberg. There they met up with General Smuts and his *commando* of 300 seasoned fighters, also bent on a flying raid into the Cape, in order to relieve the pressure in the north, and perhaps scout the ground for a major invasion in the future.

On their trek, this *commando* was ambushed by an equal force of mounted Basuto yeomanry, armed with battle-axes and assegais and knobkerries as well as rifles. Among the stragglers, Reitz had to gallop for his life along a deep creek or *spruit*, leaving some of his comrades to be mutilated 'for medicine'. Then Smuts and his men overran a camp of 200 of the 17th Lancers, a crack regiment, and they were transformed into 'giants refreshed. We had ridden into action that morning at our last gasp and we emerged refitted from head to heel. We all had fresh horses, fresh rifles, clothing, saddlery, boots and more ammunition than we could carry away, as well as supplies for every man.'

Such living off the enemy had its present dangers, as Reitz recounted in his next chapter, called 'Moss-trooping' after the Scots Border raiders. The *commando* now wore red and khaki cavalry kit, and joked that they were 'English-killing Dragoons'. Lord Kitchener issued a proclamation ordering the death penalty for all Boers caught in British uniforms. They were shelled by an armoured train, crossing the *veldt*, as the Cossacks of the White Army would be on the steppes by the Reds after the Russian Revolution. Skirmishing towards Cape Town, they fell ill on unripe fruit and were forced back over the mountain gorges by an enemy force with artillery and machine-guns. From the peaks, they saw the Indian Ocean at last, and they foraged down the valleys.

A patrol of three men was captured and executed for the wearing of the khaki. The survivors broke out to the north, slaughtering English scouts on the way back to the cactus of the Karroo. Saved by the masquerade of his uniform from a swarm of English troopers, the lone Reitz galloped back on his grey pony to alert his comrades and hold up the enemy charge. Both sides dismounted for an exchange of rifle-fire. In quick retreat, Smuts and his *commando* scattered in order to avoid hot pursuit, hoping to reunite on a later day.

Such was 'Moss-trooping' in the Boer War. The tactics of the *commandos* were those of the Reivers – mobility, harrying, dispersal, ambush, surprise attack, raiding and living off the land. Even so, 'Lord Kitchener's relentless policy of attrition was slowly breaking the hearts of the *commandos*'. General Smuts was summoned to a peace conference, as was Reitz's father among other delegates from the Transvaal and the Free State. A peace treaty was a foregone conclusion.

Every representative had the same disastrous tale to tell of starvation, lack of ammunition, horses and clothing, and of how the great blockhouse system was strangling their efforts to carry on the war. Added to this was the heavy death-roll among the women and children, and the universal ruin that had overtaken the country. Every homestead was burned, all crops and livestock destroyed, and there was nothing left but to bow to the inevitable.

Of the sting of defeat, Reitz would not speak, but there was no whining. All the *commandos* accepted the verdict of the Peace Conference stoically. Required to surrender their weapons, the 'moss-troopers' fired away their ammunition and smashed their rifle-butts and signed an undertaking that they would abide by the terms of the treaty, if they wished to remain in South Africa. Reitz and his father refused to sign and were sent into exile in Portuguese East Africa. The father ended in America, the son and his brother in French-occupied Madagascar with a company of Senegalese soldiers, sent against rebels in 'lakes and forests; swamps teeming with crocodiles, and great open plains grazed by herds of wild cattle'. *Plus ça change, plus c'est autre chose.* Disgusted with this new imperialism, the two brothers Reitz eked out a living, transporting goods by ox-cart in fever-stricken forests and across mountains, sodden by eternal rain. In his spare time in 1903, the author wrote this forgotten masterpiece about the man and the horse and their land, on which they both had to survive.

Two superb cavalry campaigns put an end to the tactics of the Reivers before the impact of artillery and the machine-gun, the aeroplane and the tank. One was in the Holy Lands of Arabia and Palestine, the other was where eastern Europe merged into the Russian steppes. The fame of Lawrence of Arabia and his camel raiders permeated the whole world. In a preliminary assault on Mesopotamia in 1914, the British cavalry of the Indian army had performed poorly against the Turkish forces. A cavalry brigade supported by two infantry divisions managed to capture Basra and advance up the biblical Tigris and Euphrates rivers towards Baghdad, but they were driven back to Kut-el-Amara, and besieged there. After five months, they surrendered, trapped as rabbits in a warren. Although the Indian Army later took Baghdad, the best of the horsemen were transferred to General Allenby's attack from Egypt up towards Syria along the Mediterranean coast.

The guerrilla exploits of Lawrence of Arabia with his mounted camel marauders became legendary in history. He was a romantic writer as much as he was a bonny fighter. Yet he fuelled a real Arab resistance after the sack of the Awali suburb outside Medina by a Turkish general, who had already practised his atrocities against Armenians in the north – a matter of rape and butchery and fire. As Lawrence described the onslaught, led by Sharif Feisal as the Arab commander:

The first rush on Medina had been a desperate business. The Arabs were ill-armed and short of ammunition, the Turks in great force. At the height of the crisis the Arabs were thrust out beyond the walls. The Turks then opened fire on them with their artillery; and the Arabs, unused to this new arm, became terrified . . . [After Awali, the] bitter taste of the Turkish mode of war sent a shock across Arabia; for the first rule of Arab war was that women were inviolable: the second that the lives and honour of children too young to fight with men were to be spared: the third, that property impossible to carry off should be left undamaged. The Arabs with Feisal perceived that they were opposed to new customs, and fell back out of touch to gain time to readjust themselves. There could no longer be any question of submission: the sack of Awali had opened blood-feud upon blood-feud, and put on them the duty of fighting to the end of their force: but it was plain now that it would be a long affair, and that with muzzle-loading guns for sole weapons, they could hardly expect to win.

Lawrence was instructed to organise a war in the Hejaz, supporting the Arab raiders with machine and light automatic Lewis guns against an enemy, supplied by the Germans with heavy artillery. He knew what he was taking on among the hill tribes. 'Their acquisitive recklessness made them keen on booty, and whetted them to tear up railways, plunder caravans, and steal camels; but they were too free-minded to endure command, or to fight in team. A man who could fight well by himself made generally a bad soldier.' The only things which stood against their eventual roving triumph were the big guns. Even if the rocky barren country suited the style of snipers and camel-raiders against an entrenched enemy, which had no stomach for a rough-and-tumble war, the Arabs were frightened of artillery. 'They thought weapons destructive in proportion to their noise. They were not afraid of bullets, nor indeed overmuch of dying: just the manner of death by shell-fire was unendurable.'

Lawrence had brought across to the Red Sea coast four Krupp mountain and ten machine-guns, rolls of barbed wire and two tons of explosives, 8,000 rifles and three million rounds of ammunition. With 5,000 outriders and 400 more camels in the baggage train and another 5,000 men on foot, the little army under Feisal moved towards the vital Hejaz railway and its terminus at Aqaba port. As Lawrence noted:

The Arab war was geographical, and the Turkish Army an accident. Our aim was to seek the enemy's weakest material link and bear only on that till time made their whole length fail. Our largest resources, the Bedouin on whom our war must be built, were unused to formal operations, but had assets of mobility, toughness, self-assurance, knowledge of the country, intelligent courage. With them dispersal was strength. Consequently we must extend our front to its maximum, to impose on the Turks the longest possible passive defence, since that was, materially, their most costly form of war.

The tactics were a supreme guerrilla strategy. Outside Ma'an, where the telephone and telegraph lines were cut, the Arabs fought on the hillsides under a cruel sun. 'We ran up and down to supply our lack of numbers by mobility.' The enemy's enclosed valley was even hotter than the open hills. 'They were Turks, men of white meat, little apt for warm weather. So we clung to them, and did not let them move or mass or sortie against us cheaply.' The Arabs now laughed at the little mountain guns firing above them, the shells bursting uselessly in air. 'They could do nothing valid in return. We were no targets for their rifles, since we moved with speed eccentrically.'

With such a description of modern mounted Reiver tactics, Lawrence summed up millennia of skirmishing strategy. Move, surround, snipe, escape. Using arrows or bullets, nothing had changed for the rider, although armoured cars were now coming. General Allenby provided two Rolls Royce mechanical monsters with tyres, which found the desert terrain more difficult to penetrate than did the hooves of camels. The British commander was praised by Lawrence. 'He was full of Western ideas of gun power and weight – the worst training for our war – but, as a cavalryman, was already half-persuaded to throw up the new school, in this different world of Asia . . . along the worn road of manoeuvre and movement.'

Under the command of Allenby, the Egyptian Expeditionary Force took no new road to Jerusalem. In the words of one war correspondent, who accompanied the soldiers and the camels, the horses and the armoured cars:

We fought on the fields which had been the battlegrounds of Egyptian and Assyrian armies, where Hittites, Ethiopians, Persians, Parthians, and Mongols poured out their blood in times when kingdoms were strong by the sword alone. The Ptolemies invaded Syria by this way, and here the Greeks put their colonising hands on the country. Alexander the Great made his route to Egypt. Pompey marched over the Maritime Plain and inaugurated that Roman rule which lasted for centuries; till Islam made its wide irresistible sweep in the seventh century. Then the Crusaders fought and won and lost, and Napoleon's ambitions in the East were wrecked just beyond the plains . . . When the Commander-in-Chief had to decide how to take Jerusalem, we saw the British force move along precisely the same route that had been taken by armies since the time when Joshua overcame the Amorites and the day was lengthened by the sun and moon standing still till the battle was won. Geography had its influence on the strategy of today as completely as it did when armies were not cumbered with guns and mechanical transport.

General Allenby advanced near the coastline towards Gaza and beyond in the last great cavalry campaign of modern warfare, using the mobility and shock charge of his horsemen as Godfrey de Bouillon and King Richard the Third of England had done. The Australian Light Horse would gallop into the Turkish ranks with their sabres, shouting, 'Allah, you bastards, we will give you Allah,' in their version of the Templar battle cry of 'Beauséant'. At Huj, the Warwickshire and Worcestershire Yeomanry charged mountain and machine-guns, hacking the Turkish loaders into silence with fearful losses. The Dorset and Buckingham and Berkshire Yeomanries repeated that suicidal assault to take the Mughar-Katrah Ridge They were emulating the berserk gallops of the Military Orders into Muslim defences in the time of the Kingdom of Jerusalem.

Lawrence of Arabia had enlightened Allenby on how his mounted guerrillas could harass the Turkish flanks as Saladin had the Crusaders, while the general's favourite reading strategy of ancient campaigns in the Middle East was the Old Testament and the *Historical Geography of the Holy Land*. In those texts, there were many warnings against leaving the coastal plains for the Judean Hills, where manoeuvre was limited and ambush was probable. But finally, the mountains had to be crossed to take Jerusalem, where the German commander von Falkenhayn had set up his headquarters in the German hospice on the Mount of Olives, while the Turkish headquarters were in the French hospice of Nôtre Dame. For the German and the Turkish forces had set up a defensive line at Nebi Samuel, where the prophet Samuel was now buried beneath the dome of a mosque, and where King Richard had turned back from reaching the Holy City on the Third Crusade.

Allenby did not intend to repeat the tragedies of the past. He would force the surrender of Jerusalem in December, 1917, without an assault. There would be no new massacre in the Holy City. The Allied cause could not stand such bad propaganda. As he instructed his commanders: 'On no account is any risk to be run of bringing the City of Jerusalem or its immediate environs within the area of operations.' He did not know that von Falkenhayn had orders not to be besieged in the Holy City and risk its sacred treasures. Hand-to-hand fighting on the ridges and failed Turkish counterattacks allowed Allenby's divisions almost to surround Jerusalem, leaving an escape route for the enemy forces, which abandoned their base.

Allenby refused to tell the world press that his capture of Jerusalem was a Crusade, although he was universally hailed as the Last Crusader. He was not only dependent on his Muslim troops from India, but on the Arab irregulars owing allegiance to Sharif Feisal, whom Lawrence called the Armed Prophet. Jerusalem had fallen peacefully, all the holy places were protected. Now the military objective was to advance on Damascus and Aleppo. Again Allenby followed crusading strategy, using his cavalry supported by sea power to progress along the shoreline, taking Acre and Haifa on the way north.

There was no new defeat at the Horns of Hittin, for Tiberias was evacuated before the Christian advance. There was a final great cavalry battle over the ruins of Megiddo, or Armageddon, prophesied as the site of the millennial struggle. In the advance on Damascus, Lawrence of Arabia had already been transferred from camel to armoured car. The Royal Air Force now turned the Turkish retreat into a rout. So Lawrence described the finale of Reiver strategy, a slaughter which would be repeated time and again until the recent Gulf Wars against Iraq:

> The holocaust of the miserable Turks fell in the valley by which Esdraelon drained to the Jordan by Beisan. The modern motor road, the only way of escape for the Turkish divisions, was scalloped between cliff and precipice in a murderous defile. For four hours our aeroplanes replaced one another in series above the doomed columns: nine tons of small bombs or grenades and fifty thousand rounds of Small Arms Ammunition were rained upon them. When the smoke had cleared it was seen that the organization of the enemy had melted away. They were a dispersed horde of trembling individuals, hiding for their lives in every fold of the vast hills. Nor did their commanders ever rally them again. When our cavalry entered the silent valley next day they could count ninety guns, fifty lorries, nearly a thousand carts abandoned with all their belongings. The R.A.F lost four killed. The Turks lost a corps.

After the iniquitous treaties in the wake of the First World War, the meat of the Near East was mainly carved up between the colonial powers of Britain and France. In relatively independent Transjordan, however, the enclave under the control of Feisal's brother Sharif Abdullah, the Bedouin raiders would have to learn the last lessons of their compromise with modern times. British army officers set up a Reserve Mobile Force, which was later called the Arab Legion. Under the successor to Lawrence, a certain John Glubb Pasha, even the Bedouin were mostly persuaded, as the Borderers had been in the 17th century, to give up camel- and sheep-raiding and blood-feuds for a more legal existence. Yet as riches lay in the size of the herds, rustling had been a form of income redistribution. As Glubb wrote: 'We had thought the abolition of raiding would increase the security of desert life, but we discovered, unexpectedly, that raiding had not only been a pastime for the chivalry of Arabia, but also a social-security system, of which our ill-timed intervention had destroyed the balance.'

The discovery of oil would change the values of wealth, while the modern weapons introduced by Allenby would make the camel charge redundant. The advent of the machine-gun and the armoured car and the aeroplane would end the four millennia which had been ruled by securing water and food supplies for hoof and hide and rider. 'To the Bedouin,' Glubb testified once more, 'grazing for his camel is life and soul; he will, and daily does, risk death to secure it.' Now petroleum would take the place of grass as the fuel and fodder of diplomacy and strategy.

The transition would be demonstrated in the ultimate Cossack wars of the Russian Revolution. When the British backed the White Army of General Denikin in the Ukraine, their target was the oil riches of Baku on the Caspian Sea. The Cossacks had been the strike fist of the Tsar's police, but now they joined both the Red and the White armies, while marauding as Green bandits between the opposed forces. These latterday Reivers were led by 'Papa' Makhno, a warlord who lived on plunder. His irregulars were anarchists as well as bandits, and they did hold sway in the Southern Ukraine for three years. Power lay in agrarian peasant communes, which were set against all authority, and these had to be eliminated by the centralised Communists in the end. As Makhno was told by his supporters: 'After we threw out the fool Nicky Romanoff, they said, another fool tried to take his place, Kerensky, but he had to go too. Who will now play the fool at our expense? The Lord Lenin? . . . We cannot do without some fool. The towns have no other purpose than this. Their system is bad. They favour the existence of the government.'

The Lord Lenin in Moscow, however, provided Trotsky with his armoured trains, and the fire power of these weapons of mass destruction persuaded many bands of the freebooters to become Communist 'moss troopers', somewhat under the control of commissars. One of their leaders, Budyonny, would even serve as a Marshal in the Red Army in the later era of tanks and heavy artillery. As Trotsky wrote: 'the guerrilla movement was a necessary and adequate weapon in the first period of the Civil War. The fight against the counter-revolution, which had not yet found itself and could put no compact armed masses into the field, was waged with the assistance of small, independent bodies of troops. This kind of warfare demanded self-sacrifice, initiative and independence. But as the war grew in scope, it gradually came to need proper organisation and discipline.'

Although Trotsky had initially been opposed to the recruitment of Cossack bands for the socialist cause, in 1918 his slogan had changed to 'Proletarians, to horse!' The mounted guerrillas under the converted Budyonny and Makhno proved effective against Denikin's Cossack rebels, and both the White armies in southern and eastern Russia were destroyed by a combination of cavalry and armoured trains, transporting fanatical infantry. Yet the invasion of Poland by the new Soviet Union in support of a further revolution in Germany proved a disaster. Although the Red Army deployed some 800,000 men, of which 150,000 were on a horse, they were defeated by Marshal Pilsudski and the Polish cavalry.

At first, Pilsudski underrated the Red Cossacks, writing that the victories of Budyonny's horsemen 'in previous Soviet theatres of war were due rather to internal disintegration of their opponents' forces than to any real value in their fighting methods'. In fact, the Red Cossacks did well on the south-western front in Poland, which Pilsudski abandoned to its fate, while concentrating his forces on the Vistula river in the defence of Warsaw against the main Red Army. Too bent on plunder to attack the Poles in the rear, Budyonny and his Cossacks lost the war by cantering through Galicia, looting and burning all the way. By the time they returned to be decimated in futile charges against the Polish fortifications at Lvov, the rest of the Red Army was already in full retreat back over the borders towards the eastern plains. As one recorder stated of Budyonny and this last mounted attack force:

His cavalry army was an ingenious combination of Genghis Khan's tactics with the elements of modern warfare. His conglomerated groups of horsemen fought with rifles and machine-guns that were carried in the old primitive waggons of the steppes. Their offensive power lay in the onslaughts they made with couched lanches and brandished sabres. Mounted on the small breed of steppe horses or on bloodstock from the Ukraine studs, they hurtled through the enemy's lines at breakneck speed as they charged over the vast steppes, whose grass sang the story of how:

> On many a night of stars and cloudy day,
> Budyonny's horse charged bravely in the fray.

And finally, they would be put back to pasture by the fire-power of the new mobile machines of war on land and in the air.

CHAPTER EIGHTEEN

The Machine and the Hunt

At the beginning of the British Industrial Revolution and the French Revolution before the Napoleonic Wars, the Prime Minister, William Pitt the Younger, took a wise precautionary decision. The British workers at the new powerlooms and the booming ironworks and coal mines might well be influenced by the Jacobin cry of 'Liberty, Equality and Fraternity', ranted across the Channel. In all the major cities, barracks began to be constructed for housing the infantry and the local Yeomanry. These were mostly built in the form of a hollow square, the usual formation of the Redcoats on the defensive in battle. This plan allowed for a barricade, if the army quarters were surrounded; it also prevented the garrison from deserting or going too easily over the wall. And in the case of an insurrection, similar to the Parisian mob storming the Bastille, and in the absence of a local police force, there would be armed men nearby, ordered to put down any disturbance under the terms of the anti-Jacobite Riot Act, which allowed the military to disperse any group of more than twelve people.

Another Wellesley, the later Duke of Wellington, had not much use for the cavalry during his victories in Spain, except at the Battle of Salamanca, where he complimented the commander of a dashing charge with the words: 'By God, Cotton, I never saw anything so beautiful in my life: the day is *yours*.' Generally, Wellington growled about his horsemen, writing after the end of hostilities that his dragoons were inferior to the French, for 'they could gallop, but they could not preserve their order'. They might win a brief advantage, but they could not rally against a counter-attack. The preferred weapon of the light horse was still the short sabre; the new carbines were rarely used.

In the final climactic Battle of Waterloo, indeed, the French hussars could not break the British squares. There had been a dashing charge of the Scots Greys against a whole army corps of *cuirassiers*, but a French hussar counter-assault had slashed their scattered ranks to ribbons. The other mounted Brigade of the Household Cavalry, the Reds and the Blues with the Dragoon Guards, performed better, routing their opponents, but retiring in good order. English musketry and artillery broke Marshal Ney's attack on the Redcoat squares with his heavy horse, while the last throw of the Imperial Guard into the guns fared no better. With the Prussian army already closing on his right flank, Napoleon's army disintegrated in a panic. The Emperor's *Official Bulletin* showed no remorse about the collapse, which he ascribed to his men:

> Noticing the astonishing disorganization, the enemy immediately attacked with their cavalry and increased the disorder, and owing to night coming on, such was the confusion that it was impossible to rally the troops and point out their error to them . . . all was thrown away by a moment of mad terror.

The folly of a charge against artillery, also the bond between man and horse in war, was told with pity in a *Journal of the Waterloo Campaign* by Cavalié Mercer, the commander of a troop of horse artillery. Each of his field pieces fired 700 rounds from red-hot barrels at two assaults of the French squadrons. 'Suddenly a dead mass of cavalry appeared for an instant on the main ridge, and then came sweeping down the slope in swarms, reminding me of an enormous surf bursting over the prostrate hull of a stranded vessel, and then running, hissing and foaming, up the beach . . . There were lancers, amongst them, hussars, and dragoons – it was a complete *mêlée*.' Protected by two squares of Redcoat infantry, the gunners continued to fire:

> The effect was terrible. Nearly the whole leading rank fell at once; and the round-shot penetrating the column, carried confusion throughout its extent . . . Those who pushed forward over the heaps of carcasses of men and horses gained but a few paces in advance, there to fall in their turn . . . like grass before the mower's scythe. When the horse alone was killed, we could see the *cuirassiers* divesting themselves of the encumbrance and making their escape on foot . . . Many cleared everything and rode through us; many came plunging forward only to fall, man and horse, close to the muzzles of our guns, but the majority again turned . . . The same confusion, struggle amongst themselves, and slaughter prevailed as before, until gradually they disappeared over the brow of the hill.

The Duke of Wellington also knew that the aftermath of victory was worse than the winning of it. From his troop, Mercer had lost two-thirds of his 200 horses and a third of his gunners. He watched some of the wounded move, but the sight was heart-rending. There were also horses to claim his compassion, 'mild, patient, enduring. Some lay on the ground with their entrails hanging out, and yet they lived. These would occasionally attempt to rise, but, like their human bed-fellows, quickly falling back again, would lift their poor heads'. One animal had lost both his hind legs and sat on his tail, neighing with melancholy throughout the night. Although Mercer knew that killing the horse would be merciful, he could not bring himself to do it. 'Blood enough I had seen shed in the last six-and-thirty-hours, and sickened at the thought of shedding more. There, then, he sat as we left the ground, neighing after us, as if reproaching our desertion of him in the hour of need.'

The defeat of Napoleon and the restoration of the Bourbon monarchy encouraged another massive and bleeding repression in England. There were only four years between Waterloo and what was called 'Peterloo' in Manchester, the killing and maiming, mostly by a vanguard of the local mounted Yeomanry, of hundreds of a large crowd of unemployed weavers, gathered to listen to a speech by Henry 'Orator' Hunt, pressing for a Reform Bill to ensure an increase in Parliamentary Suffrage. Unlike the regular Hussars there, the Yeomanry were recruited from mill-owners and merchants, shop- and inn-keepers. At least, eleven of the crowd were killed, while some 500 protestors were wounded, mainly by sabre cuts or horses' hooves. As one witness recorded: 'They cut down and trampled down the people; and then it was to end just as cutting and trampling the furze bushes on a common would end.'

The instigator, Henry Hunt, was forced to run the gauntlet between the clubs of special officers, led by the infamous Deputy Constable, Joseph Nadin, who was accused of profiting from the sale of Tyburn tickets, a reward system for securing higher sentences for suspect criminals. He was also thought to have provoked the largest death toll of the Luddites in Lancashire, when after more arson, seven of them had been killed by the military. This act of gratuitous violence at Peterloo, however, was to produce outrage across the nation, also protest songs and a poem of hatred, hardly equalled since the troublesome query of the medieval Peasants' Revolt:

> When Adam delved and Eve span,
> Who was then the gentleman?

Sung to the tune of 'The Battle of Waterloo', the Luddites or machine-breakers of the period, came up with a ballad against the Deputy Constable and the Yeomanry:

'Twas on the sixteenth day of August, Eighteen hundred and nineteen,
A meeting held in Peter Street was glorious to be seen,
Joe Nadin and his bulldogs, which you might plainly see,
And on the other side stood the bloody cavalry.

> With Henry Hunt we'll go, my boys,
> With Henry Hunt we'll go.
> We'll mount the cap of Liberty,
> In spite of Nadin Joe.

The exiled Percy Bysshe Shelley was more bitter about the mass transportation and death penalty inflicted by the 'Framebreakers' Bill' of 1812 on the Luddites. To the poet, the Foreign Secretary under Lord Liverpool, Viscount Castlereagh, and the King were responsible for an early form of genocide.

> I met Murder on the way –
> He had a mask like Castlereagh –
> Very smooth he looked, yet grim;
> Seven blood-hounds followed him:
>
> All were fat; and well they might
> Be in admirable plight,
> For one by one, and two by two,
> He tossed the human hearts to chew
> Which from his wide cloak he drew . . .
>
> Last came Anarchy: he rode
> On a white horse, splashed with blood;
> He was pale even to the lips,
> Like Death in the Apocalypse.
>
> And he wore a kingly crown;
> And in his grasp a sceptre shone;
> On his brow this mark I saw –
> 'I AM GOD, AND KING, AND LAW!'

> With a pace stately and fast,
> Over English land he passed,
> Trampling to a mire of blood
> The adoring multitude.

Riots of the early 19th century in England were against the two mechanical revolutions in industry and agriculture, which were causing mass unemployment, exacerbated by the post-war depression. The Luddites were the hand loom weavers and spinners, thrown out of work by water-powered spinning-jenny frames, and gig-mills, which replaced the raising of the nap of woven cloth by the teazle, a dried thistle top. Another street ballad sang of their unrest:

> O, cropper lads of great renown,
> Who love to drink good ale that's brown
> And strike each haughty tyrant down,
> With hatchet, pike and gun.

> What though the specials still advance,
> And soldiers nightly round us prance,
> The cropper lads still lead the dance,
> With hatchet, pike and gun.

> O, the cropper lads for me,
> And gallant lads they be,
> With lusty stroke the shear-frames broke,
> The cropper lads for me.

Weavers and shearers smashed more than a thousand engines, and they torched some of William Blake's 'dark satanic mills'. As a discharged soldier wrote to his Member of Parliament: 'The burning of factorys or setting fire to the property of people we know is not right, but Starvation forces Nature to do that which he would not, nor would it reach his thoughts had he sufficient employ.' After one incident in 1816, when machines for making bobbin nets were destroyed and a watchman was wounded, seven men were hanged, and three transported. The sentences were so severe that the rural agitator, William Cobbett, even argued in his 'Letter to the Luddites' in favour of the new technology. But with the widespread agricultural revolts of 'Captain Swing' and the farm labourers against threshing-machines and low wages and high food prices, Cobbett changed his tune in the *Political Register*:

> I said that millions of people could not starve; that it was impossible for things to go on till the highways were strewed with dead bodies . . . There are great numbers of Englishmen who are insurgents, savages, villains, monsters. There is no getting out of this dilemma. The fact is, they are people in *want*. They are people who have nothing to lose, except their lives; and of these they think little, seeing that they have so little enjoyment of them.

A surprising fact about these industrial and agricultural revolts was that they caused little bloodshed, unlike the *jacqueries* in France. As with the Reivers at the end of the centuries of conflict on the Borders, transportation to the colonies was the preferred solution, no longer to Ireland or America, but to the far-flung Antipodes. The figures for those sentenced to convict hard labour in Australia was some 22,000 men and women between 1793 and 1815, while during the next riotous decade, the number rose to 78,400 deportees, including later, those famous early trade unionists, the Tolpuddle Martyrs. And the means of repression were curiously similar to the American *posse* of good citizens, sworn to hunt down outlaws. In both nations, the militia was largely disbanded, while a powerful force of police constables was hardly yet hatched. In England, to support the military, the volunteer Yeomanry, officered by the gentry and manned by tenant farmers and merchants and smallholders, acted against those who were held to disturb the peace. Numbering some 15,000 troopers across the shires, they were hated after Peterloo, being in the opinion of General Sir Charles Napier, 'over-zealous for cutting and slashing'. As for the Duke of Wellington, then the Lord Lieutenant of Hampshire, he raised a private force of mounted men to chase the agitators in the county:

> I induced the magistrates to put themselves on horseback, each at the head of his own servants and retainers, grooms, huntsmen, game-keepers, armed with horse-whips, pistols, fowling pieces and what they could get, and to attack in concert, if necessary, or single, these mobs, disperse them, and take and put in confinement those who could not escape.

Such part-time policemen on horseback were necessary and effective. In 1822, the Suffolk labourers from the villages near Diss smashed every threshing-machine on the nearby farms. When dispersed by the mounted gentry, they scattered to assemble again and renew their attacks. After ten days of scattered raids, they were caught in a body 'by a party of gentlemen, farmers and others, accompanied by the Eye Yeomanry Cavalry'. Thirty of the rebels were seized and imprisoned in Norwich castle, awaiting the Assizes; but when the Suffolk Cavalry trotted out in the streets after their exploits, 'they were received with a shower of stones and brickbats, and were stoned completely throughout the city'.

Four years later, even the military could not quell the 'Powerloom Riot' of the Lancashire weavers. They were pelted as they tried to guard the mills, and they could not prevent the rebels from destroying the machines with their Enochs, their giant hammers as large as that of John Henry, the black ballad hero of the American South-west. At Chadderton mill, seven more were killed and dozens were transported, but their protests against the machines and the iniquity of the Corn Laws even earned the sympathy of *The Times*, which asked: 'What has the Government done? They have sent soldiers to quell the riot. Have they sent nothing else? It is hard to give men who ask for bread, bullets and bayonets, and only bayonets and bullets.'

In reply, the local authorities accused the rioters of resorting to a form of blackmail, and demanding protection money as the Reivers had done. In the chief year of the agrarian revolt under 'Captain Swing', 1830, an Andover magistrate complained to Lord Melbourne, then the Home Secretary, that 'the Peasantry have not only dictated a rate of wages, not only destroyed all agricultural machinery, and demolished iron foundries, but have proceeded in formidable bodies to private dwellings to extort money and provisions – in fact, have established a system of pillage'.' These exactions, however, were quelled by the arrival of a troop of the 9th Lancers, who seized several prisoners. And so, 'the greatest agitation and alarm' was succeeded by 'peace and penitence'.'

This would be the last major revolt of the agricultural labourers in England. The rebels were chiefly the marginal folk, the youths without jobs, the shepherds, and above all, the poachers with their centuries of struggle against the savage Game Laws. In his *Swing Unmasked*, Edward Gibbon Wakefield saw the agitators as rural paupers, 'strong, intelligent and upright . . . driven to poaching and smuggling by the futility of the Poor Law'. The smallholder, and the farm labourer by day and the poacher by night, were often covert allies. 'Swing' mobs were escorted by armed poachers in East Sussex, while Sixpenny Handley on Cranbourne Chase, a warren of poachers, produced a riot of machine-breakers.

Before the days of Robin Hood, the outlaw had always contended against royal and feudal authority in the taking of game, particularly the deer. And indeed, since the beginnings of horse culture, the original Mongol hunters had all beasts at their will to kill. Only with the rise of kingship in Europe were Game Parks enclosed, solely to gratify the court's pleasure in the pursuit. In the case of the Reivers, a whole Border battle was fought over aristocratic hunting 'rights' at Chevy Chase. And with the wide-ranging enclosures of the 18th century and the Black Act of 1723 condemning poachers to death, the villagers' means of supplementing their diet with wild meat was condemned. And with the French Revolution, any loosening of the severe Game Laws appeared to be a form of social levelling as well as an attack on the 'rights' of property and possession. As Alexander Pope had observed in 'Windsor Forest':

> Proud Nimrod first the bloody Chase began,
> A mighty Hunter, and his Prey was Man.

In the Victorian age, the pursuit of a stag, except on Exmoor, was chiefly a matter of stalking the beast on foot with a rifle. And fox-hunting saw the transfer of the chase from total aristocratic control to the beginnings of a community sport. The Duke of Beaufort still controlled his Hunt by hereditary right, with Badminton as the centre of those, who loved horse and hound. The Duke of Rutland was usually Master of the Belvoir, Earl Spencer of the Pytchley, and Lord Willoughby de Broke of the Warwickshire. But the huge expenses of maintaining the Hunts and the stables and the kennels forced the Masters to ask for subscriptions from the wealthy to cover the expenses. By the start of the next century, indeed, one enthusiast noted that hunting was no longer the exclusive sport of the landed interest, but two-thirds of every field were 'businessman of sorts . . . redolent of money'.

The other new fox-hunters were tenant farmers, who had to be woo'd and included, so that they would allow the Hunts to cross their lands and would not put up barbed wire, as the farmers did in the American West to keep out the cattle of the ranchers. As a result, the prosperous sheepmen of Leicestershire, were followers of the Quorn, while seventy tenant farmers, 'clad in scarlet and all beautifully mounted', rode with the Brocklesby over the Wolds. For one historian, a common 'desire to love and cherish the fox and a desire to chase and kill it . . . was a fact which, perhaps more than any other, gave vitality, cohesion and stability to county society'.

The long weeks at country houses were also the occasions for political and social bonding, or even international misunderstanding. If anyone made riding to hounds the most fashionable sport in all of Europe, it was the Empress Elisabeth of Austria. Taught to ride as well as a circus performer by her father in Bavaria, she became estranged from her husband the Emperor Franz Josef the Second, and she pursued her hunting in Hungary and England and Ireland. Renowned as one of the greater beauties and best horsewoman of her age, she rode with the Pytchley on Bravo, her favourite mount.* A local ballad praised her arrival:

> 'The bright star of Europe' her kingdom has left,
> And Austria mourns of its Empress bereft.
> Firm seat in the saddle: light hands on the reins,
> As e'er guided steed over Hungary's plains:
> She has come – with her beauty, grace, courage and skill
> To ride, with our hounds, from old Shuckburgh Hill.

An international incident occurred in 1879, when she was hunting with the Royal Meath on Irish turf. An exhausted stag leapt through a breach in the wall around the Catholic seminary of Maynooth College. The hounds and the Empress followed in hot pursuit, and she was welcomed by the priests. She returned there to hear Sunday Mass, performed by the Vicar Capitular of Dublin. The events were widely reported. Known already for her support for Hungarian independence within the Habsburg Empire, her behaviour at Maynooth appeared to approve of the struggle of the Catholic masses against their Protestant rulers. No act of hers could have done more to inflame religious and nationalist feelings in Ireland, where the situation was becoming more explosive because of another potato blight affecting the poor, as at the time of the Great Hunger thirty years before. Then, evictions by 15,000 extra troops and mass starvation had led to some 1,500,000 deaths with nearly another million people emigrating to America, while the personal insecurity of all property owners was 'so hideous that the impression is of being in an *enemy country*'.

Nothing endeared, however, the British aristocracy so much to the masses as Racing. The development of the sport at Newmarket and Epsom Downs, particularly the classic founded by Lord Derby, produced huge crowds and a carnival atmosphere. Most remarkably, all modern racehorses were recently discovered to be bred from only twenty-eight animals, imported to Britain some 300 years ago. Most of the male thoroughbreds can trace their genesis back to the Middle

Eastern stallion, the Darley Arabian, shipped over from Aleppo at the beginning of the 18th century, while the rest derive from the Byerley Turk, captured at the Battle of Buda, and the Godolphin Barb, born in the Yemen. These three Arabs covered twenty-five mares, and their foals engendered all of the country's bloodstock. The great-great-grandson of the Darley Arabian, Eclipse, only was raced for two seasons after 1767 and won eighteen times without being whipped or spurred. As the adage went: 'Eclipse first, the rest nowhere.'

Yet with the coming of modern technology in transport and weaponry, the primal bond between man and horse in hunting and warfare would be lost. The country squires began to bemoan the trains that were making their retreats so accessible, and were turning whole villages into weekend cottages for city dwellers. And in war, heavy artillery and the carbine rifle were rendering the cavalry charge into a mincemeat of folly. The most celebrated of these gallant forays were executed in the Crimea, where an unnecessary war was fought against Russia by an army, left to wither of neglect and cholera, much as the Irish had been in the Great Hunger. Curiously enough, the Crimea was the home of Tartars, descended from the Mongol Golden Horde, some of them serving as Cossacks for the Tsar. Aided by the French, a British expeditionary force of some 25,000 men with a Heavy and a Light Brigade of cavalry landed in 1854 near Balaclava, a fishing village over the mountains from Sebastopol, the naval dockyard for the enemy Black Sea fleet. After an initial infantry battle at the Alma river, where the Hussars and the Lancers failed to purse the routed Russians, the Tsarist commander, Prince Menschikov, decided to counter-attack and destroy the British supply base.

So developed at Balaclava the two celebrated cavalry actions of Victorian times. With 25 infantry battalions and 34 squadrons of cavalry and 78 cannon, the Russians advanced to try and seize the British field guns on Causeway Heights. The Heavy Brigade was ordered to reinforce the few Highlanders still holding the redoubts. Seeing a mass of 2,500 Russian horsemen standing in a wall against them, a mere 300 men of the Inniskilling Dragoons and the Scots Greys galloped into the enemy line and were swallowed within the seething mass. The reserve of the Royals and two more regiments of Dragoons now hurled themselves into the *mélée* and hacked the Russians into retreat, although a quarter of their strength. The Light Brigade on their flank would not join in the action. Its commander, Lord Cardigan, insisted that he had to obey orders, even though he remarked: 'Those damned Heavies, they will have the laugh on us this day.'

So it happened. The Highlanders and the Heavy Brigade had to withdraw from the Heights, leaving their field pieces to the enemy. Cardigan was now commanded to prevent the Russians from carrying off the guns. In front of the Light Brigade lay a valley; either side bristled with batteries and riflemen; at the end, stood a line of brass cannon, backed by a mounted regiment. Into this suicidal trap, Cardigan led the Light Brigade, first at a walk, then at a canter, then at the gallop. Of 673 men, only 230 would reach the Russian guns and cavalry, and 195 would return from a bloody shambles of riders and horses, making a crimson heaving on the valley floor.

Cardigan himself passed the Russian battery and then decided to ride slowly back again. The survivors behind him split around the enemy cannon and engaged the opposing cavalry and retired, supported by French *Chausseurs* on their left flank. The Heavy Brigade was not allowed to aid in the retreat; too many men had already been sacrificed. They could only note that the fire going back was more severe than going in. The wounded remnants staggered by in ones and twos. 'Such a smash was never seen.' The only apology Cardigan could give to his shattered Brigade was: 'Men, it was a mad-brained trick, but . . . no fault of mine.'

Certainly, as went the glorified poem of 'The Charge of the Light Brigade', it was true that cannon to left of them, cannon to right of them, volleyed and thundered, while into the jaws of death rode the gallant Six Hundred. But for Lord Cardigan, there was to reason why, and not to do and die. What was untrue was the remark of a French officer, that the action was magnificent, but it was not war. Especially for the watching army wives on a safe hill, the action was horrific, and it was war, an epitaph on the folly of the cavalry charge into artillery. A more judicious poem came from the pen of Alfred, Lord Tennyson, praising the success of the gallop of the Heavy Brigade in two successive charges into the Tsarist ranks:

> 'Lost one and all' were the words
> Mutter'd in our dismay;
> But they rode like Victors and Lords
> Thro' the forest of lances and swords
> In the heart of the Russian hordes,
> They rode, or they stood at bay –
> Struck with the sword-hand and slew,
> Down with the bridle-hand drew

The foe from the saddle and threw
Underfoot there in the fray –

Ranged like a storm or stood like a rock
In the wave of a stormy day;
Till suddenly shock upon shock
Stagger'd the mass from without,
Drove it in wild disarray,
For our men gallopt up with a cheer and a shout,
And the foemen surged, and waver'd, and reel'd
Up the hill, up the hill, up the hill, out of the field,
And over the brow and away.

Glory to each and to all, and the charge that they made!
Glory to all the three hundred, and all the Brigade!

While Sebastopol was eventually taken by many artillery barrages and infantry assaults, far more men, stricken with disease and without tents in the winter snows, died in camp in the Crimea or in the appalling conditions of the Barrack Hospital at Scutari, where even Florence Nightingale and her nurses could not save them. When she left, she declared: 'I stand at the altar of the murdered men, and while I live I will fight their cause.' Back in Britain, however, the governments were mobilising a light horse for police work against agitators, as the Tsar had done with the Cossacks. The mass movement of the Chartists was the new quarry, with their demand for universal suffrage and more rights for the people. By the Metropolitan Police Act of 1829 and the Municipal Corporations Act of 1835, all boroughs were required to set up some form of police system, overseen by a Watch Committee and subsidised by local rates. The response to the legislation was spotty and poor, but after huge Chartist disturbances, the 'Obligatory Act' of 1856 compelled local authorities to maintain a force of constables, some of them mounted for crowd control.

In the case of riots, special constables could be sworn in, while the Yeomanry and the military remained on standby. In the Chartist scare during the revolutionary year of 1848 in Europe, the powers in London recruited 170,000 special constables, and another 110,000 in 1867 during the Fenian outrages, while in the wake of 'Bloody Sunday' in 1887, over 30,000 citizens were engaged in temporary duties. They were not always of much use. The Mayor of Exeter complained: 'Special Constables are of no great avail in any sudden tumult, even if they are got together and sworn in, there is no means of distinguishing them from the Roughs and if they do not fight each other, they do not act much in concert.'

The Chartist uprisings were larger, but less dangerous, than those of the Luddites and 'Captain' Swing, and certainly of the Rebecca movement in Wales and the Plug-plot disturbances of 1842 in the northern shires. The mounted Rebecca rebels, disguised in women's clothes, demolished tollgates and houses and hayricks, and they were rarely caught. The Plug-plot risings of strikers in their campaign of factory arson, took over whole towns such as Stockport and Bolton, where the Town Hall was set on fire with special constables inside its walls. They also rose in Birmingham, where the Bull Ring was invaded and warehouses burned down and shops plundered. Only the intervention of the Dragoons and a few policemen prevented the sack of the centre of that industrial city.

The many demonstrations of the Chartists were distinguished by their moderation. Although Lenin was later to call them the 'first broad, truly mass and politically organised proletarian revolutionary movement', they were more addicted to dissenting Methodism than early Bolshevism. In their confrontations with the London police in 1848 in Bonners Fields and Clerkenwell Green and Trafalgar Square, their weapons were flung stones and stakes against constables, armed with cutlasses and truncheons. Rushes by the policemen managed to disperse the milling mobs; there was no question of a repetition of the burning of the capital, as in 1780 in the Gordon riots, 'When the rude rabble's watchword was destroy / And blazing London seemed a second Troy.' The Chartists did not put torches to Newgate prison; they only presented to Parliament a Petition, signed by millions of workers, who wanted to improve the conditions of their lives.

Although the Fenian terrorist campaign of 1867 struck at gasworks and railways, while two of the captured Irish rebels were liberated on their way to goal, the hanging of three of their rescuers still took place. An explosion outside Clerkenwell prison wall, to free more Fenians, resulted in twelve deaths of innocent bystanders. Yet despite the anger of Queen Victoria, who wrote that she began to wish 'that these Fenians should be thought lynch-lawed and on the spot' because their trials broke down, no insurrection in London actually occurred. The city seemed proof against any revolutionary attack. For the Pall Mall affair of the year before had already been seen off by the constables alone, after the windows of the Carlton Club and a few others were broken, *pour encourager les autres* manifestations. Frederick Engels himself despaired of these rioters, calling them a 'stray rabble rather than unemployed workmen [who] had brought further discredit upon socialists'.

As for the labour demonstration in 1887 in Trafalgar Square on 'Bloody Sunday', Irish Nationalists showed the most resistance, as they would on another 'Bloody Sunday' in Londonderry nearly a century later. Wearing red and green armbands and chanting the 'Marseillaise' and 'Starving for Old England', they fought the police at Westminster Bridge; twenty-six injured people ended up in St Thomas's Hospital. The tens of thousands of protesters who reached Trafalgar Square were soon dispersed by the hooves and bayonets of the Brigade of Guards. 'You should have seen that high-hearted host run,' George Bernard Shaw wrote. 'Running hardly expresses our collective action. We skedaddled, and never drew rein until we were safe on Hampstead Heath or thereabouts . . . it was the most abjectly disgraceful defeat ever suffered by a band of heroes outnumbering their foes a thousand to one.'

In the papers of the socialist leader John Burns, an unnamed eyewitness, on top of a horse-drawn bus, told of the effectiveness of the Household Cavalry against the agitators. He saw the Horse Guards march up to the West End of the Square and begin to walk very slowly round. Then the troop officer gave a command:

> The soldiers began to walk at a much quicker pace. All around from every part of the square the booing and the screaming was fearful. Again at the very same spot he gave another command and they began to trot. The screams and the shrieks that I then heard were in my ears for months. Again at the same spot he gave command. It was a wild cavalry charge around the square. The panic-stricken people tried to get away but loud above the clattering of the horses' hoofs and the rattling of their accoutrements were the frightened mad screams of the poor people. The square was now thinned indeed . . .

In the affray, 200 were wounded, two died. John Burns was sentenced to six months in Pentonville prison for provoking an armed assault on the police, although the mob only had sticks as weapons. When he was released, Burns gave a speech on Bastille Day, saying he was ashamed and disgusted with the working classes. They were not educated as they ought to be, and that was due mostly to their own apathy and indifference. He wanted Trafalgar Square to become a serial revolutionary *rendezvous*; from there, the mob could storm the new Bastille, Pentonville prison, and release the other captives and convicts. The radical reformer William Morris also complained that political agitators could not strike a spark out of the bulk of the people on any subject whatsoever, although his utopian novel *News from Nowhere* forecast a socialist millennium, heralded by a massacre of workers in Trafalgar Square, leading to a General Strike and the collapse of the government, a wrong prophecy of events to come.

The first elected Labour leader, Keir Hardie, deplored in 1903 'the fatalistic patience' of the unemployed in London. To him, 'these crowds of helpless atoms' had no fight left in them. In the words of the popular music-hall ditty, they would do nothing but 'wait till the work comes round'. Even in the actual General Strike of 1926, they would prove themselves more collaborators with capitalism than combatants against its evils. And in all of that 20th century, the London mounted police would prove time and again that the quarters and hooves of the horse could break up large demonstrations more effectively than the swing of the truncheon.

Until the coming in 1914 of the Great War, which would stem, in mud and machine-gun and barbed wire, any cavalry charge on the European front, one American hero and President kept alive the tradition of the light horsemen in *posse* and combat. While running in New York for mayor and president of the Board of Police Commissioners, Theodore Roosevelt spent his summers becoming a dude rancher in the Dakotas. His courage and character were in no doubt, although his glasses and short-sight gave him the name of 'Four-Eyes'. In the Cuban War of 1898, he recruited and led a 'jim-dandy regiment' of Rough Riders in the 'San Juan charge' up Kettle Hill, surviving a hailstorm of bullets.

When in 1901 Roosevelt unexpectedly became President of the United States, he was true to his assumed cowboy identity, both creating the first National Parks to preserve the wilderness, and attacking the railroad trusts and Wall Street 'robber barons', who were exploiting the western farmers and the ranchers. His aggression was shown by the construction of a Great White Fleet and the building of the Panama Canal in a puppet state. A big-game hunter, he survived an assassination attempt, but inspired the ballad, 'The Teddy-Bears Picnic'. When the Great War came, he begged the President, Woodrow Wilson, to send him with a regiment to the trenches in Flanders. He was refused. As in the Crimean Charge of the Light Brigade, cavalry surges on the Western Front were up obsolete murder alleys. Past his time, Theodore Roosevelt died with the signing of the Peace at Versailles. As the writer of *The Hero in America* proclaimed, in Roosevelt's legend was something heroic. 'He was our last great American on horseback.'

The Great War or First World War in Europe saw the obliteration of the cavalry by the battle tank. The horseman was useless against mortar and howitzer, barbed wire and machine-gun, shell-hole and dug-out. Even when 375 of the new armoured machines ground ditches over the German lines in 1916 at Cambrai, the reserve cavalry could not move forward quickly enough to break through to the rear of the enemy. The metal track had taken over from the horseshoe, the iron turret from the hide saddle. Only Field Marshal Douglas Haig stood out against the Prime Minister, Lloyd George, who declared that 'cavalry would never be used in France'. He agreed with Winston Churchill that its personnel should be transferred to aircraft or tanks or armoured cars. Haig protested, pointing out 'the ease with which cavalry could be moved from one sector to another and then be dismounted'. Referring to some medieval tactics, Haig insisted 'that the British cavalry resembled highly trained mobile infantry rather than the old cavalry arm'.

A compromise was reached. Two more cavalry regiments were sent to Palestine, where they proved most effective, while twenty were unscrambled on the Western Front. The result was that Haig now commanded three divisions of light horse, rather than five; these Brigades, each backed by twelve Vickers machine-guns, constituted 16,200 men, of which only one-third were still mounted. Yet this Reserve was in place to achieve its last chance of glory in 1918 during the final German Spring offensive, which drove the Allies back to the Marne river.

At Villers-Bretonneux, the retreating British infantry was saved by cavalry charges into machine-gun fire. The Australian and Canadian Brigades were particularly expert and foolhardy. At Collézy, the 3rd Dragoon Guards, the 10th Hussars and the Royals charged into the opposing machine-guns and infantry. According to the regimental historian, the dragoons cheered and the sabres came down to 'the sword in line'. The Germans 'either put their hands up or else bolted into the copse. This did not save them, for once cavalry had been launched, it was always for the enemy either to run or to make placatory gestures. They were ridden down and a hundred sabred.'

After this action, a staff officer wrote that 'the cavalry barometer stands very high again. It was very low a month ago.' And at Moreuil Wood – what shades of the imperial cavalry – Lord Strathcona's Horse Royal Canadians came in, so that galloping steeds seemed 'to magnify in power and number; it looked like a great host sweeping forward over the open country. . . ' The commander, John Seely, also noted in his memoirs, *Adventure*: 'The air was alive with bullets, but nobody minded a bit. It was strange to see the horses roll over like rabbits, and the men, when unwounded, jump up and run forward, sometimes catching the stirrups of their still mounted comrades.'

On top of a steep bank, two lines of the enemy with machine-guns in the centre and on the flanks confronted the Canadian cavalry with their sabres. They repeated the folly of the Charge of the Light Brigade. They rode through the stormshot of fire, then wheeled to kill on the return, leaving seventy Germans dead by the sword. 'In those brief moments,' Seely wrote of the fanatical bravery of his men, 'we lost over eight hundred horses, but only three hundred men killed and wounded'. The dismounted survivors held the position, until they were relieved by more cavalry, with a pair of British aviators dropping bombs and using aerial gunfire in support. This was the ultimate mounted charge of the British empire in modern war. As Haig summed up: 'Cavalry is a special arm, and it is not every occasion on which it can be used; but when it is wanted, it is wanted very badly.'

The elegant Siegfried Sassoon pronounced the requiem on such cavalcades in his *Memoirs of a Fox-hunting Man*. A notable rider to hounds, he had joined the Yeomanry in 1914 in anticipation of the looming struggle. 'The cloudless weather of that August and September need not be dwelt on; it is a hard fact of history; the spellbound serenity of its hot blue skies will be in the minds of men as long as they remember the catastrophic events which were under way in that autumn when I was raising the dust on the roads with the Yeomanry.' A riding accident, followed by a training period, took time to bring Sassoon to the back of the trenches as a transport officer, overseeing pack animals for supply wagons. By the end of the Great War, indeed, nearly a fifth of Britain's horses were mobilised, producing 500,000 mounts with 200,000 mules from overseas. Interminably, the Yeomanry Colonel preached 'open warfare' and a 'Big Push' next spring. Yet Sassoon ended in the muddy trenches and the shell-holes of a no man's land. All he wanted to do was to kill or to die. 'In the circumstances there didn't seem anything else to be done.' Wounded and invalided with shell-shock, Sassoon returned to the mud and the blood. Somehow he survived the war to become an aesthete in the New Generation, which abhorred the slaughter that had dispatched tens of millions of soldiers on the forking trails of bullet or whizz-bang or disease to one kind of death or another.

CHAPTER NINETEEN

Dressage

Many thousands of horses lived through the massacres on the Western Front, indeed long enough to appear in a Veterans Parade in 1934 at London's Olympia in an International Horse show. *Sic transit gloria equi*. Pride of place was the bay mare Kitty, who belonged to Lord Digby of the Coldstream Guards; she was not put down until she was thirty-one years old, at the beginning of the Second World War. Except in its colonies, however, Britain had gotten rid of its cavalry in favour of armoured vehicles. When the war broke out in 1939 with the Nazi attack on Poland, the defenders were some of the last to use cavalry against Panzers. Thirty-eight mounted regiments fought against the *Blitzkrieg*. Although the Polish light horse did not charge unsupported into German tanks, for it was backed by artillery and machine-guns, the dive-bombers did their dirty work from the air. In the first month of the war, the Pomeranian Cavalry Brigade lost two-thirds of its mounts in thirty minutes. 'The best horses in the world could not withstand the demoralising attacks of the Stukas . . . Along the road to Warsaw lay thousands of dead and dying Polish-Arab horses.'

Curiously enough, the forces of Adolf Hitler were employing some 800,000 horses for their advance into Russia, once war was declared in 1941 on the former ally. Opposing them were the last brigades of the legendary Cossacks. The Russians deployed thirty cavalry divisions and used 1,200,000 horses as pack animals in their campaigns. Near Musino Village, north-west of Moscow, the 44th Mongolian Cavalry Division galloped into the artillery and automatic fire of the foe. Without one casualty, the Germans killed or wounded 2,000 Mongols and their mounts. History was overturned. Where was the Golden Horde except in the bloody snow? Machines now unmade men and their horses.

With the peace or Cold War, only the Chinese People's Republic and the Soviet Union employed three divisions of cavalry with carbines on their disputed frontiers in Siberia and Mongolia, while the Indian army maintained two regiments of horsed and camel riders to patrol the Rajastan desert on the frontier with Pakistan. There, so often, all had gone wrong in the old imperial days. As for the British, hanging on to their last dependencies, a Royal Exodus Hunt after desert foxes and wolves was still run from Habbaniyah for the Iraq Levies and a Royal Air Force regiment. In British Somaliland, a Camel Corps and Scouts still dealt with sporadic cattle rustling and tribal raiding, until their means of transport were converted into lorries and armoured vehicles. The Sudan Defence Force, the heirs of the Dervish riders who had fought so bravely against General Gordon and Kitchener at Khartoum, maintained a Camel Corps and three squadrons of mounted rifles called the Shendi Horse, later converted to dragging howitzers through the scrub and sand in a successful campaign against the Italian army in Abyssinia in the Second World War. And indeed, in Darfur to this day, camel riders with Kalashnikov rifles raid and rape and slaughter the rival tribes as though nothing had changed, except the killing power of the weaponry, in a thousand years.

In much of the rest of the world, horse culture had become a sport rather than a battle. Fox-hunting and show jumping and racing put the steed on display in all its speed and grace. Since the 12th century, dogs had been used in Europe to purse game, mastiffs for the deer, greyhounds for the hare, while the hunters rode behind the pack. In the 18th century, fox-hounds were specifically bred at the Quorn for the chase. With the coming of the Victorian age and with the new plutocracy joining the aristocracy in a social pursuit, which included tenant farmers, whose land had to be crossed, a golden age of fox-hunting began as a ritual in every shire. In the eyes of a Swiss visitor, England was the most horse-mad country in Europe, 'a sort of island of the Houyhnhnms' from *Gulliver's Travels*. The costumes were somewhat military with pink and black tunics and white britches, while the Master was the commander in the field. By including the local people, who loved their horses, the Hunts were changing this royal and gentry pastime into a community bonding. 'If it ever presents the appearance of exclusiveness,' the wise Lord Willoughby de Broke observed, 'the whole fabric will dissolve.'

Until the demise of the cavalry in the Great War, hunting had also been seen as military training. 'I will not enlarge upon the political advantages of encouraging a sport which propagates a fine breed of horses,' James York had written in 1802 to the Countess de Grey, 'and prevents our young men growing quite effeminate in Bond Street, nor upon the high reputation of the English horse abroad, which are perhaps the only cavalry that ever won whole battles against a very superior force of horse and foot.' Lord Cardigan, indeed, led the Charge of the Light Brigade as he had the Melton Mowbray Hunt. And after the Boer War, a rider with the Old Berkshire exclaimed: 'How many of that first batch of gallant Yeomen who sprang to arms five years ago in the hours of their country's difficulty, and who did such splendid service for their native land in South Africa, were trained in the hunting field.'

For the villagers, both tradesmen and farm labourers, the Meet was a great social occasion. On the Boxing Day event in 1841 of the Pytchely, 1,500 enthusiasts followed the Hunt on foot. Even the radical William Cobbett remembered running from the hop-garden, where he worked as a child, 'scores of times to follow the hounds, leaving the hoe to do the best that it could to destroy the weeds'. Before a national obsession with football, and to a lesser degree with cricket, hunting foxes in the saddle and on foot, also hare-coursing with lurchers and greyhounds, provided rural entertainment. There was also an element of risk and danger in the show. The riders broke their necks and bones, while their prey often escaped to earth. There was one superb description by the hunting correspondent Nimrod of a fall, while out with the Hambledon in Hampshire:

Morant went brilliantly up to the last ten minutes, when he and No Pretender were missing. Can I ever forget the state we found them in, after we had killed our fox? No – nor can many of his friends now alive. He was sitting still in his saddle under a blackthorn hedge, a sad example of mis-spent time. He was minus his hat, his face was torn and bloody, and his clothes were rent. No Pretender's tongue was hanging out of his mouth, black from pressure on his bit, and very woe-begone did he look. But here was one of the good traits of the man; he had not a spark of jealousy about him, and joined in the laugh his appearance created. 'Well,' said he; 'a *very pretty* thing indeed, I am glad you killed him, for the hounds deserved him. *I should have liked to have seen the finish*, but somehow or other the old horse shut up.'

Until the last century before the millennium, however, criticism of what were called blood sports was limited. The reason that it arose as a tidal wave was the shift of the population to the city and suburbia, until nine in ten Britons had forsaken a rural ride. Proud of outlawing bull-baiting and cock-fighting, although not professional boxing, the reformers wished to end the many thousands of years of hunting on horseback. For them, the supermarket had ended the need to kill game or vermin in such a barbaric way. There had been only a few protestors, particularly in 'The Task' by the poet William Cowper, who loathed 'the reeking, roaring hero of the chase':

> Detested sport,
> That owes its pleasure to another's pain;
> That feeds upon the sobs and dying shrieks
> Of harmless nature . . .

And indeed, one observer, who knew the slums, remarked on the kennels and stables at Badminton: 'It is not right to see hounds lodged better than human beings.'

The modern arguments against hunting are most convincing when they are psychological. 'Blooding' by the brush of a dead fox is seen as a ritual murder. A communal participation in the death of a beast is an enjoyment of the sacrifice of the innocent. To Maureen Duffy in *Animals, Men and Morals*, the desire to kill or to take part in killing lurks in most of us.

> Troops taking a village in Vietnam go berserk and massacre the inhabitants; tourists queue for the bullfight; American, and at one time British, slaughterhouses welcome visitors; the curious paid the keeper to see snakes at the zoo swallow live food when feeding was withdrawn from public view; children torment insects; public executions were enjoyed by many.

The arguments of the lovers of the chase are based on the view halloo that man is a hunting animal as well as a social one. That is a quality he shares with other animals which he may hunt, such as the fox. When our original societies began, we were hunters and gatherers. We hunted for meat and fish, we gathered wild fruit and roots and seeds. We respected what gave us life. After killing a deer, the Mayan archer would kneel to beg the forgiveness of the stag. He needed to take its life to keep his family. He respected its place in nature as much as his own.

Good hunters preserve the stocks of game. They do not destroy these, for then they may not hunt. Although man may dominate nature and has interfered with its processes, he is part of its ways. He has become its gamekeeper. He maintains the killing grounds of the larger cats, the tigers and the lions, in reserves. He has made pets of the smaller cats and delivered to them all the birds and mice of the cities to torment in their claws. He recognises a right to hunt in those animals which tickle his fancy, wild and tame.

Without the preservation of food, there would be little preservation of animals. Packets and tins allow us to keep ourselves and our dogs in comfort in winter. Both species do not have to eat the rats and the elephants in the zoo, as the French did in Paris when it was under Prussian siege. Only canning and distributing food in modern urban society has made us capable of living well without hunting at all. And this was not so until a century ago. Thousands of years had to pass before the primitive hunters and gatherers were assaulted by the kings and warlords of the new cities. The forests were cleared for farms, the rivers used for fields and aqueducts and sewers for townsfolk. With the hunters fled the wild animals. For they knew each other and lived by each other. The city was their enemy and their destroyer.

The long march of the urban frontier was aided by the railways and the highways and the forces of the factories. Where the Sioux and the Apaches had ridden beside and eaten and worn and worshipped the buffalo, still grazing in their millions on the red grass of the prairies, the Colt revolver and the Winchester rifle and barbed wire soon decimated the tribes and the herds. If another age felt it had to conserve the remnants of the American tribes as well as a few of the noble beasts, the action came too late. A perfect balance in nature had been tipped over. Greed and technology was driving the last of the hunters to the edges of civilisation. There they could be examined as the Savage in Aldous Huxley's *Brave New World*, a few specimens still allowed to kill an occasional seal or whale because they knew no better. The representatives of the most ancient ways in human history were reduced to an ethnic curiosity.

But did the people of the cities and the suburbs really know better? Did the incomers to the villages and the countryside, the accusers of the hunters who were often farmers too, did they respect the traditions and the skills of those who had preserved the green spaces for thousands of years? No, for they were wiser. Although human beings went on killing each other during the 20th century in tens of millions, hunters should stop killing wild predators. Modern man could wash his hands of mass murder of his own kind, but not of the blood of the fox.

Yet the jungle had quit the Amazon and had come to Manhattan. The ghetto was more dangerous for mankind than the rainforest, which was being felled, anyway, to the destruction of the remaining peoples, who lived there on game. Each year, thousands were killing each other with guns in the streets of the capitals of the world. Hundreds of thousands were poisoned annually by narcotics. Millions were butchered in Rwanda and the Congo, yet the West walked away from trial or judgement. Stalin had died in his bed, although he had killed tens of millions in his *gulags*. As a species, our crimes against ourselves stained the last century. Our crimes against our fellow animals hardly weighed down the scales of suffering.

When we stop killing one another, we may try to become more humane to the rest of nature. But verdicts, like charity, begin at home. We must cleanse our own natures before we dare to meddle too much with the ways of creation and human history. We are what we are, and we should not forget it. If we want to behave differently, we must first change ourselves. Otherwise, we merely spread our flaws like muck over the whole earth.

We deny what we call 'rights' to the majority of humanity, yet some of us complain that we deny 'rights' to our animals. This is not the meaning of the word 'rights'. In the Bible, right conduct was doing good or well. 'The Rights of Man' inspired the American and French Revolutions. That radical and recent idea led to the triumph of nationalism and democracy. In fact, social man still had as many duties as 'rights'. And he only could claim these rights as an individual or as a member of the human race. Now 'rights' are claimed for groups and genders and causes and ages and sexual preferences and differences in the colours of our skin. And for animals, and even for trees.

These categories have no rights, or not in the meaning of the biblical or revolutionary sense. They have no rights, because they are not persons or humanity. They have no rights, because they have no obligations. They demand to take from the rest of society, but to give nothing back, because their group or gender or whatever has been wronged. They seek to borrow a noble word and a living from those who mean what they do and provide the food for us all.

If animals do not have rights, yet we may choose the duty of treating them as well as we can. We should not abuse them, as we do in factory farms or by transportation almost as bad as the wagons once used to take human beings to the concentration camps. As long as we eat meat, a gentle rearing and carrying of our food is both righteous and wise. As long as we have slaughterhouses, the animals should reach them in the best condition and be killed as quickly as possible. Their suffering should be short. That is what most government regulations are about. These have nothing to do with morals or rights. But they have to do with the rightful concept of ourselves as creatures of some mercy.

That leads to the best argument of those who wish to ban hunting, or what they call 'blood sports'. They claim that if these rural pursuits are eliminated, the human nature of country people will be improved. They will be saved from their darker side, their blood lust. Yet this is nonsense. How can one piece of legislation alter the instincts of history? How can a modern cause repeal the habits of the millennia? How can city people condemn a sport that makes communities of so many country people? And how in our democracy can a group of our elected representative dare to try and suppress the activities of the folk, who dwell in nine-tenths of the land and were called its backbone and its tillers of the soil before becoming its underpaid providers on the supermarket shelves?

Hunting with dogs was banned in 2004 in spite of the opposition of the House of Lords. The House of Commons, whose members mainly represented the cities, insisted upon it. So the urban majority chose to oppress the rural minority, who knew the truth of tradition and country management. Stags must be culled, for instance, to preserve the strength of the herd. Most people agree to that. Even in a stag hunt, when the prey is at bay, the huntsman reckons its stay of execution is, at the most, a minute. It is the same story with foxes. Poisoning prolongs their pain. Shooting them often only wounds. Traps maim in a sorry death. Yet they would kill wantonly all the farmer's hens on a free range, if they were not kept in check. Hunting with hounds does so. And in terms of the suffering of the predators, they expire in the shortest way. For the huntsman usually dispatches the fox before the other carnivores, the hounds.

Yes, dog does still eat dog, among humans and beasts. We cannot change the nature of foxes, even if we try to domesticate dogs and cats. These pets still eat any lesser beast that they can catch, be it a mouse or a rat or a sparrow. Yet we are told we can alter in human beings the traditions and instincts of all the millennia and more of hunting.

History is often irony. Prescribed by the British Parliament, the riders to hounds of the 250 Hunts in Britain now carry an occasional harrier hawk or Golden Eagle on their wrist. So the Mongolians did, when the tale of horse culture had its beginnings. Now the ultimate bird of prey descends once again on the fox in England's green and pleasant land, because its talons can evade the clutches of the law. How kill a beast? Is that really the question? We are rather better at killing each other in our tens of millions than in our record of slaughtering animals. So we will continue to the end of our existence as living beings, who persist in massacring each other. To moralise about what is our nature is a mere hypocrisy about our means of survival. We must recognise ourselves as primal predators, in need of a great deal of civilisation. We may mend our ways, but only over a long time.

Whatever the *mots justes* or *faux pas* which have plagued the sport of fox-hunting, it was mass gambling that saved the sport of thoroughbred Racing. The global attraction of the Grand National steeplechase even silenced the protests of the Animal Rights activists on the Aintree course, in their concern that too many hunters broke their legs on the high jumps such as Becher's Brook. The death by heart failure in 2005 before the last fence at Exeter of Best Mate, who had rivalled Arkle in winning the Cheltenham Gold Cup three times, led to headlines and widespread weeping. There was no question of the bond between the public and a beloved racehorse. The aristocratic side of racing, the Royal Enclosure at Ascot, had become irrelevant in an age of world-wide spectator communications. No longer could Lady Randolph complain about the change at Newmarket from late Victorian to Edwardian times:

> When I first went there, only the old stands existed, some of which date back quite two hundred years. The ladies who came were *habituées*, and did not muster a dozen at the outside. Among them were Caroline, Duchess of Montrose, who was a large owner of horses, the Duchess of Manchester (now Duchess of Devonshire), and Lardy Cardigan, who would drive up in an old-fashioned yellow tilbury, in which she sat all day.

> It was the fashion to ride, those who did not appearing in ordinary country clothes. Nowadays velvet and feathers are worn by the mob which throngs the stands, many not knowing a horse from a cow, but coming because it is the fashion . . .

Given the huge capital costs of maintaining a racing stable, and the ruin of the aristocrats after the Great War and the Depression and a Second World War, at the end of which they were declared to be 'lower than the vermin' they hunted, the gambling mob in the stands and telecommunications and oil-rich *sheikhs* saved the Jockey Club from extinction. A Reivers' Trail now led back to the deserts of Dubai and the breeding of the Arab horses, which had become the fastest in all the world.

Two sports remaining the *nonpareil* of wealthy horse culture – polo and show-jumping. Where once the Mongols, riding bareback, had knocked about with their lances a severed human or goat's head, now the rich and the well-connected played their *chukkas* in country-house estates, slamming a leather ball between the posts. The heirs of the *gauchos* from South America proved the most hardy of the professional players, as always celebrated as much for their virility as their skill.

Still the Mecca of show-jumping, Badminton retained its past glories. The sport, indeed, attracted the royal family, with Princess Anne marrying a top rider, and their daughter spending years with a National Hunt jockey. Both mother and child would appear for their country in the Olympic Games, where the discipline and the dressage of leaping log fences in a restricted ring replaced the chariot-race round the ancient Greek stadium. In modern times, however, royalty was not forgiven its faults, although the Emperor Nero was judged the winner of his Olympic race, even after falling off his racing vehicle.

And so, the bond between mount and rider survived over its many trails, which led from a marginal nomad existence to the luxury of racetracks and flamboyant shows. Yet in the end, the horses bred by men for their wars and their transport were often misused by men for their politics and their pleasures. The testament to the noble beast was written by George Orwell in his satire, which marked the end of the Second World War, *Animal Farm*. The tale begins with Old Major, a prize Middle White boar, addressing the creatures on the Manor Farm, and singing a song, 'Beasts of England', to a tune, something between the sentimental cowboy ditty, 'O my darling Clementine', and the more revolutionary 'La Cucaracha':

> Soon or late the day is coming,
>> Tyrant Man shall be o'erthrown,
> And the fruitful fields of England
>> Shall be trod by beasts alone . . .
>
> For that day we all must labour,
>> Though we die before it break;
> Cows and horses, geese and turkeys,
>> All must toil for freedom's sake.

The anarchist Old Major dies, the tyrannical Napoleon and the Trotsky pig Snowball and the spin-doctor Squealer take over. For their strength, they need the two cart-horses, Boxer and Clover, known to have minimal brains for their size. These two faithful disciples 'had great difficulty in thinking out anything for themselves, but having once accepted the pigs as their teachers, they absorbed everything they were told, and passed it on'. Of the new commandments written on the barn wall after a successful rebellion, one stated that all animals were equal, while the leading slogan was: FOUR LEGS GOOD. TWO LEGS BAD.

In the unremitting labour required to turn the rebel land into a going concern, 'Boxer was the admiration of everybody. Now he seemed more like three horses than one; there were days when the entire work of the farm seemed to rest on his mighty shoulders . . . His answer to every problem, every setback, was "I will work harder".' In a human counter-attack on the place, Boxer reared up on his hind legs and struck out with his great iron-shod hoofs like a stallion, stunning a stable-lad. In another assault, he broke open three heads of the intruders. He wasted all his strength on lugging up stores to rebuild a destroyed windmill, meant to provide power for the farm, now taken over by Comrade Napoleon and his pigs and attack dogs.

Until his decline, fallen with bloody lungs in the cart-shafts, Boxer was a believer in Mussolini's slogan: 'If Comrade Napoleon says it, it must be right!' Only when taken away in a van, painted with *Horse Slaughterer and Glue Boiler, Dealer in Hides and Bone Meal*, did Boxer drum his hoofs in despair on the metal walls of his hearse. The pigs, now trotting on two legs and more equal than other beasts, pronounced Boxer a revolutionary hero, then joined in a human alliance at a drunken feast, where the creatures outside looked from pig to man, and from man to pig, and it was impossible to say which was which.

In all the worldwide trails, which have spread the equine culture through so many laborious and forking paths, it is indisputable that the horse has done more for man than man has done for the horse. Yet, as with the Centaur, the bond between the beast and the human being had made them, in myth and literature, one flesh-and-blood. And their ways have covered the earth and reached to the stars, where Sagittarius still shines above. The heir of the Borderers, Neil Armstrong, made a giant step for the Reivers, if not for mankind, by standing on the moon. What, after all, is the difference between the saddle and the spacecraft in the ultimate ride towards eternity?

Appendix

The Border Clans

The principle of clanship had been reluctantly acknowledged by the Scottish legislature, not as a system approved of, but as an inveterate evil, to cure which they were obliged to apply extraordinary remedies. By the statute 1581, it was declared, that the clans of thieves, keeping together by occasion of their surnames, or near neighbourhood or society in theft, were not subjected to the ordinary course of justice; and therefore it was made lawful, that whatever true and obedient subject should suffer loss by them, might not only apprehend, slay, and arrest the persons of the offenders, but of any others being of the same clan. And thus the whole sept was rendered jointly answerable, and liable to be proceeded against, in the way of retaliation, for the delinquencies of each individual.

But to render the recourse of the injured parties more effectual, an elaborate statute, made two years afterwards, proceeding on the same melancholy preamble of waste and depredation committed on the Borders and Highlands, directs that security shall be found by those landlords and bailies on whose grounds the offending clansmen dwelt, that they would bring them in to abide process of law when complained of, or otherwise drive them from their grounds. It was further decreed, that the clans, chiefs, and chieftains, as well on the Highlands as on the Borders, with the principal branches of each surname who depended upon their several captains by reason of blood or neighbourhood, should find hostages or pledges for keeping good rule in time coming, under pain of the execution of these hostages unto the death, in case transgression should happen without amends being made by delivery of the criminal. These hostages were to be kept in close prison until the chiefs by whom they were entered in pledge found security that they would not *break ward,* that is, make their escape. But on such security being found, the hostages were to be placed in *free ward;* that is, were to remain prisoners on parole at their own expense, in the families of such inland gentlemen and barons as should be assigned to take charge of them respectively, the Borderers being quartered on the north, and the Highlanders on the south side of the Forth; which barons were bound, under a penalty of L.200, not to license their departure. The clans who should fail to enter such pledges within the time assigned, were to be pursued as incorrigible freebooters, with fire and sword. To render the provisions of this act yet more effectual, it was appointed that all Highlanders and Borderers should return from the inland country to the place of their birth: That all the clans should be entered in a register, with the names of the hostages or sureties, and of the landlords or bailies. Also that vagabonds and broken men, for whom no sureties or pledges were entered, as belonging to no known clan, should find security to undergo the law, under pain of being denounced rebels. Also that the security found by the feudal landlords and bailies to present such offenders as dwelt on their lands to regular trial, was distinct from, and independent of, that which should be found by the patriarchal captain, head, or chieftain of the clan, and that each subsisted and might be acted on without prejudice to the other. These securities being obtained, it was provided, that when goods or cattle were carried off by the individuals of any clan, the party injured should intimate the robbery to the chief, charging him to make restitution within fifteen days, wherein if he failed, the injured party should have action against him, and other principal persons of the clan, to the amount of his loss.

These, and other minute regulations to the same purpose, show that the clan system had become too powerful for the government, and that, in order to check the disorders to which it gave rise, the legislature were obliged to adopt its own principle, and hold the chief, or patriarch of the tribe, as liable for all the misdeeds of the surname.

The rolls which were made up in consequence of these acts of parliament, gives us an enumeration of the nobles and barons (several of whom were themselves also chiefs) who possessed property in the disturbed Border districts, and also of the clans who dwelt in them.

Roll of the Names of the Landlords and Bailies of Lands Dwelling on the Borders, where broken Men have dwelt and presently dwell. A.D. 1587

MIDDLE MARCH

The Earl of Bothwell (*formerly Hepburn, then Stuart.*)
The Laird of Fairnyherst (*Kerr*)
The Earl of Angus (*Douglas*)

The Laird of Buccleuch (*Scott*)
The Sheriff of Teviotdale (*Douglas of Cavers*)
The Laird of Bedroule (*Turnbull*)
The Laird of Wauchop
The Lord Herries (*formerly Harries, then Maxwell*)
The Laird of Howpaisley (*Scott*)
George Turnbull of Halroule
The Laird of Littledene (*Kerr*)
The Laird of Drumlanrigg (*Douglas*)
The Laird of Chisholme (*Chisholme*)

WEST MARCH

The Lord Maxwell (*Maxwell*)
The Laird of Drumlanrigg (*Douglas*)
The Laird of Johnston (*Johnstone*)
The Laird of Applegirth (*Jardine*)
The Laird of Holmends (*Carruthers*)
The Laird of Gratney (*Johnstone*)
The Lord Herries (*Maxwell*)
The Laird of Dunwiddie
The Laird of Lochinvar (*Gordon*)

The Roll of the Clans that have Captains and Chieftains on whom they depend of times against the Will of their Landlords, and of some special Persons of Branches of the said Clans.

MIDDLE MARCH

Elliots[1] (*Laird of Lairistoun*)
Armstrongs (*Laird of Mangertown*)
Nicksons[2]
Crossers

WEST MARCH

Scotts of Ewesdale[3]
Beatisons, or Beatties

Littles (*chief unknown*)
Thomsons (*chief unknown*)
Glendinnings (*Glendonwyne of that Ilk*)
Irvings (*Irving of Bonshaw*)
Bells (*believed to be Bell of Blacket House*)
Carruthers (*Laird of Holmends*)
Grahames[4]
Johnstones (*Laird of Johnstone*)
Jardines (*Laird of Applegirth*)
Moffatts (*chief unknown, but the name being territorial, it is probably an ancient clan*)
Latimers (*chief unknown*)

A little work, called *Monipenny's Chronicle*, published in 1597 and 1633, gives, among other particulars concerning Scotland, a list of the principal clans and surnames on the Borders not landed, as well as of the chief riders and men of name among them. From this authority, we add the following list of *foraying or riding* clans, as they were termed, not found in the parliamentary roll of 1587. It commences with the east marches, which being in a state of comparative good order, were not included under the severe enactments of 1587.

EAST MARCHES

Bromfields (*chief, Bromfield of Gordon Mains, or of that Ilk*)
Trotters (*chief unknown*)
Diksons (*chief unknown*)
Redpath (*Laird of Redpath*)
Gradens (*Laird of Graden originally their chief*)
Youngs (*chief unknown*)
Pringles (*believed to be Pringle of Galashiels*)
Tates (*Tait of Pirn*)
Middlemast (*chief unknown*)
Burns (*chief unknown*)
Dalgleishes (*Dalgleish of that Ilk*)
Davisons (*Davison of Symiston*)
Pyles (*Pyle, or Peele, of Milnheuch*)
Robisons (*chief unknown – a Cumberland clan*)
Ainslies (*chief unknown*)
Olivers (*chief unknown*)

Laidlaws (*chief unknown: It is said by tradition the family came from Ireland, and that the name was originally Ludlow*)

LIDDESDALE

Parks (*chief, John of Park*)
Hendersons (*chief unknown*)

WEST MARCHES

Carliles (*Lord Carlile*)
Romes (*Clans now almost extinct – chiefs unknown* Gasses)

An equally absolute authority is the enumeration which is put by Sir David Lindsay of the Mount, in his very curious drama called the *Partium*, into the mouths of Common Thrift, a Borderer, and who, being brought condign punishment, takes leave of his countrymen and companions in iniquity:

> Adieu, my brother Annan thieves,
> That helpit me in my mischieves . . .
> The Scots of Ewesdail and the Graemes,
> I have na time to tell your names;
> With King Correction be ye fangit,
> Believe right sure ye will be hangit!
> SIR WALTER SCOTT

Notes

1 The Elliots and Armstrongs inhabited chiefly Liddesdale.
2 The Nixons and Crossers might rather be termed English than Scottish Borderers. They inhabited the Debateable Land, and were found in Liddesdale, but were numerous in Cumberland.
3 It is not easy to conjecture whether one part or branch of this numerous surname is distinguished from the rest, or whether it must be understood to comprehend the whole clan. The chief of the name was Scott of Buccleuch.
4 The chief of the Grahames is unknown. The clan were rather English than Scottish. They inhabited the Debateable Land.

Acknowledgements

The sources for quotations are given in the Notes. Where permissions are necessary, every effort has been made to trace copyright holders. Any omissions brough to the attention of the author will be remedied in future editions. The same applies to the illustrations. Their sources are ackowledged in their captions, where the provenance is known. Many of the photographs are by the author, otherwise in public domain.

Notes

CHAPTER ONE

From Asia to King Arthur

The inspiration for this book comes from Walter Prescott Webb's seminal *The Great Plains* (New York, 1931). He was indebted to Emerson Hough, *The Way to the West* (New York, 1922), but more significantly to Clark Wissler, *The American Indian* (New York, 1922), also to his *Man and Culture* (New York, 1923). From them came the idea of the spread of a 'horse culture' from Mongolia to Asia and Africa through Europe to Britain and the Americans.

For information on the Greeks and Romans, the superb *Oxford Classical Dictionary* (Oxford University Press, 1999) contains most of the relevant information on the classical world. Highly readable and informative are A.R. Burn, *Alexander the Great and the Hellenistic Empire* (London, 1947); E.A. Thompson, *The Early Germans* (Oxford, 1965), and P.B. Ellis, *Celt and Roman: The Celts of Italy* (London, 1998). Useful on the *auxilia* is G.L. Cheesman, *The Auxilia of the Roman Imperial Army*; on the Parthians, M.A.R. Colledge, *The Parthian Period* (London, 1986); on the Scythians, R. Rolle, *The World of the Scythians* (tr. London, 1989) and *Scythians and Greeks* (David Braund ed., University of Exeter, 2005); on the Sarmatians, T. Sulimirski, *The Sarmatians* (London, 1970); on the Goths, H. Wolfram, *History of the Goths* (London, 1988); and on the Huns, E.A. Thompson, *A History of Attila and the Huns* (1948) and O.J. Maenchen-Helfen, *The World of the Huns* (London, 1973). Also essential are Peter Heather, *The Goths* (Oxford, 1996) and Thomas S. Burns, *A History of the Ostrgoths* (Indiana University Press, Bloomington, 1984).

The recent discovery of the mosaics of mounted heroes at Palmyra was reported in *The Times*, July 8, 2005. Sheppard Frere wrote an illuminating book for the History of England series, *Britannia: A History of Roman Britain* (rev. ed., London, 1987), while in Arthurian studies, most important is John Morris, *The Age of Arthur: A History of the British Isles from 350 to 650* (London, 1973). Authoritative on its subject is Nick Aitchison, *The Picts and the Scots at War* (Stroud, Gloucs., 2003). Also see Adomnán, *Life of Columba* (tr. A.O. & M.O. Anderson, rev. ed., Oxford, 1991).

CHAPTER TWO

Islam and Norman

From the vast literature on the Arabs, I would select Bernard Lewis, *The Arabs in History* (rev. ed., London, 1970); E.W. Bovill, *The Golden Trade of the Moors* (rev. ed., Oxford, 1970); and P.H. Newby, *Saladin in His Time* (London, 1983), from which comes the quotation about Saladin's army. For their concepts of geography and its influence on culture, I am indebted to Ibn Khaldun, *History of the Berbers* (tr. De Slane, Algiers, 1852), and to Fernand Braudel, *The Mediterranean and the Mediterranean World in the Age of Philip II* (rev. ed., 2 vols., London, 1972–73).

The quotation on the two traditions of horsemanship is taken from E. Wissler, *Man and Culture, op. cit.* Also essential is P.H. Blair, *Anglo-Saxon England* (rev. ed., Cambridge, 1995). G.N. Garmonsway made the excellent translation of *The Battle of Brunanburh*. The extraordinary Curator at the Royal Library, Copenhagen, Sigfús Blöndal, wrote *The Varangians of Byzantium* (Cambridge, 1978). He translated Haraldr Hardrada, while the translation from *Beowulf* is from this author. The *Head-ransom* of Egil Skalla-Grímsson is taken from *English Historical Documents*, I, c.500–1042 (D. Whitelock ed., London, 1979), while Charlemagne is quoted by E.L. Gonshof, 'Charlemagne's Army', *Frankish Institutions under Charlemagne* (New York, 1970).

In his seminal work, *War and Human Progress* (London, 1950), John U. Nef argued that weaponry changed cultures through industrial advances. Most useful on tactics and weapons are J.F.C. Fuller, *Decisive Battles: Their Influence upon History and Civilisation* (2 vols., London, 1939); E.S. Creasy, *The Fifteen Decisive Battles of the World* (London, 1852); A.H. Burne, *More Battlefields of England* (London, 1952); and Peter Young and John Adair, *Hastings to Culloden* (London, 1964).

The best introduction to Mongol civilisation is Ralph Fox, *Genghis Khan* (London, 1936), followed by Walter Heissig, *A Lost Civilisation: The Mongols Rediscovered* (London, 1966). Definitive are Leo de Hartog, *Genghis Khan: Conqueror of the World* (London, 1989); B.F. Manz, *Tamerlane: His Rise and Rule* (Cambridge, 1989); and Morris Rossabi, *Khubilai Khan: His Life and Times* (University of California Press, 1988). The translation of Cavafy's poem, 'Expecting the Barbarians' is by Rae Dalven in *The Complete Poems of Cavafy* (New York, 1948).

CHAPTER THREE

Crusade and Cossack

All inquiries into the crusades still begin and end with Sir Stephen Runciman, *A History of the Crusades* (3 vols., Cambridge, 1951–4). Generally useful on the subject is Richard Barber, *The Knight and Chivalry* (London, 1970). Jonathan Riley-Smith is admirable on the motives of the crusades in *The Crusades: Idea and Reality 1095–1294* (London, 1982), while Norman Housley, *The Later Crusades, 1274–1580: From Lyons to Alcazar* (Oxford, 1992) is fine. The passage from Richard of Devizes, *Chronicles of the Crusades*, is quoted by Alfred H. Crosby in his provocative *Ecological Imperialism: The Biological Expansion of Europe, 900–1900* (Cambridge, 1986). Amin Maalouf, *The Crusades Through Arab Eyes* (London, 1984) is an admirable corrective to the Christian chroniclers and quotes the opinions of Arab historians of the time. Zoé Oldenburg in *The Crusades* (London, 1965) is second only to Runciman in her understanding of that religious phenomenon. Most valuable in his analysis is Hans Eberhard Mayer, *The Crusades* (Oxford, 1972). Most important on the Crusades and European colonisation is Robert Bartlett, *The Making of Europe: Conquest, Colonization and Cultural Change 950–1350* (London, 1993).

Jonathan Riley-Smith is also admirable in *The First Crusade and the Idea of Crusading* (London, 1933), as is his edition of *The Atlas of the Crusades* (London, 1991). Also useful in its ideas is J.J. Saunders, *Aspects of the Crusades* (Christchurch, N.Z., 1962). And I am indebted to Desmond Seward, *The Monks of War* (rev. ed., London, 1995). A most important book on frontier conflicts is *Medieval Frontier Societies* (R. Bartlett and A. Mackay eds., Oxford, 1989).

For the Cossacks, I have relied on Philip Longworth, *The Cossacks* (London, 1969), also Albert Seaton, *The Horsemen of the Steppes: The Story of the Cossacks* (London, 1985), from whom I have taken the long quotation on the change in three generations of Cossacks. Richard Pipes writes well in *Russia Under the Old Regime* (New York, 1974), as does William Sunderland, *Taming the Wild Field: Colonization and Empire on the Russian Steppe* (Cornell University Press, 2004). The Cossack observers are P.S. Pallas, *Travels through the Southern Provinces of the Russian Empire in the Years 1793-94* (2 vols., London, 1802–3), and S. Purchas, *Hakluytus Posthumus, or Purchas His Pilgrimes* (3 vols., London, 1625).

CHAPTER FOUR

The Creation of the Reivers

Sir Walter Scott's 'Essay on Border Antiquities' and on 'Provincial Antiquities of Scotland', was published in *The Miscellaneous Prose Works* (Vol. 7, Edinburgh, 1834). He quotes both Froissart's *Chronicles* and Walter Bower's *Scotichronicon* (S. Taylor, D.E.R. Watt & B. Scott eds., 9 vols., Aberdeen, 1987–98), although the verse from that work has been modernised. He also had translated Bishop Lesley (Leslie), *De Origine, Moribus, et Rebus gestis Scotorum*, which was published by the Bannatyne Club in 1830. Ailred's description of the Battle of the Standard was translated from the Latin by A.O. Anderson, *Scottish Annals from English Chronicles, AD 500 to 1286* (London, 1902). Ronald McNair Scott has written a fine biography of *Robert the Bruce: King of Scots* (London, 1982), while essential reading is Matthew Strickland & Robert Hardy, *The Great Warbow: From Hastings to the Mary Rose* (Stroud, Gloucs., 2005), also Keith Durham, *The Border Reivers* (Oxford, 1995). For the medieval armaments industry, Jean Gimpel, *The Medieval Machine: The Industrial Revolution of the Middle Ages* (London, 1971) is important.

Generally useful are W. Croft Dickinson, *Scotland from the Earliest Times to 1603* (rev. ed., Oxford, 1977); E.M. Barron, *The Scottish War of Independence* (Inverness, 1934); G.W.S. Barrow, *Robert Bruce and the Community of the Realm of Scotland* (London, 1965) and *The Kingdom of the Scots* (London, 1973); E.LG. Stones ed., *Anglo-Scottish Relations, 1174-1328* (London, 1965); R.L. Graeme Ritchie, *The Normans in Scotland* (Edinburgh, 1954); T.C. Smout, *A History of the Scottish People 1560–1830* (London, 1969); and John Laffin, *Scotland the Brave: The Story of the Scottish Soldier* (London, 1963). James Craigie edited *Basilikon Doron* in 1942 for the Scottish Text Society, while the observer of the Scots factions was Fynes Morrison in 1598, quoted in P. Hume Brown, *Early Travellers in Scotland* (Edinburgh, 1891).

On Border warfare, George MacDonald Fraser, *The Steel Bonnets* (London, 1971) is definitive, although he is brief on its origins in the 13th century. I am indebted to John E. Morris, *Bannockburn* (Cambridge, 1914), who quotes extensively from contemporary chroniclers. Also important are R. Borland, *Border Raids and Reivers* (Glasgow, 1910); J.C. Bruce, *Handbook to the Roman Wall* (Newcastle, 1947); J. Nicolson and R. Burn, *History and Antiquities of Westmoreland and Cumberland* (London, 1977); James L. Mack, *The Border Line* (Edinburgh, 1926); and George Ridpath, *The Border History of England and Scotland* (Berwick, 1858).

The chroniclers quoted come from John Barbour, *The Brus* (G. Eyre Todd ed. and tr., London, 1907); John of Fordun, *Chronicles of the Scottish Nation* (W.F. Skene ed., F.S.H. Skene tr., 2 vols., Edinburgh, 1871–72); *Chroniques de Froissart* (Simeon Luce ed., 15 vols., Paris, 1869–99). *The Chronicle of Lanercost, 1272–1346* (Sir Herbert Maxwell tr., Glasgow, 1913); *Les Vraies Chroniques de Messire Jehan Le Bel* (L. Poulain ed., Brussels, 1863); Geoffrey le Baker, *Chronicon* (E.M. Thompson ed., Oxford, 1889); and Andrew of Wytoun, *Orygynale Cronykil of Scotland* (D. Laing ed., 3 vols., Edinburgh, 1872–1879).

CHAPTER FIVE

Harry and Burn

I remain grateful to *The Great Warbow: From Hastings to the Mary Rose*, *op. cit.*, for its excellent analyses of battles and use of contemporary medieval accounts. Particularly useful have been *English Historical Documents, 1327–1485* (A.R. Myers ed., London, 1969) for the Bridlington and other chronicles; Robert Lindsay Piscottie, *The Historie and Chronicles of Scotland* (Aeneas, J.G. Mackay ed., 3 vols., Edinburgh, 1899-1911), which quotes the words of Johnie Armstrong to his king. Also invaluable in the Reivers is Sir Walter Scott, 'Tales of a Grandfather' and 'Border Minstrelsy', *The Prose Works* (Vol. 1, Edinburgh, 1836). John T. White, *The Death of a King, being extracts from contemporary accounts of the Battle of Branxton Moor September 1513* (Edinburgh, 1970) and *Trewe Encountre of Batayle Lately Don Betwene Englande and Scotlande* (London, 1513). See also George Buchanan, *History of Scotland* (James Aitken tr., 3 vols., Glasgow, 1827); Ranald Nicholson, *Scotland: The Later Middle Ages* (Edinburgh, 1989); Alexander Grant, *Independence and Nationhood, Scotland 1306-1469* (Edinburgh, 2001); C.J. Rogers, *War, Cruel and Sharp: English Strategy Under Edward III, 1327-1360* (Woodbridge, 2000); George Ridpath, *The Border History of England and Scotland* (Berwick, 1810); and the admirable Peter Reese, *Flodden: A Scottish Tragedy* (Edinburgh, 2003).

The ironic ballad, 'The War-Song of Dinas Vawr' comes from Thomas Love Peacock, *The Misfortunes of Elphin* (London, 1828). For many versions of Border and American ballads, no praise is enough for the magisterial collection made by MacEdward Leach, *The Ballad Book* (New York, 1955). John Major, a Lowland Scots writer, described in 1527 the equipment of the Highlander in *Historia Majoris Britanniae, A History of*

Greater Britain (A. Constable tr., Scottish Historical Society, 1892). Lord Hume's remarks at Flodden are quoted in James Taylor, *The Great Historic Families of Scotland* (2 vols., Edinburgh, 1889), while Father Richard Augustin Hay, *Genealogie of the Sainteclaires of Rosslyn* was first published in 1835 in Edinburgh.

CHAPTER SIX

Ballads of Circumstance

In this chapter, I have found valuable *Scotland from the Earliest Times to 1603* (*op. cit.,*) and the excellent Jamie Cameron, *James V: The Personal Rule 1528–1542* (East Lothian, 1998). Also important in the Scottish Record Office for this period are the *Acts of the Lords of Council* and the *Acts of the Lords of Council and Session*, and the *Acts and Decreets*, as they will be in the succeeding chapters of this book. To be consulted are William Drummond, *History of Scotland from the Year 1423 until the year 1542* (London, 1861); A.H. Dunbar, *Scottish Kings: A Revised Chronology of Scottish History 1005–1625* (Edinburgh, 1906); David Hume, *The History of the House and Race of Douglas and Angus* (Edinburgh, 1748); R.K. Hannay and D. Hay (eds.), *The Letters of James V* (Edinburgh, 1954); and W.C. Dickinson (ed.), *John Knox's History of the Reformation in Scotland* (Edinburgh, 1949); C. Bingham, *James V: King of Scots* (London, 1971); P.D. Anderson, *Robert Stewart, Earl of Orkney, Lord of Shetland: 1533–1593* (Edinburgh, 1982); and Amstael's edition of the *Johnstoni Historia,* quoted by Sir Walter Scott. George Neilson fully deals with the question of the *Repentance Tower and its Tradition* (Edinburgh, 1890).

CHAPTER SEVEN

The Prickly Pride

I have found most informative W.A. Armstrong, *The Armstrong Borderland* (North Berwick, 1969); I.B. Cowan and D. Shaw (eds.), *The Renaissance and Reformation in Scotland* (Edinburgh, 1983); Pamela E. Ritchie, *Mary of Guise in Scotland, 1548–1560* (East Lothian, 2002); W. Ferguson, *Scotland's Relations with England: a Survey to 1707* (Edinburgh, 1977); N. Macdougall, *James III: A Political Study* (Edinburgh, 1982) and *James IV* (Edinburgh,

1989); C. McGladdery, *James II* (Edinburgh, 1990); S. Ross, *The Stewart Dynasty* (London, 1993); M.W. Stuart, *The Scot who was a Frenchman; being the life of John Stewart, Duke of Albany in Scotland, France and Italy* (London, 1940).

The Patten chronicle is quoted in G. Dickinson, 'Some Notes on the Scottish Army in the First Half of the Sixteenth Century', *Scottish Historical Review, xxviii*, 1949. As late as 1669, an English clergyman, James Brome, was commenting on the antiquated Highland battledress; he is quoted in the thorough book by J.T. Dunbar, *History of Highland Dress* (Edinburgh, 1962), as Lord Scrope is quoted in the judicious *The Border Reivers, op. cit.* The best descriptions of the Border feuds remain in Sir Walter Scott's works and in George MacDonald Fraser's *The Steel Bonnets, op. cit.* Buchanan made his comment on Buccleuch's barbarity in his *Admonitioun to the trew lordis*, 1571. I have slightly adapted for better modern understanding the texts of the Border ballads, printed in Sir Walter Scott, *Minstrelsy of the Scottish Border* (T.F. Henderson ed., Edinburgh, 1902); Scott quoted from John Cleland's *Poems.*

Invaluable is the admirable biography by Antonia Fraser, *Mary, Queen of Scots* (London, 1969). She also quotes William Patten, *Diary of Somerset's Campaign, 1547*. Also important is Gordon Donaldson, *All the Queen's Men: Power and Politics in Mary Stewart's Scotland* (London, 1983) and *The Reformation in Scotland* (Cambridge, 1960); G. Seton, *A History of the Family of Seton* (2 vols., Edinburgh, 1896); J.K. Cameron, *The First Book of Discipline* (Edinburgh, 1972); Duncan Shaw (ed.) *Reformation and Revolution* (Edinburgh, 1967); D.H. Willson, *James VI and I* (London, 1956); D.L.W. Tough, *The Last Years of a Frontier* (Oxford, 1928); and William Forbes-Leigh S.J., *Narratives of Scottish Catholics under Mary Stewart and James VI* (Edinburgh, 1885). Another important source was the *Basilikon Doron* (James Craigie ed., Scottish Text Society, 1942), while the observer of Scots factions was Fynes Morrison in 1598, quoted in P. Hume Brown, *Early Travellers in Scotland* (Edinburgh, 1891). The translation from Dante's 'Paradiso' is my own.

CHAPTER EIGHT

Women of Courage and Circumstance

I am dependent again on Sir Walter Scott for his *Border Antiquities* and *Ballads* and *Minstrelsy*, and also for the extracts from the *Memoirs* of Sir Robert Carey and the trial of Willie of Westburnflat. The quotation about Widsith comes from my *The Sword and the Grail, op. cit.* The whole question of the role and feelings of women among the Reivers is hardly documented outside ballad and song.

CHAPTER NINE

Kirk and Destruction

Worth noticing is the famous Curse upon the Reivers made by the Archbishop of Glasgow in a *Monition*, parts of which are reproduced. The common traitors, Reivers, thieves of Teviotdale, Eskdale, Nithsdale and Annandale were subject to an *anathema*. 'Men, wiffis, and barnys . . . are part murdrist, part slayne, brynt, heryit, spulezeit and reft, oppinly on day licht and under silens of the nicht, and their takis and landis laid waist.' Therefore, the Archbishop denounces, 'proclamis, and declaris all and sindry the commitaris of the said saikles murthris, slauchteris, brinying, heirchippes, reiffis, thiftis and spulezeis . . . of their evil dedis generalie CURSIT, waryit, aggregeite, and reaggregeite, with the GREAT CURSING'.

See William Law Mathieson, *Politics and Religion: A Study in Scottish History from the Reformation to the Revolution* (2 vols., Glasgow, 1902). He also quotes Lindsay, *True Narrative of the Perth Assembly* and provides his own comments. Also essential is David Stevenson, *The Origins of Freemasonry: Scotland's Century, 1590–1710* (Cambridge, 1988). See also Sir Richard Maitland and Alexander, Lord Kingston, *The History of the House of Seytoun* (Edinburgh, 1829), and Lord J. Somerville, *Memorie of the Somervills; being a history of the baronial house of Somerville* (Sir Walter Scott ed., 2 vols., Edinburgh, 1815); Scott also quotes Satchells, *History of the Name of Scott* in his *Minstrelsy of The Scottish Border, op cit.*, and the *Mercurius Politicus*. David Stevenson has also written two excellent books: *The Scottish Revolution 1637–1644: The Triumph of the Covenanters* (Newton Abbot, 1973), and *Revolution and Counter-Revolution in Scotland, 1644–1651* (London, 1977). The quotations from Robert Baillie are taken from *The Letters and Journals* (D. Laing ed., 3 vols., Edinburgh, 1841–1842); see also F.N. McCoy, *Robert Baillie and the Second Scots Reformation* (London, 1974). The turncoat with the dangerous maxim was James Turner, who persecuted the Covenanters whom he knew well, after the Restoration.

Important are G. Burnet, *History of my Own Times* (O. Airy ed., 2 vols., Oxford, 1897–1900), also *The Hamilton Papers* (S. R. Gardiner ed., London, 1880), also P. Gordon of Ruthven, *A Short Abridgement of Britane's Distemper* (J. Dunn ed., Edinburgh, 1844). E. Hyde, the Earl of Clarendon, *The History of the Rebellion and Civil Wars in England Begun in the Year 1641* (W.D. Macray ed., 6 vols., Oxford, 1888) remains indispensable. See also G. Wishart, *The Memoirs of James, Marquis of Montrose, 1639–50* (Edinburgh, 1893), and *Montrose* (London, 1931) by John Buchan, who comments on his hero. Relevant are W.S. Douglas, *Cromwell's Scotch Campaigns, 1650-51* (London, 1898): J.K. Hewison, *The Covenanters* (2 vols., Glasgow, 1913); W.M. Lamont, *Godly Rule, Politics and Religion, 1603–1660* (London, 1969); C.S. Terry, *The Life and Campaigns of Alexander Leslie, First Earl of Leven* (Edinburgh, 1899); *Memorials of the Great Civil War* (H. Cary ed., 2 vols., London, 1842); and Stuart Reid, *Battlefields of the Scottish Lowlands* (Barnsley, 2004).

CHAPTER TEN

The Social Bandits

Eric Hobsbawm completed his important early book on *Primitive Rebels* (Manchester, 1959) with his seminal *Bandits* (4th rev., ed., London, 2000). The quotations about the *Haiduks* are taken from him. Christopher Hibbert wrote on *Highwaymen* (London, 1967), also on *The Road to Tyburn: Jack Sheppard and the 18th Century Underworld* (London, 1957). See also William Pope, *The Mémoires of Monsieur Du Vall, containing the History of his Life and Death* (London, 1670), and *The Newgate Calendar* (A. Knapp and W. Baldwin eds., 4 vols., London, 1828). Patrick Pringle also wrote *Stand and Deliver: The Story of the Highwayman* (London, 1951) and *The Thief-takers* (London, 1958). Very useful is Rayner Heppenstall, *Tales from the Newgate Calendar* (London, 1981), while the last word on *Robin Hood* (rev. ed., London, 1989) is by J.C. Holt, whose translations of Wyntoun and Langland and Chaucer are gratefully used in this text.

Henry Mayhew published his *London Labour and the London Poor* in 1851, while the 1685 broadsheet of the 'Life, Trial, & Execution of William Nevison, The Highwayman, at York Gaol' was reproduced in *A Collection of 'Ballads on a Subject '* Charles Hindley ed., vol.2, London, 1927). *The Beggar's Opera* by John Gay was first performed in 1728, while Bertolt Brecht's *Threepenny Opera (Dreigroschenoper)* was shown in 1928 in Germany; his *Threepenny Novel* was translated by Desmond I. Vesey with verses translated by Christopher Isherwood, and published in 1958 in London. James Sharpe is discerning on *Dick Turpin: The myth of the English highwayman* (London, 2004). Harrison Ainsworth's account of how *Rookwood* was written occurs in a 'Preface' of 1849, usually reprinted in editions of the novel printed after that date. *Jack Sheppard* was first published in 1839; Thackeray wrote in *The Times*, 2 September, 1840; Professor Aytoun and Sir Theodore Martin wrote *Flowers of Hemp: or the Newgate Garland* in the same year, while Thomas de Quincey was quoted in Rayner Heppenstall, *Tales from the Newgate Calendar, op. cit.* Also important are Paul Vanderwood, *Disorder and Progress: Bandits, Police and Mexican Development* (Lincoln, Nebraska, 1981); Friederich Katz, *The Life and Times of Pancho Villa* (Stanford, Ca., 1999); and Pearl Buck's translation of *Shuihu Zhuan: All Men Are Brothers* (New York, 1937).

CHAPTER ELEVEN

The American Horse

See Andrew Sinclair, *The Naked Savage* (London, 1991). These accounts of the reaction of the Mexican Indians to the coming of the Spaniards can be found in Miguel Leon-Portilla's admirable compilation of the Indian chroniclers, *The Broken Spears* (Boston, 1962). I have used an early English version of Antonio de Herrera's book translated by Captain John Stevens and published in London in six illustrated volumes in 1740 under the title of *The General History of the Vast Continent and Islands of America, Commonly called, The West Indies, from the First Discovery thereof: with the best Accounts the People could give of their Antiquities.* (As in other early translations, I have modernised the spelling and the overuse of capital letters.) Victor W. von Hagen has edited a work on Inca Peru taken from the writings of Pedro de Cieza de Leon, *The Incas* (Norman, Oklahoma, 1959). The quotations come from his judicious introduction, and from Portilla, *The Broken Spears*, See also Bernal Diaz del Castillo, *The Discovery and Conquest of Mexico, 1517–1521* (New York 1956). Also see Francisco López de Gómara, *Cortes, The Life of the Conqueror by His Secretary* (Berkeley, 1966).

The urbane Edward Bancroft in his *Essay on the Natural History of Guiana, in South America* (London, 1769) probably has the last word on the dispute over the savagery of European massacre compared with Indian cannibalism. 'It is certainly more unnatural to kill each other by unnecessary wars, than to eat the bodies of those we have killed: the crime consists in killing, not in eating, as the worm and vulture testify, that human flesh is by no means sacred. But tho' civilized nations abhor eating, they are familiarised to the custom of killing each other, which they practise with less remorse than the savages. But custom is able to reconcile the mind to the most unnatural objects.'

Before Columbus even reached America, the Spanish historian Azurara noted the disdain which the Neolithic Canary Islanders had for precious metals. 'They have no gold or silver, nor any money, nor jewels, nor anything else artificial, save that which they make with the stones that serve them as knives, and so they build the houses in which they live. They disdain gold, silver, and all other metals, making mock of those that desire them; and in general there are none of them whose opinion is different. No quality of cloth pleases them, and they make mock of those who desire it. . . But they greatly value iron, which they work with their stones, and of this they make hooks for fishing.' From Azurara, *The Chronicle of the Discovery of Guinea* (1448), as reprinted in V. de Castro e Almeida ed., *Conquests and Discoveries of Henry the Navigator*, (London, 1936). See also William H. Prescott, *History of the Conquest of Mexico and History of the Conquest of Peru* (Modern Library ed., vol. 1, New York, 1956).

I remain in debt to Henry Nash Smith's seminal work, *Virgin Land: The American West as Symbol and Myth* (Cambridge, Mass., 1950). The quotations are those of B. O'Fallon, an Indian agent, and Captain Randolph D. Marcy; both are taken from W.P. Webb, *The Great Plains, op. cit.* Major Stephen H. Long first called the plains, 'the Great American Desert' in his report of 1821. He declared that the area 'is almost wholly unfit for cultivation, and of course uninhabitable by a people depending upon agriculture for their subsistence. Although tracts of fertile land considerably extensive are occasionally to be met with, yet the scarcity of wood and water, almost uniformly prevalent, will prove an insuperable obstacle in the way of settling the country'. Although cattle ranching and intensive farming has been developed on the Great Plains, too often the prairie has ended as a dustbowl in the wake of the plough and the wind. And unless the problem of water is finally solved in that arid area, it may yet revert to the Great American Desert of its original name.

For an admirable description of the life of the Mountain Men, see Ray Allen Billington, *The Far Western Frontier, 1830–1860* (New York, 1956). The best study of the tragedy of the Donner expedition is George R. Stewart, *Ordeal by Hunger: The Story of the Donner Party* (New York, 1936). Essential reading is W. Eugene Hollon, *The Great American Desert* (Oxford, 1966); he quotes Pedro de Castañeda. Also important is Joe B. Frantz and Julian Ernest Choate, Jr., *The American Cowboy: The Myth and the Reality* (Norman, University of Oklahoma, 1955). The quotation from J. Frank Dobie is from 'The First Cattle in Texas and the Southwest Progenitors of the Longhorns,' *Southwestern Historical Quarterly* (Vol XLII, January, 1939).

The wise historian is John R. Alden in *The History of Human Society* series, *Pioneer America* (J.H. Plumb ed., London, 1966). The quotations are taken from Charles Howard Shinn, *Mining Camps: A Study in American Frontier Government* (rev. ed. by R.W. Paul, New York, 1965). Dr John C. Lord delivered his lecture on the 'American Borderer' in Buffalo, February, 1849. Invaluable on early European and indigenous American relations is Lewis O. Saum. *The Fur Trader and the Indian* (Seattle, University of Washington Press, 1965); he gives the quotation from Henry Boller. Also see Walter Prescott Webb, 'Ended: 400 Year Boom, Reflections on the Age of the Frontier', *Harper's Magazine*, October, 1951, and Frederick Jackson Turner, *The Frontier in American History* (New York, 1920). Also deterministic in his view of American Western pioneers is the quoted Henry Bamford Parkes, *The American Experience*, (New York, 1947).

CHAPTER TWELVE

The Scotch-Irish

For the emigration of the Lowland Scots to Ulster and the Scots-Irish to North America, followed by the Highlanders, see the excellent James G. Leyburn, *The Scotch-Irish: A Social History* (Chapel Hill, North Carolina, 1962); I am grateful to him for some contemporary quotations. Also important are Charles A. Hanna, *The Scotch-Irish, or the Scot in North Britain, North Ireland, and North America* (2 vols., New York, 1902); Henry Jones Ford, *The Scotch-Irish in America* (Princeton, New Jersey, 1915); William E.H. Lecky, *Ireland in the Eighteenth Century* (2 vols., London, 1883); and Ian C.C. Graham, *Colonists from Scotland; Emigration to North America, 1707–1783* (Ithaca, 1956).

Alan Lomax is definitive in *The Folk Songs of North America in the English Language* (London, 1960). Of many books on the American Revolution, I am most indebted to George F. Scheer & Hugh F. Rankin, *Rebels and Redcoats* (New York, 1957) for their many eye-witness accounts. Se also A. Sinclair, *An Anatomy of Terror* (London, 2002) and Theodore Roosevelt, *The Winning of the West* (2 vols., New York, 1904). See also Cormac McCarthy, *Cities of the Plain* (New York, 1995).

CHAPTER THIRTEEN

Warriors into Outlaws

On the American conflict, I have chiefly used the magisterial Edward Hagerman, *The American Civil War and the Origins of Modern Warfare* (Bloomington, Indiana, 1988), although he plays down the importance of the mobility of cavalry in search-and-destroy operations. I have also found valuable Stephen Z. Starr, *The Union Cavalry in the Civil War* (Leicester, 1979); Edward G. Longacre, *Grant's Cavalryman: The Life and Wars of General James H. Wilson* (New York, 1996); and Colonel Harry Gilmor, *Four Years in the Saddle* (New York, 1866). The quoted US Federal Telegrapher was W.F. Bassett, to be found in the riveting accounts of western outlaws in James D. Horan, *Desperate Men* (New York, 1949). He used extensive extracts from the Pinkerton files. Also evocative were Frank C. Lockwood, *Pioneer Days in Arizona: From the Spanish Occupation to Statehood* (New York, 1932), and Pat F. Garrett, *The Authentic Life of Billy the Kid* (Norman, Oklahoma, 1954). The quotation about the 'pastoral epoch' is taken from Marshall Fishwick, 'Billy the Kid: Faust in America', *Saturday Review*, 11 October, 1952. See also William Settle, *Jesse James Was His Name* (Columbia, Mo., 1966); Stephen Tatum, *Inventing Billy the Kid: Visions of the Outlaw in America, 1881–1981.* (Albuquerque, 1982); and Richard White, 'Outlaw Gangs of the Middle American Border: American Social Bandits', *Western Historical Quarterly*, Vol. XII, October, 1981.

CHAPTER FOURTEEN

Print the Legend

As stated before, this book is wholly indebted to the seminal work of Walter Prescott Webb in *The Great Plains*. Also significant are W. Eugene Hollon, *The Great American Desert: Then and Now* (New York, 1966); Richard Rhodes, *An Evocation of the American Middle West* (New York, 1970); and William T. Hornaday, 'The Extermination of the American Bison, with a Sketch of Its Discovery and Life History' *Smithsonian Report*, 1887. Also see James G. Bell, 'A Log of the Texas-California Cattle Trail', *South-western Historical Quarterly*, Vol. XXXV, January, 1932, and Joseph G. McCoy, *Historic Sketches of the Cattle Trade of the West and the Southwest* (Glendale, Ca., 1940), along with Colonel Richard I. Dodge, *The Plains of the Great West*

(New York, 1877), an extraordinary contemporary description of social life on that shifting frontier. For a full later account, see Ernest S. Osgood, *The Day of the Cattleman* (University of Minnesota Press, 1929). For the cowboy's origins and social order, the quotation is from Dana Coolidge, *Old California Cowboys* (New York, 1939), and the code is from Charles Siringo, *Riata and Spurs* (New York, 1927).

The quotation about the California Trail is from the rich book by Joe B. Frantz and Julian E. Choate Jr., *The American Cowboy: The Myth and the Reality* (University of Oklahoma Press, 1955). John Young's testimony was recorded by Frank Dobie and left to the Barker Texas History Center, Austin. Edward Everett Dale, *The Range Cattle Industry: Ranching on the Great Plains from 1865–1925* (University of Oklahoma Press, 1930) is detailed on the rise of the cattle syndicates. Jack Weston, *The Real American Cowboy* (New York, 1985) has original and illuminating insights, but is marred by an effort to discover class consciousness, where it hardly existed. There is an excellent analysis of the dime novel and popular Western fiction in Henry Nash Smith, *Virgin Land: The American West as Symbol and Myth* (Howard University Press, 1950). Although sometimes accused of tweaking his recorded ballads, as did Sir Walter Scott, the lifework of Alan Lomax, *The Folk Songs of North America in the English Language* (London, 1960) has preserved a whole skein of history.

William F. Cody claimed to have written *The Life of Hon. William F. Cody, Known as Buffalo Bill, the Famous Hunter, Scout and Guide. An Autobiography.* (Hartford, Conn., 1879), while Richard J. Walsh did write, *The Making of Buffalo Bill: A Study in Heroics* (Indianapolis, 1928). Also see Larry McMurtry, *The Colonel and Little Missie: Buffalo Bill, Annie Oakley, and the Beginnings of Superstardom in America* (New York, 2005); Louis S. Warren, *Buffalo Bill's America: William Cody and the Wild West Show* (New York, 2005); and R.W. Rydell and R. Kroes, *Buffalo Bill in Bologna: The Americanization of the World, 1869–1922* (University of Chicago Press, 2005). The quotation on the mythical cowboy comes from F. Baumann, 'On a Western Ranch', *Fortnightly Review*, Vol. XLVII, 1887. See J. Fenimore Cooper, *The Prairie* (Boston, 1827), and Owen Wister, 'How Lin McLean Went East', *Harper's New Monthly Magazine* (Vol. LXXXVI, December, 1892, and *The Virginian* (New York, 1931). Andy Adams wrote *The Log of a Cowboy* (Boston, 1903), and Zane Grey, *The Lone Star Ranger* (New York, 1915).

For the Western film, see Andrew Sinclair, *John Ford: A Biography* (New York, 1979), also William K. Everson, *A Pictorial History of the Western Film* (New York, 1969); George N. Ferris and William K. Everson, *The Western from Silents to the Seventies* (rev. ed., New York, 1973); Will Wright, *Six Guns and Society; A Structural Study of the Western* (UCLA, 1975); and William W. Savage, *The Cowboy Hero: His Image in American History and Culture* (New York, 1979). 'Buffalo Bill' is taken from E.E. Cummings, *Poems, 1923–1954* (New York, 1954).

CHAPTER FIFTEEN

Horse Culture

Equine mythology is cleverly treated in M. Oldfield Howey, *The Horse in Magic and Myth* (London, 1923). Excellent on the *condottieri* are Frances Stonor Saunders, *Hawkwood: Diabolical Englishman* (London, 2004) and Anthony Mockler, *Mercenaries* (London, 1970). Important studies are Philippe Soupault, *Paolo Uccello* (Paris, 1929), and Enzo Carli, *All the Paintings of Paolo Uccello* (tr. Marion Fitzallan, London, 1964). Pietro C. Morani, *Leonardo da Vinci: The Complete Paintings* (New York, 2003) is important. On George Stubbs, see Malcolm Warner & Robin Blake, *Stubbs & the Horse* (Yale University Press, 2004); Robin Blake, *George Stubbs and the Wide Creation* (London, 2005); and Martin Myrone, *George Stubbs* (Tate Publishing, 2002). For 18th-century painting, Michael Levey, *Rococo to Revolution* (London, 1966) remains significant.

On Pushkin, I have relied on his texts, also on Svetlana Evdokimova, *Pushkin's Historical Imagination* (Yale University Press, 1999), and on Waclow Lednicki, *Pushkin's Bronze Horseman: The Story of a Masterpiece* (Westport, Conn., 1978). The quotations from Lord Byron are taken from Canto VIII of *Don Juan* and *Mazeppa*. See Mikhael Lermontov, *A Hero of Our Own Times* (tr. Eden & Cedar Paul, London, 1940). A significant work is Edward B. Greenwood, *Tolstoy: The Comprehensive Vision* (London, 1975). I have preferred *The Collected Stories of Isaac Babel* (ed. & tr. Walter Morison, intro. Lionel Trilling, London, 1957) to later editions of his works. His *1920 Diary* was published by the Yale University Press in 1995. See also two important articles in *The New York Review of Books*: Alfred Kazin, 'A Jew on Horseback', June 22, 1995, and John Bayley, 'The Hard Hitter', April 11, 2002. Jorge Luis Borges, *Collected Fictions* (tr. Andrew Hurley, London, 1999) contains all his known work. I have also used the translation by Anthony Kerrigan of *The End* and *The South* in *Ficciones* (New York, 1962).

CHAPTER SIXTEEN

Outback and Backlands

Excellent on border conflicts in Australia is Henry Reynold, *Frontier: Aborigines, Settlers and Land* (London, 1996). I have quoted from his book, also from L. Fison and A.W. Howitt, *Kamilaroi and Kurnai* (Oosterhout, 1967); H. Melville, *The History of the Island of Van Diemens Land* (London, 1835); and the Papers of Sir George Arthur in the Mitchell Library, Australia. Although wrong-headed about Frederick Jackson Turner's Frontier thesis, John Greenway makes useful comparisons between American and Australian experiences and folksongs and cattle trails in *The Last Frontier* (London, 1972); the long quotation on the music of the two continents is his work. I am indebted to Russell Ward, *The Australian Legend* (Melbourne, 1958) for his observations, while Charles White, *History of Australian Bushranging* (2 vols., Sydney, 1900, 1906) is outstanding on its subject. He has provided the quotations on the bushrangers and the eye-witness accounts of Glenrowan. I am also grateful to Samuel Putnam for his introduction to and excellent translation of *Os Sertões* by Euclides da Cunha, now entitled *Rebellion in the Backlands* (Chicago, 1944). Although too Marxist in his interpretations, E.J. Hobsbawm has written the definitive text on *Primitive Rebels* (Manchester, 1959). I am grateful to him for the ballads about Captain Limpião and Antonio Silvino.

CHAPTER SEVENTEEN

Commandos and Camels

For a particular and contemporary account of campaigns on the north-western frontier of India, I am indebted to Colonel Lewis Robert Stacy, *Narrative of Services in Beloochistan & Affghanistan in the Years 1840, 1841 & 1842* (London, 1848). His account of the use of light horse in a British army advance through a hostile landscape is a prophecy of the eventual supremacy of artillery. I have also found useful Willem Vogelsang, *The Afghans* (Oxford, 2002) and Leigh Maxwell, *My God – Maiwand!: Operations of the South Afghanistan Field Force, 1878–80* (London, 1979).

Of the hundreds of histories and accounts of the Boer War, I have found most useful C.E. Vulliamy: *Outlanders: A Study of Imperial Expansion in South Africa, 1877–1902* (London, 1938) and Deneys Reitz, *Commando: A Boer Journal of the Boer War* (London, 1929). I have quoted gratefully from both texts, also from the anonymous colonial horseman, reported in John Laffin, *Digger: The Story of the Australian Soldier* (London, 1969), which carries on the history of horse culture to Allenby's campaign in Palestine in the First World War.

Both of T.E. Lawrence's accounts of the Turkish War of 1917, *Revolt in the Desert* (London, 1927) and *Seven Pillars of Wisdom* (mass ed., London, 1935) are essential reading. The war correspondent who accompanied the Egyptian Expeditionary Force was W.T. Massey, who wrote of his experiences in *The Desert Campaigns* (London, 1918) and *How Jerusalem was Won: Being the Record of Allenby's Campaign in Palestine* (London, 1919). David L. Bullock, *Allenby's War: The Palestine-Arabian Campaigns, 1916–1918* (London, 1988) is good on strategy. For the decline of Bedouin cattle-raiding between the two World Wars, James Lunt, *The Arab Legion* (London, 1999) is important, as is J.B. Glubb, *The Story of the Arab Legion* (London, 1948) and *A Soldier with the Arabs* (London, 1957). The final quotations are taken from Erich Wollenberg, *The Red Army* (London, 1938), while the autobiography should be read of Nestor Makhno, *La Révolution Russe en Ukraine. Mars 1917–Avril 1918* (Paris, 1927).

CHAPTER EIGHTEEN

The Machine and the Hunt

For the Battle of Waterloo, I have been chiefly informed by Colonel H.C.B. Rogers, *Wellington's Army* (London, 1979), and David Hamilton-Williams, *The Fall of Napoleon: The Final Betrayal* (London, 1994). Napoleon's *Official Bulletin* was published in *Le Moniteur*, 21 June, 1815, and General Cavalié Mercer's *Journal of the Waterloo Campaign* in 2 volumes (Edinburgh, 1870). The letter of a discharged soldier to his Member of Parliament was printed in J.L. and B. Hammond, *The Skilled Labourer* (London, 1919), while Graham Wallas, the witness to Peterloo, was quoted by E.P. Thompson in his definitive *The Making of the English Working Class* (rev. ed., London, 1968). The quotation from the Duke of Wellington is cited by David Williams, *John Frost* (Cardiff, 1939).

Most important is Malcolm Thomis and Peter Holt, *Threats of Revolution in Britain, 1789–1848* (London, 1977). I am most grateful to the unsigned essay, 'The Luddites in the Period 1779–1830' in *The Luddites* (Lionel M. Munby ed., London, 1971), especially for its use of contemporary quotations, while the street ballads come from John Miller's essay in that collection, 'Songs of the Labour Movement'. The Andover magistrate's letter to Lord

Melbourne is part of the supreme study of the agrarian revolt, E.J. Hobsbawm and George Rudé, *Captain Swing* (London, 1969).

For the Game Laws and wars, essential reading are Roger B. Manning, *Hunters and Poachers: A Cultural and Social History of Unlawful Hunting in England 1485–1640* (Oxford, 1993); Harry Hopkins, *The Long Affray; The Poaching Wars in Britain* (London, 1985), quoting 'The Fine Old English Labourer'; D. Hay *et alii*, *Albion's Fatal Tree* (London, 1975); E.P. Thompson, *Whigs and Hunters: the Origin of the Black Act* (London, 1975); and E. Gibbon Wakefield, *Facts Related to the Punishment of Death in the Metropolis* (London, 1831). For the favourable comment on the merits of fox-hunting in country society, see F.M.L. Thompson, *England Landed Society in the 19th Century* (London, 1963). Also significant are David Cannadine, *The Decline and Fall of the British Aristocracy* (Yale University Press, 1990); G.E. Mingay, *The Gentry – the Rise and Fall of a Ruling Class* (London, 1976); S. Longrigg, *The English Squire and his Sporting Ways* (London, 1910); R.S. Surtees, *The Hunting Tours* (London, 1821-34); and A. Sinclair, *Death by Fame: A Life of Elisabeth Empress of Austria* (London, 1998), while Alexander Pope published in 1713 his 'Windsor Forest'.

The figures of death and emigration, also the quotation on *The Great Hunger: Ireland 1845–9* are taken from the book title of that name by Cecil Woodham-Smith, published in 1962 in London. I am most grateful to Mark Henderson, 'Elite 28 that gave birth to the sport of kings', *The Times*, 6 September, 2005, for all the information on the genetic heritage of British bloodstock. Of many works on the Crimean War, I have chiefly used Peter Gibbs, *Crimean Blunder* (London, 1960) and John Harris, *The Gallant Six Hundred* (London, 1973). See also A.W. Kinglake, *The Invasion of the Crimea* (8 vols., Edinburgh, 1863–87), also Cecil Woodham-Smith, *Florence Nightingale* (London, 1950).

Most useful on the Victorian police force are F.C. Mather, *Public Order in the Age of the Chartists* (Manchester, 1959) and Donald C. Richter, *Riotous Victorians* (Ohio University Press, 1981), which quotes the Mayor of Exeter on Special Constables and the eyewitness to 'Bloody Sunday'. For the rebel cause, see W.S. Smith, *The London Heretics, 1870–1914* (New York, 1968). Alfred Lord Tenyson's poem, 'The Charge of the Heavy Brigade' appeared in *Tiresias and Other Poems* (London 1858). Dixon Wecter wrote *The Hero in America* (New York, 1941). Indispensable is The Marquess of Anglesey, *A History of the British Cavalry 1816–1919* (Vol. 8, London, 1997), especially for his quotations from Field Marshal Haig and other officers. Also important is J.E.B. Seely, *Adventure* (London, 1933). Siegfried Sassoon, *Memoirs of a Fox-hunting Man* was published in 1928 in London.

CHAPTER NINETEEN

Dressage

I am most grateful to J.M. Brereton, *The Horse in War* (Newton Abbott, 1976), from whom I have quoted. Also significant is James Lunt, *Imperial Sunset: Frontier Soldiering in the 20th Century* (London, 1981). For the countryside appreciation of fox-hunting, consult J.V. Beckett, *The Aristocracy in England 1660–1914* (Oxford, 1986); David Cannadine, *Aspects of Aristocracy: Grandeur and Decline in Modern Britain* (Yale University Press, 1994); Phyllida Barstow, *The English Country House Party* Wellingborough, 1989); and David C. Itzkowitz, *Peculiar Privilege: A Social History of English Foxhunting 1753–1885* (Hassocks, Sussex, 1977), a book which excels in contemporary sources. The Swiss visitor was Louis Simond, *Journal of a Tour and Residence in Great Britain, during the Years 1810 and 1811* (2 vols., Edinburgh, 1817). William Cobbett's *Rural Rides in the Counties* . . . was published in 1830 in London, while Charles James Apperly's articles for the *Sporting Magazine* were collected and published as *Nimrod's Hunting Reminiscences* (London, 1926). The observer at Badminton was quoted in R. Carr, *English Fox Hunting: A History* (Oxford, 1976). Maureen Duffy wrote 'Beasts for Pleasure' in *Animals, Men and Morals* (S. & R. Godlovitch and J. Harris eds., London, 1971); Lady Randolph Churchill had her *Reminiscences* printed in 1908 in London, while George Orwell's influential *Animal Farm* was first published in 1945 in London.